The Road to Louisiana

The Saint-Domingue Refugees
1792-1809

The Road
to Louisiana

The Saint-Domingue Refugees
1792-1809

edited and annotated by
Carl A. Brasseaux and Glenn R. Conrad

with translations by
David Cheramie

University of Louisiana at Lafayette Press

Library of Congress Catalog Number: 92-71305
ISBN Number: 978-1-935754-60-2

Copyright 1992

University of Louisiana at Lafayette Press
P.O. Box 40831
Lafayette, LA 70504-0831
http://ulpress.org

CONTENTS

Introduction

This anthology constitutes the first attempt to fill comprehensively one of the most enduring lacunae in Louisiana historiography—the French-Antillian migration to the lower Mississippi Valley. Generations of Louisiana historians have neglected this influx, involving more than 10,000 Saint-Domingue refugees between 1792 and 1810. These newcomers were subsequently joined by far smaller numbers of French citizens from Guadeloupe and Martinique. Not only were these immigrants largely responsible for the establishment and success of the state's sugar industry, but they also gave New Orleans many of its most notable early institutions—the French opera, newspapers, schools, and colleges—and ultimately its antebellum French flavor. The refugees also contributed Creole cuisine, Creole language, okra, and voodoo to their adopted homeland.

Despite their significance, the refugees have attracted remarkably little scholarly attention. Louisiana's pioneer historians—François Xavier Martin, Charles E. A. Gayarré, and Alcée Fortier—and their successors have generally accorded them only passing mention.[1] The articles assembled in this anthology are the first to document the migrations and resettlement of these unfortunate people and to assess their impact upon New Orleans. Three of the four articles have appeared earlier in various scholarly journals, some of which are now defunct.[2] Two of the articles have

---

[1]François X. Martin, *The History of Louisiana from the Earliest Period* (1882; reprint ed., New Orleans, 1963), p. 346; Alcée Fortier, *A History of Louisiana*, 4 vols. (New York, 1903), III, 60-61. Gayarré offers a more comprehensive account in *History of Louisiana*, 4 vols., 4th ed. (1903; reprint ed., New Orleans, 1965), IV, 214-220.

[2]Gabriel Debien, "Les Colons de Saint-Domingue Réfugiés à Cuba (1793-1815)," *Revista de Indias*, XII (1953), 559-605; XIV (1955), 11-36; Gabriel Debien and René Le Gardeur, Jr., "Les Colons de Saint-Domingue Refugié à la Louisiane," *Louisiana Review*, IX (1980), 101-140; X (1981), 11-49, 97-141; Paul F. Lachance, "The 1809 Immigration of

been translated from the original French by David Cheramie to make them accessible to English-speaking historians and genealogists, who had previously been unable to extract and utilize the wealth of information presented by the authors.

The authors, widely recognized for their lasting contributions to the field of Saint-Domingue studies, trace the refugees' long, hard road to Louisiana. Thomas Fiehrer, an expert on the French Antilles, provides an overview of Louisiana's historical Caribbean connection. Gabriel Debien, dean of the French-Antillian historians, investigates the temporary relocation of the Saint-Domingue refugees in Cuba (1793-1815). Debien and the late New Orleans historian and genealogist René LeGardeur recount the small-scale migration of refugees into southern Louisiana preceding the massive, early nineteenth-century influx, analyzed by noted Canadian historian Paul Lachance.

Because the 1809 immigrants literally doubled the size of New Orleans within a three-month period, absorbing in the process the native Creole population, the few extant studies of the refugees have understandably tended to concentrate on their Crescent City experiences. The refugees' influence upon rural Louisiana, however, is less well known. Though the participation of Saint-Domingue refugees in Pointe Coupée's abortive 1795 slave insurrection is amply documented, historians have overlooked the mundane experiences of the more typical refugees who tended to blend quietly into their cultural and economic milieu. In the absence of secondary literature on these rural folk, historians have been content to merely speculate about the size and significance of the Antillian community in the rural parishes.

Yet, evidence regarding the rural refugees abounds in national, regional, state and local archives, particularly Louisiana's civil and ecclesiastical parish repositories. These materials clearly suggest that most Antillian immigrants remained in New Orleans, but that the few refugees who relocated in the rural parishes exerted a degree of political, economic, and cultural influence that belied their small numbers. Within ten years of their arrival, several Saint-

Saint-Domingue Refugees to New Orleans: Reception, Integration and Impact," *Louisiana History*, XXIX (1988), 109-141.

Domingue refugees had achieved political positions of regional and statewide importance. (See below, Table I.)

TABLE I
Political Positions
Held by Saint-Domingue Refugees
Louisiana's Rural Parishes,
1805-ca. 1820

NAME	POSITION	LOCATION	DATE
Bailly, Pierre	commandant	Iberville Dist	1805
	judge	Iberville Dist	1805
Bry, Henry	representative, leg. council	Terr. of Orl.	1810
Dechanet-Desassarts, Denis-Richard	clerk of court	St. John Par.	1806
	assessor	1st Mun., NO	1809
Dubourg de la Loubère, Arnould-Louis	judge	Plaquemines Par	1815
Moreau-Lislet, Louis-Marie-Elis.	interpreter	Terr. of Orl.	1805
	civil code	Terr. of Orl.	1806
	regent	College of Orl.	1811
	representative /senator	Louisiana	1820s

Other refugees made notable contributions to local medicine and education. Denis-Richard Dechanet-Desassarts, son of an actor from the Comédie Française, arrived at New Orleans around January 15, 1794. After working as a tutor in the Crescent City for several years, Dechanet-Desassarts moved to the German Coast area, where he became a farmer. In the August 13, 1806, issue of the *Moniteur de la Louisiane* he started a public subscription for funds to construct a schoolhouse in the Second German Coast. In addition, François-Marie Prévost, a Port-de-Paix public health officer who migrated to Louisiana in 1801, performed Louisiana's first cesarean section at Donaldsonville (Ascension Parish).[3]

Such anecdotal accounts of the notables, however, provide a circumscribed view of the elite and thus are not necessarily

[3]See below, pp. 157-159, 210-211.

representative of the rural refugees as a whole. Nor do they provide an accurate view of demographic patterns of migration and resettlement outside New Orleans. Louisiana's Catholic church records suggest a limited and very gradual diffusion of Antillian refugees into the established population of the rural parishes. Paul Lachance located approximately 1,150 Saint-Domingue refugees in the New Orleans church records for the period ca. 1803-ca. 1820; only eighty-seven are identified in Louisiana's rural church parishes for the period 1803-1830. Louisiana's first federal census corroborates the ecclesiastical data. Of the refugees named in Lachance's list, fourteen appear as residents of the rural parishes in the 1810 census of the Territory of Orleans, while only twelve are listed in the Louisiana census ten years later. The paucity of refugee listings was due in part to the immigrants' poverty. Having generally arrived with little or nothing, the refugees were forced to rent accommodations from established settlers and thus were not named in the census reports, which identified only property-holding heads of households (a situation which existed in New Orleans as well).3 Identification of refugees in the rural parishes is complicated still further by the presence of large numbers of French natives who may—or may not—have settled briefly in the Antilles before the onset of the French Revolution and its attendant servile insurrections. Southwest Louisiana church registers list 254 such French immigrants for the early nineteenth century alone. In the absence of biographical data linking these individuals with the French Antilles, they have not been included in this study. Saint-Domingue refugees in the 1810 and 1820 censuses reinforce the impressions conveyed by the Catholic church records. Roughly eighty to ninety percent of all Saint-Domingue refugees remained in the Crescent City in the decades immediately following their arrival in Louisiana.

Table II
Demographic Distribution of Saint-Domingue Refugees
New Orleans and Louisiana's Rural Parishes
1803-1830

Census Reports, 1810-1820

Location	Pct.
New Orleans	78
Rural Parishes	22

Church Records, 1803-1830

Location	Pct.
New Orleans	93
Rural Parishes	07

Most of the rural refugees initially tended to congregate in two areas—St. Martin Parish, which then also contained present-day Lafayette and Vermilion parishes, and the French-speaking river parishes, from Pointe Coupée in the north to St. James Parish in the south. (See below, Table III.) Many were merchants evidently lured to embryonic towns of the hinterlands by the region's emerging sugar economy. An overwhelming majority (eighty-five percent) of these individuals were natives of Saint-Domingue who had migrated from Cuba to New Orleans in 1809. (See below, Table IV.) Approximately seven percent of the refugees were born at either Cuba or Jamaica, where their parents first sought refuge from the black revolution. Most (sixty-four percent) were young men. (See below, Table V.) All of the refugees listed in Louisiana's published early nineteenth-century church records were white. Contemporary civil records for southwestern Louisiana also make no mention of free persons of color among the refugees. The presence of French Antillian-born, Creole-speaking slaves can only be surmised by the existence of small pockets of black Creole-speakers in St. Martin and Assumption parishes. Identification of slaves born in the sugar islands is difficult because of the absence of published ecclesiastical slave registers, the tendency of slave vendors to conceal the Caribbean origin of their human chattel, and by the failure of the 1850 census, the first to identify all counted individuals by name, to identify the birthplace of enumerated slaves. In the absence of such data, positive determination of the Creole dialect's origins (white or black refugees, or even independent, indigenous development) and means of transmission is virtually impossible.

Table III
Saint-Domingue Refugees
Appearing in Ecclesiastical Records
Louisiana, 1803-1830

	No.	Pct.
Southwest Louisiana	35	40.5
St. Landry Parish	7	
St. Martin Parish	26	
St. Mary Parish	2	
River Parishes	42	48.0
Ascension Parish	8	
East Baton Rouge Parish	11	
Iberville Parish	5	
Pointe Coupée Parish	5	
St. James Parish	13	
Lafourche Basin	9	10.5
Assumption Parish	5	
Lafourche Parish	2	
Terrebonne Parish	1	
Unknown	1	
North Louisiana	1	1.0
Natchitoches Parish	1	
Total Refugees	87	

Table IV
Birthplaces of Rural Refugees

	Southwest Louisiana	River Parishes	Lafourche/ Terrebonne	North Louisiana	Pct.
St. Domingue	24	41	8	1	85
Cuba	2	1	1	0	5
Pennsylvania	3	0	0	0	3
Jamaica	2	0	0	0	2
Maryland	2	0	0	0	2
Guadeloupe	1	0	0	0	1
Martinique	1	0	0	0	1

Table V
Composition of the Rural Refugees
by Gender

Sex	No.	Pct.
Male	56	64
Female	31	36

Despite its deficiencies regarding slaves, the 1850 census sheds considerable light regarding the fate of the free rural refugees, both white and black. Though it enjoyed broader geographic distribution than in the first decades of the nineteenth century, the rural refugee community remained small, overwhelmingly white, and poor. Most of its gainfully employed members remained farmers and artisans catering to the agricultural sector, though they counted a few professionals among their number. Its racial and gender characteristics, however, changed slightly over the years, as women increased in number and as a few free persons of color began to take their first tentative steps toward the countryside. The census lists only 112 natives of the French Antilles in the rural parishes. Nearly half (forty-eight percent) of these individuals were female, while eighty-nine of them (seventy-nine percent) were white. Refugees in the twenty-five free black households were overwhelmingly mulatto (eighty-eight percent). These free persons of color were concentrated in Jefferson Parish (twelve households), with a few individuals scattered about the southern half of the state: Iberville (one household), Plaquemines (four households), Pointe Coupée (one household), Rapides (one household), St. Bernard (one household), St. Landry (four households), and St. Tammany (one household). Forty-seven percent of all rural refugee households owned no real estate in 1850; seventy-five percent of all free black refugees owned no real property. Approximately twenty-three percent of all rural refugees owned more than $1500 in real property, with a small number of them counted among the economic elite in their respective parishes. Twelve refugees were legitimate planters, owning at least $10,000 in real estate. One of these refugee planters, Manuel Britton (probably Breton), was a Cuban-born merchant residing in Pointe Coupée Parish. Six of refugee planters owned at least $50,000 in real property, the wealthiest, P.M. Lapice of St. James Parish, claiming $150,000 in prime farmland. As one would expect, the refugee planters were concentrated in riverbottom parishes—Assumption (3), Ascension (1), Jefferson (1), Madison (1), Natchitoches (3), Pointe Coupée (1), St. James (1), and St. Landry (1).

Many of those who prospered were not among the first wave of island immigrants to venture into the country parishes. Census lists suggest, and church records verify, that many of the first refugees to wander into the countryside died untimely deaths, usually falling victim to myriad endemic diseases. Others appear to have eventually returned to New Orleans after failed attempts at farming. These medical and economic casualties were replaced by a small, but persistent trickle of refugees from New Orleans. The latter refugees, already acclimated to the Louisiana climate, tended to remain in the countryside. But, as in the early nineteenth century, nearly nine-tenths of French Antilles natives continued to reside in New Orleans, primarily in the First Municipality (the Vieux Carré)[4] and the Third Municipality (Faubourg Marigny)[5] which boasted fifty-seven and thirty-one percent of the refugees respectively. (See below, Table VI.)

Table VI
Distribution of French Antilles Natives in the 1850 Census of Louisiana

Parish	Hhds 858	Pct.	Persons 1212	Pct.
Ascension	5	1	9	1
Assumption	3	0	4	0
Avoyelles	1	0	2	0
E. Baton Rouge	0	0	0	0
W. Baton Rouge	2	0	2	0
Bienville	0	0	0	0
Bossier	0	0	0	0
Caddo	0	0	0	0
Calcasieu	0	0	0	0
Caldwell	0	0	0	0
Carroll	1	0	1	0
Catahoula	0	0	0	0

[4]The present-day French Quarter.

[5]The area of New Orleans immediately downstream from the French Quarter.

Parish	Hhds	Pct.	Persons	Pct.
Claiborne	1	0	1	0
Concordia	1	0	1	0
DeSoto	0	0	0	0
E. Feliciana	0	0	0	0
W. Feliciana	0	0	0	0
Franklin	0	0	0	0
Iberville	3	0	3	0
Jackson	0	0	0	0
Jefferson	26	0	31	3
Lafayette	0	0	0	0
Lafourche	2	0	2	0
Livingston	0	0	0	0
Madison	1	0	1	0
Morehouse	0	0	0	0
Natchitoches	6	1	7	1
Orleans (rural)	9	1	12	1
1st Municipality	487	57	690	57
2nd Municipality	15	2	25	2
3rd Municipality	258	30	373	31
Ouachita	1	0	2	0
Plaquemines	6	1	6	0
Pointe Coupée	3	0	3	0
Rapides	1	0	1	0
Sabine	0	0	0	0
St. Bernard	7	1	12	1
St. Charles	0	0	0	0
St. Helena	0	0	0	0
St. James	7	1	12	1
St. John	1	0	1	0
St. Landry	8	1	8	1
St. Martin	0	0	0	0
St. Mary	1	0	1	0
St. Tammany	2	0	2	0
Tensas	0	0	0	0
Terrebonne	0	0	0	0
Union	0	0	0	0
Vermilion	0	0	0	0

The transient nature of the first rural refugees diminished the group's social, cultural, and demographic impact on rural French Louisiana's general population. The newcomers' illusory presence was compounded by the tendency of many island immigrants to marry outside their group. This is particularly true of the first refugees to relocate in the country parishes after 1809. Fifty percent of these individuals married Louisiana Creoles or Acadians, and an additional twenty-one percent married French immigrants. (See below, Table VII.)

This trend continued throughout the antebellum period, and the 1850 census indicates that only eight percent of all refugees remaining in Louisiana had a refugee spouse.

Table VII
Spouses of Rural Saint-Domingue Refugees
1803-1830

	No.	Pct.
Creole (Louisiana)	28	40
French Immigrant	15	21
St. Domingue refugee	12	17
Acadian	7	10
Anglo-American	5	7
Isleño	1	1
English	1	1
Free Woman of Color	1	1

The Antillian refugees also tended to blend into their new economic surroundings. Refugee men, both black and white, tended to remain mostly farmers, artisans catering to the needs of the agricultural community, and day-laborers. But emotionally and physically drained by their flight from Saint-Domingue, their heroic attempt to reestablish their way of life in Cuba, and by their second forcible dispersal at the hands of their reluctant hosts,[6] most of these farmers remained poor, owning little or no real estate. Ninety-eight of the one hundred and twelve rural refugees (87.5 percent) owned less than $500.00 in real property. Those fortunate enough to acquire farms generally remained only moderately prosperous, though three refugees ascended to lofty economic heights in both Assumption and Natchitoches parishes. These agriculturalists were complemented by a small coterie of professionals, including physicians, teachers, and attorneys.

Table VIII
Professions of Rural Refugees, 1850

	No.	Pct.
Accountant	1	2
Butcher	1	2

[6]See below, pages 1-113.

	No.	Pct.
Carpenter	6	13
Cigar maker	2	4
Clergy	1	2
Clerk	1	2
Cooper	1	2
Doctor	5	11
Engineer	1	2
Farmer	12	27
Fisherman	3	7
Laborer	3	7
Lawyer	2	4
Merchant	2	4
Speculator	1	2
Tailor	1	2
Teacher	2	4

Table IX
Birthplaces of the Refugees, 1850

	No.	Pct.
Saint-Domingue	66	58.92
Cuba	20	17.86
Martinique	15	13.39
Jamaica	4	3.57
West Indies	4	3.57
Guadeloupe	3	2.67

The integration of the rural Antilles refugees stands in stark contrast to the their urban haven along the Mississippi River. Though living in socially and racially integrated neighborhoods which, like those of the countryside, threatened to overwhelm them, the Saint-Domingue refugees appear to have been far more culturally and linguistically resilient than their country cousins. Their ethnic persistence is due in part to the social network that they appear to have established in the Crescent City's First and Third Municipalities. Refugee families, often allied by intermarriage in the early nineteenth century, often resided in proximity to one another, forming homogeneous clusters in culturally, linguistically and racially heterogeneous neighborhoods. Many urban men kept alive their economic ties to the islands through their employment in New Orleans mercantile houses. Such professional contacts appear to have kept alive the refugees' long-cherished hope of returning to the islands, and, as the 1850 census strongly suggests,[7] many Saint-Domingue and Martinique natives appear to have returned to the birthplaces in sporadic, but consistently unsuccessful, attempts to reclaim their families' estates. These failed resettlement attempts diminished, but never fully extinguished, the smouldering embers of island identity in the New Orleans area. Many early twentieth-century New Orleans Creoles of refugee ancestry still cherished portraits of refugee ancestors, still attended the French Opera, and still considered themselves a people set apart from their neighbors by culture, language and class.[8] For their now fully assimilated country cousins, however, the refugee influx was a distant and largely forgotten episode in their oral tradition.[9]

[7]The ages and birthplaces of many Caribbean natives in the 1850 census of Louisiana indicate that numerous refugee families attempted unsuccessfully to reestablish themselves in the islands at least once following the end of the Haitian revolution.

[8]See Leonard V. Huber, *Creole Collage: Reflections on the Colorful Customs of Latter-Day New Orleans Creoles* (Lafayette, La., 1980), *passim*.

[9]Only the Domengeaux family of southwestern Louisiana appears to have maintained any oral account of the influx. The Domengeaux tradition maintains that the widowed head of the family fled Saint-Domingue with her young son in order to avoid becoming Toussaint L'Ouverture's mistress.

The Road to Louisiana

The Saint-Domingue Refugees
1792-1809

From La Tortue to La Louisiane:
An Unfathomed Legacy

by Thomas Fiehrer

After biological and social reproduction, migration is undoubtedly the most characteristic fact of human existence. Migration is the motor of social change and the leaven of culture. It is the wild card of politics and the handmaiden of history. The peopling of North America during the past five centuries makes this all too obvious, though not all sources of migration to that fortunate continent have been treated by demographers. Some immigrant groups are known only to themselves—if that. Others—the American Irish and the Canadian French, for example—are studied in minute detail. For many periodic migrations, the push in migratory flow (what motivates it) and the pull (what directs it to specific destinations—chain migration by kin-group, for example) are only vaguely known.[1]

Among American cities, New Orleans, with its fertile hinterland and booming nineteenth-century port (whose commerce in Jacksonian times outstripped even New York's), was the recipient of nearly all major migratory movements to North America: French, Spanish, British Isles, German, Italian (Sicilian), Yugoslav, Latin American, Canadian, and of course African. Internally, New Orleans always attracted commercial adventurers from New England and New York.

In the early nineteenth century, prior to mass European migration to Canada, the United States, Argentina and Brazil, a number of major uprootings occurred within the Americas. The Acadian diaspora or "grand dérangement" that accompanied the Seven Years War (1756-1763) was one of the largest human displacements to that time. It sent many thousands of French colonial people out of Nova Scotia and back to maritime France, to the eastern seaboard, the Gulf Coast and as far south as Haiti and Guiana. The stock cliché has it that the bulk of that long

---

[1]A succinct view of contemporary Caribbean migration is in Orlando Patterson, "Migration in Caribbean Societies," in William H. McNeill and Ruth S. Adams, eds., *Migration: Patterns and Policies* (Bloomington, Ind., 1978), pp. 106-145.

1

wandering population eventually found haven in rural South Louisiana, though the exact destiny of a large proportion of exiled Acadians is far from certain.[2]

Two decades later, another French colonial population found itself involuntarily on the move. Just after the American Revolution, settler/planters were forced from the Windward Islands by the British navy, to resettle in Trinidad, a neglected Spanish territory off Venezuela.[3] Soon thereafter, the French Revolution shook the foundations of Western Europe and reverberated to the West Indies, whence the inhabitants of Saint-Domingue, France's colonial jewel, got themselves to Cuba, Jamaica, the United States and Europe. Eventually Cuba and Louisiana wound up with the lion's share of Saint-Domingue's dispossessed. And thereby hangs our tale.

An abiding curiosity of American local and national history is that the details and effects of this last development—one of arguable significance nationwide, and one of major consequences in Louisiana's formative experience—has remained buried until recently in the recesses of the collective unconscious. During the lengthy process of the French Revolution, the movement of colonial settlers to the United States mainland profoundly altered the demography and culture of the Lower Mississippi watershed. While it is generally known that many of the salient personalities of early nineteenth-century New Orleans society began their careers in Saint-Domingue or Cuba, no systematic assessment of the complex effects of the diffusion of French Caribbean peoples throughout the region has as yet appeared. This phenomenon, it seems, simply fell between the cracks of Haitian historiography (the whereabouts of former white colonials were of minimal interest), accounts of the French Revolution (which focus essentially on the metropole), and popular works on the Mississippi Valley (whose authors saw nothing special in it).

We might barely imagine, in view of Haiti's perennial political

---

[2]Carl Brasseaux, *The Founding of New Acadia: The Beginnings of Acadian Life in Louisiana, 1765-1803* (Baton Rouge, 1987), chs. 1 and 2 are the best treatment to date.

[3]Louis de Verteuil, *Trinidad* (London, 1858), pp. 416-423; Bridget Brereton, *Race Relations in Colonial Trinidad* (Cambridge, England, 1979), ch. 34; Linda Newson, *Aboriginal and Spanish Colonial Trinidad* (London, 1976), pp. 183-186.

tragedies or Cuba's long pariah status vis-a-vis the United States, that two short centuries back, those insular societies were the centerpieces of both French and Spanish overseas trade and navigation, and staging areas for expeditions of exploration and settlement that enriched a bewhigged maritime bourgeoisie at home.[4] Nantes and Bordeaux lived from Saint-Domingue's rich estates, while Havana and Santiago breathed life into Barcelona and Seville.

But North America was also involved, first and clandestinely, as a major commercial supplier of both Cuban and Saint-Domingue traders, and an importer of rum and molasses; secondly as a needy ally of France during the American Revolution, which depended for its success upon the deployment of troops from Saint-Domingue. The Comte de Grasse and Rochambeau arrived at the Chesapeake in August of 1781.[5] Simultaneously, Cuban troops attacked the British in West Florida, as Spanish Governor Bernardo de Gálvez supplied George Washington with cannon and other hardware via the Mississippi. Consequent American triumphs indirectly encouraged the popular struggles in France, so that by 1792, Saint-Domingue's insurgent slaves were about to demolish the structure that had absorbed two-thirds of French foreign commercial interests.[6] Cuba then, would be the initial recipient of many thousands of fleeing French merchants and planters. Once again, propinquity was destiny.

The shock waves of the French Revolution were widely felt. From Paris they radiated out to all Europe, and from Saint-Domingue they shook the planter communities of the Old South and Spanish America, even reaching the remote post of Natchitoches, far up Louisiana's Red River.[7] French colonials

[4]For a case study of official U.S. complicity in the underdevelopment of Haiti between the Wars, see Thomas Fiehrer, "Political Violence in the Periphery: The Haitian Massacre," *Race and Class*, XXXII (1990), 1-22.

[5]Claude Manceron, *The Wind from America, 1778-1781* (New York, 1978), pp. 435-515, *passim*.

[6]Eric Wolf, *Europe and the People Without History* (Berkeley, 1982), p. 151.

[7]Thomas Fiehrer, "Ça ira et Carmagnole: les tentatives espagnoles pour refrener le mouvement révolutionnaire à la Louisiane, 1789-1803," in Danielle Begot, ed., *Révolution et contre-révolution dans le monde créole* (Basse-terre, Guadeloupe, [forthcoming]).

fled in various directions—to Europe, to the American East
Coast, to Jamaica (with the British evacuation), and to nearby
Baracoa and Santiago de Cuba. The latter were the largest single
concentrations of Saint-Domingue refugees. In the course of the
next fifteen years or so, about half of these wound up sailing to
New Orleans. By 1815, well over 11,000 refugees (that we know
of) had regrouped there from disparate points in Europe and the
Americas.[8]

This sketch is actually the last chapter of a tale that begins far
back in the mists of early French and Portuguese experience
on the west coast of Africa, in the basins of the Congo and
Senegal rivers. There, through the course of the sixteenth and
seventeenth centuries, many European groups sought slaves and
mineral wealth to trade in Europe and the Americas. In time a
"contact" or elementary pidgin language based on fragments of
Portuguese, French and African languages emerged in trading
posts and aboard ship.[9] Known as Crioullo or Creole, it diversified
into a complete language as it diffused from the Indian Ocean to
the Cape Verdes to Senegal, and from the Guianas to Martinique,
Saint-Domingue and New Orleans—a sort of lingua franca of
the South Atlantic, binding the French maritime world together
across great expanses of land and sea.[10] The carriers of the Creole
language, from the Indian Ocean to the recesses of Louisiana,
were a correspondingly new people—the product of trade contacts
among three continents, and the vanguard of the French empire
in the tropics. (One of these, Jean-Baptiste Pointe du Sable, born
in Saint-Domingue about 1750, was reputedly the founder of

[8]Paul Lachance and Thomas Fiehrer, "Effects of the French Revolution in Louisiana,"
(working paper).

[9]Philip Curtin, *Economic Change in Pre-Colonial Africa: Senegambia in the Era of the
Slave Trade* (Madison, Wis., 1975), pp. 117-122; also the extraordinary research in Joseph Miller, *Way of Death: Merchant Capitalism and the Angola Slave Trade, 1730-
1830*; André Villard, *Histoire du Sénégal* (Dakar, 1943), pp. 62-66; Paul Gaffarel, *Le
Sénégal* (Paris, 1890), pp. 71-82.

[10]Alexander Hull, "Evidence for the Original Unity of North American French Dialects,"
Revue de Louisiane, III (1974), pp. 59-70; Hull, "Creole," in *Encyclopedia of Southern
Culture* (Chapel Hill, 1989), pp. 770-771.

Chicago; another, Alexandre Dumas, was born there in 1762.) A French-Indian-African race was in the making throughout the seventeenth century, from Canada, to the Mississippi to the West Indies.[11] Because of the thinly dispersed character of French overseas settlement, this people, vaguely known as Creoles, was never fully acknowledged — in either Europe or America—as a distinct ethno-cultural entity, whose very existence was owed to the overseas expansion of the French state.[12]

Thus, though France only acquired Saint-Domingue toward the end of the seventeenth century, island society was already old in the sense that its sources reached far back to first French encounters in Africa and early Huguenot attempts to settle Brazil and Florida.[13] When French imperial interests in Africa and the Caribbean were violently set back by the Revolution, as represented in the last years of Saint-Domingue, the consequent out-migrations further dispersed the Creole society into two, much larger populations (Cuba and the United States), from which it has been difficult to extract.

Three points in tandem, then, require reiteration before considering the outlines of Saint-Domingue's development: first, Saint-Domingue was an old society in 1789. Settlements further south, in the lesser Antilles, were simply removed either westward to Trinidad, or northward to Hispañola, through the course of the eighteenth century, following British aggression in Grenada and other islands, and the decline of Martinique, the crucible of French Creole culture in the Caribbean.[14] Second, we

---

[11]Gayatri Spivak, "Race Before Racism: The Disappearance of the American," *Plantation Society in the Americas*, III, no. 2 (1992), 100-115; Patricia Woods, *French-Indian Relations on the Southern Frontier, 1699-1762* (Ann Arbor, Mich., 1980), ch. 3.

[12]Roger Mercier, "L'Amérique et les Américains dans 'l'Histoire des deux Indes' de l'Abbé Raynal," *Revue Française d'Histoire d'Outre-Mer*, LXV (1978), No. 240, 309-323.

[13]A splendid, comprehensive, though brief account is in Philip P. Boucher, *Les Nouvelles Frances: French in America, 1500-1815, An Imperial Perspective* (Providence, R.I., 1989); see especially pp. 74-82, 85-96, 98-104.

[14]Robert Louis Stein, *The French Slave Trade in the Eighteenth Century: An Old Regime Business* (Madison, Wis., 1979), pp. 32-33; Dale W. Tomich, *Slavery in the Circuit of Sugar: Martinique and the World Economy, 1830-1848* (Baltimore, 1990), chs. 1-2.

note that the antiquity and eventual complexity and maturing of the Creole language testify to the existence of a language community dispersed over an immense space, linked by sailing ships, and sharing a common life and reference to core cultural assets derived from various regions of France, and Africa—east and west.[15] Though the standard works on the early French Caribbean do not forthrightly say as much, they do imply the presence of a new ethnos, a new Atlantic people, in the dramatic activities of the age of piracy.[16] Third, we ought not assume that the Saint-Domingue migrations (as they affect Louisiana) were mere random occurrences. The United States government did not favorably view the ingress of "foreign" slaveholding people into its newly acquired territory The refugees sought asylum in Louisiana because many had contacts there dating back to the founding of the Gulf Coast colony, which was long sustained by the island's resources. In ominous tones, Pierre Le Moyne d'Iberville remarked to himself: "I departed Léogane [then capital of Saint-Domingue] on December 31, 1698, at nine p.m." to establish a post at the Gulf Coast.[17] Sauvolle recounts how desperately dependent upon supplies from Saint Domingue was the French military garrison hanging on through its first season at present-day Ocean Springs, Miss.[18] From that fateful point, Louisiana

---

[15]Julien LaFontant, *France and the Black Experience* (Baltimore, n.d.); Alexander Hull, "The Origins of New World French Phonology," *Word*, XXIV (1968), 255-269

[16]References are found throughout these classic works: François Joachim Duport Du-tertre, *Histoire des conjurations, conspirations et révolutions célebres, tant anciennes que modernes* (Paris, 1762); Jean-Baptiste Labat, *Nouveau voyage aux isles de L'Amérique, contenant l'histoire naturelle de ces pays, l'origine, les moeurs, la religion et le gouverne-ment des habitans anciens et modernes, les guerres et les événemens singuliers qui y sont arrivez . . .*, 6 vols. (Paris, 1724), Guillaume-Thomas-François Raynal, *Histoire philoso-phique et politique des établissemens et du commece des Européens dans les deux Indes*, 9 vols., 2nd ed. (Avignon, 1786); Jean Meyer, *Histoire du sucre* (Paris, 1989), pp. 51-63.

[17]His objective required three voyages. See Carl Brasseaux, trans. and ed., *A Compara-tive View of French Louisiana, 1699 and 1762*, 2nd ed. (Lafayette, La., 1980), p. 11.

[18]*The Journal of Sauvole: Historical Journal of the Establishment of the French in Loui-siana*. ed., Jay Higginbotham (Mobile, Ala., 1969), pp. 30-33, 56. The dimensions of Louisiana's early rice and lumber trade with Martinique and Saint-Domingue may be gauged from Bill Barron, ed., *The Vaudreuil Papers (1743-1753)* (New Orleans, 1975), pp. 171-175, 200-201, 253-256, 391-392.

remained intimately tied through trade, communication and migration to her parent colony. Consequently, it is the exceptional character of Saint-Domingue society—a composite and synthesis of elements accumulated from pre-colonial Africa, from the indigenous West Indies, and from distinct French regions—that accounts in large measure for Louisiana's celebrated cultural singularity.

Saint-Domingue gave birth to Louisiana and sustained her to maturation. In her own dotage—as represented in the early nineteenth century migrations—Saint-Domingue sought refuge with a close branch of the Creole family, and in her debility ironically reinforced local society's distinctive character, prolonging the life cycle of the French Creole world, whose remnants—the "forgotten people" of South Louisiana—mainstream America still finds inscrutable.

Seaborne trans-frontiersmen, to borrow Franklin Knight's image, moved gradually from Jeremy Deschamps' informal "colony" on Tortuga to the adjacent country around Port-de-Paix in Spanish-controlled northwestern Hispañola through the last decades of the seventeenth century, as buccaneering gave way to commercial agriculture and stock raising throughout the Caribbean.[19] The area did not become a formal French possession until the Treaty of Ryswick in 1697, but from that date until the demise of colonial rule in 1803, population growth was steady, particularly in slaves. The French court stimulated settlement with propaganda advertising the West Indies as salubrious and fertile. By the early eighteenth century, migration to the lesser French Antilles and Guiana waned, as Europeans and other West Indians drifted in greater numbers toward the magnet of teeming ports, markets, and raucous new settlements that sprang up throughout the island.[20]

[19]Franklin Knight, *The Caribbean: The Genesis of a Fragmented Nationalism* (New York, 1978), pp. 68, 79.

[20]Gabriel Debien and Marcel Chatillon, "La propagande imprimée pour les plantations des Antilles au XVIIIe siècle," unpublished manuscript, pp. 33-34.

By the mid-eighteenth century, large sections of Saint-Domingue were under production in units of varying sizes, depending on rainfall, topography, and available capital. Sugar, cotton, tobacco, indigo, cacao, and coffee estates dotted the plateaux, the valley of the Artibonite, and the northern plain. A booming agro-export economy, tied together by a series of small coastal trading stations that linked the irregular coasts, exchanged materials (legally) with Bordeaux, La Rochelle, Nantes, and Marseilles, via a series of state-protected monopolies.[21] Timber, barrel staves, furs, and rice arrived from Louisiana, and from France came crude machine parts, housewares, hardwares, and luxuries, including the ubiquitous clarets of Bordeaux. So specialized and differentiated was the emergent colonial economy that Cap-Français (today Cap-Haïtien), the leading urban center, could support French theatre, learned societies, an active press, European entertainments, a wide range of public merriments, such as *fêtes, bals masques, charivaris,* and a stream of distinguished "tourists."[22]

The slave war that erupted against the colonists and foreign armies in 1792 was cataclysmic in its affront to the reigning mode of tropical production and its corresponding social paradigm. The dramatic revolt generated swift and stern reaction among other slaveholding societies, including the American South. [23]

The outlines of Saint-Domingue's colonial order were already fixed by the end of the seventeenth century, though the mode of production would soon absorb resources and manpower

---

[21]Gérard Mentor Laurent, *Contribution à l'histoire de Saint-Domingue* (Port-au-Prince, 1971), pp. 11-41, *passim.*

[22]Jean Fouchard, *Plaisirs de Saint-Domingue* (Port-au-Prince, 1955), pp. 80-88; Pierre de Vaissière, *Saint-Domingue: Société et la vie créole sous l'ancien régime, 1629-1789* (Paris, 1909), p. 280; Robert Cornevin, *Le Théâtre haïtiene des origines à nos jours* (Montreal, 1973), p. 39. M. L. E. Moreau de Saint-Méry, *Description . . . ,* 2 vols. (Paris, 1875), II, 200-208, lists even members of the royal families of Europe.

[23]Alfred Hunt, *Haiti's Influence on Antebellum America: Slumbering Volcano in the Carribean* (Baton Rouge, 1987).

in an unprecedented fashion in response to far-off demand. It is well to be mindful that this was a society of agriculturists, whose productivity drew forth from Europe and elsewhere the predictable range of social predators. Early census data and accounts of French chroniclers indicate, early on, the prominence of indigo to the exclusion of later, more profitable cotton, sugar, and coffee.[24] Indigo in the years 1688 through 1770 was in stiff competition with the crop of San Salvador (Guatemala) and South Carolina; the relief later occasioned by Saint-Domingue's entry into the sugar and coffee markets, which were closely interrelated on the consumption end,[25] can be imagined.

The militaristic and defensive character of the society reveals its frontier uncertainties, which in time shifted in focus from external threats (freebooters) to internal ones (Africans). Perhaps the tone was set by the striking evidence of international rivalry and brutality in the siege of Port-de-Paix in 1695, wherein no group was spared. Contradictions embedded in the caste hierarchy posed by the *Code Noir* are revealed in the arming of black and mulatto militiamen, a practice with fatal implications for the revolutionary years that lay ahead.[26]

By 1789, over 800 plantations, excluding many small *habitations* in the rugged south, were in the hands of *grands blancs*—the rich. In addition, there were 2,000 *petits blancs,* or middle class producers of coffee, 700 growers of cotton and over 3,000 small growers of indigo.[27] The island was the world's main supplier of coffee and exported more sugar than all the

[24]John G. Clark, *La Rochelle and the Atlantic Economy* (Baltimore, 1981), pp. 160-163, indicates the shift to sugar, coffee and cotton after the 1730s.

[25]Sidney Mintz, *Sweetness and Power: The Place of Sugar in Modern History* (New York, 1985), pp. 131, 157; Meyer, *Histoire du sucre*, pp. 77-90.

[26]Winston De Ville, ed., *Saint-Domingue: Census Records and Military Lists, 1688-1720* (Ville Platte, La., 1987).

[27]Michel-Rolph Trouillot, "Coffee, Color and Slavery in Eighteenth-Century Saint-Domingue," *Review*, V (1980), 331-388; M. L. E. Moreau de Saint-Méry, *Description topographique, physique, civile, politique et historique de la partie française de l'isle Saint-Domingue* (Philadelphia, 1797-1798), I, 304-311. The latter is indisputably the key colonial text. A short abridgment and translation is Ivor Spencer, *A Civilization That Perished: The Last Years of White Colonial Rule in Haiti* (Lanham, 1985).

British West Indies combined. Though published sources are not
altogether credible, it is generally supposed that by the period
of the French Revolution the colony had 450,000 or more slaves;
40-45,000 whites, including a large transient population; and at
least 32,000 *affranchis,* or freedmen, known originally as *sang-
mêlés,* and later as *gens-de-couleur libres,* a class that was not
considered quite white, but surely was not slave.[28]

The colony was administrated in three units, each
corresponding roughly to distinct ecological conditions and
productive emphases. All three possessed rich sugar plains,
surrounded by mountainous, less accessible terrain.   The
earliest established zone, the *plaine du nord,* had the largest,
most prosperous estates. Less than a fourth of the total area, it
held two-fifths of all whites and about a third of all slaves.[29] The
affranchis were less conspicuous here. The central or western
department was least developed, while the south came under
production last. The south was, unlike the Artibonite and the
north, suited to small-scale units. On the transit margins of the
colony, it likewise became a stronghold of the marginal people,
the *affranchis* whose limited wealth restricted them to cheaper,
smaller, less accessible lands. Some 6,000 free colored came
to control this area after the 1770s, developing a monopoly of
coffee production—an important fact in the coming civil war and
revolution, with implications for a succeeding century of local
politics.

The terrain inhibited road construction, forcing urbanization
to the south coast, whose many small ports ushered regional
products to markets and bound the region together through a
variety of light crafts. In the north, at Le Cap, were moored
large vessels from French Atlantic ports, from Havana, New
Orleans, and the Spanish Main; the remaining French islands
and soon the United States were added to the trade. The
maritime network was the colonial lifeline, since despite
the large individual fortunes accumulated, few goods were
produced locally that could not be more efficiently imported, to

[28]Moreau, *Description,* I, 83-89; Charles Frostin, *Les Révoltes blanches à Saint-Domingue
aux XVIIe et XVIIIe siècles (Haiti avant 1789)* (Paris, 1975), p. 28.

[29]David Nicholls, *Economic Dependence and Political Autonomy: The Haitian Experience*
(Montreal, 1974), p. 52.

the delight of metropolitan cartels and the ultimate undoing of Creole loyalty to the old regime's power structure.[30]

Saint-Domingue's population growth, best viewed in relation to similar, contemporaneous societies, shows a precipitous increase in the slave traffic to the island after 1740, followed by substantial French immigration; that is, a veritable population explosion. The relatively small proportion of *sang-mêlés* and the disproportionate number of males over females were ratios that altered dramatically toward balance during the succeeding half of the eighteenth century, but soon disappeared into folklore, absorbed by isolated maroon bands and rural concubinage.[31] Families in the island and in Louisiana shared numerous kin and business networks for a century and a half, but the reconstruction of those connections, hampered by the improbable spellings of surnames in parish and military records (among others), requires tedious searches to establish. Certain surnames do persist from the early settlement era through the Revolution and diaspora to the New Orleans area, but clear lineages are seldom left by so much successive movement.

After a century and a half of French control, Saint-Domingue's population took the form of an uneven triangle of power distribution, with the rich and officialdom at the top, the *affranchis* at one corner and the modest whites at the other. Excluded, from political participation at least, were the over half-million slaves. The relative fixity of individual inclusion in these four groups is not clear. Evidence—contemporary accounts, official reports, personal correspondence—is contradictory. The basic organic law theoretically afforded protection to each group from any of the others. The *Code Noir* (1685), article 59, conferred full citizenship on the *affranchis,* and many of them enjoyed the benefits of the social system, yet they complained of discriminatory policies and the occasional *ad hoc* laws that

[30]Laurent, *Contribution*, pp. 74-75; Alex Dupuy, "French Merchant Capital and Slavery in Saint-Domingue," *Latin American Perspectives*, XII (1985), 77-102. David Geggus, "The Major Port Towns of Saint-Domingue in the Late Eighteenth Century," in Peggy Liss and Franklin Knight, eds., *Atlantic Port Cities* (Knoxville, 1990), is invaluable.

[31]Jack D. Forbes, *Black Africans and Native Americans: Color, Race and Caste in the Evolution of Red-Black Peoples* (New York, 1988), pp. 53-54, 90, 185, 237.

impeded their entry into marriages, professions, or economic alliances of their choosing. There is evidence that the voluntary altering of individual status, implying manipulation of ethnic or racial identity, was not uncommon—that slaves could become *affranchis,* who could later convert into *petits blancs,* and these become *grands blancs,* despite the small scale of the society and its intimate, semi-feudal character. It was no casual endeavor to alter one's family history, but given the movement of peoples throughout the region and the chaos, venality, and materialism that reigned in a volatile tropical frontier, money doubtless bleached some pedigrees, as was frequent in nearby Cuba.

Some whites were sanctioned for their affinity to *affranchis* and still others disabled by marriages or other intimate connections to colored Creole families.[32] Many *petits blancs* took colored or black mistresses and/or wives; even high-ranking officials and notables patronized their colored offspring and occasionally sought to marry non-white concubines. Those with the means to arrange a stint in Europe for their colored daughters found it possible to marry them into white families, whence they lost their colonial identity.[33] Given the short lifespan of the colony, many *affranchis,* perhaps several thousand, achieved crossover status during their lifetimes; and a good number of Africans and black Creoles passed into *affranchi* status. One African-born slave achieved planter status and held a seat in the French Estates General.[34] The race-status-caste configuration was expected formally to correspond to a color spectrum, which it did only in a general way. Inevitably, some "white" Creoles had had non-white ancestry[35] and many free colored people were perceived as

[32]Gabriel Debien, *Les Colons de Saint-Domingue et la révolution* (Paris, 1953), pp. 34-40.

[33]Amélie Domignon de Brettés, unpublished memoir, 1820, p. 58, in the possession of the Count and Countess de Ste. Opportune, Château de Reiul, Reiul-en-Brie, France.

[34]David Geggus, "Racial Equality, Slavery, and Colonial Secession during the Constituent Assembly," *American Historical Review,* XCIV (1989), 1290-1308.

[35]Virginia Domínguez, *White by Definition: Social Classification in Creole Louisiana* (New Brunswick, N.J. 1986), pp. 66-69; Joseph Mossmeier Papers, Record Group 15, Louisiana Historical Center, Louisiana State Museum, New Orleans.

whites once they left the island. Manumitted slaves, like Toussaint L'Ouverture, were sometimes beneficiaries of patronage. Occasionally there were slaves whose prestige or privilege exceeded that of less fortunate *affranchis.*

By the end of colonial rule, the *affranchis,* despite their real grievances, had done well. They owned large portions of the southern region and nearly a third of all land, plus a fourth of the very valuable slaves. The hypothetical *affranchi* was approaching the wealth of the "average" white.[36] The system's volatility lay not with the excluded slaves, but with the aspiring *affranchis,* and more so with the small-holding *petits blancs*— the coffee growers, craftsmen, traders, merchants, and clerks upon whose versatility, ingenuity, thrift, and discipline about half the colonial income depended. Rather limited operators of humble beginnings, these had a smaller stake in slavery, were close to the *affranchis* by common interests and often kinship, and bitterly resented the rich, often absentee class and the metropolitan maritime monopoly. Like their colored allies, their position was exceedingly contradictory. Despite their independence as a socioeconomic group, and their greater attachment to the land and to Creole proto-nationalism, they feared that political independence would remove the only barrier between their interests and complete domination of the country by the reactionary *grands blancs.*[37]

These latter were composed of an indeterminate number, never large, of European administrative personnel, naval officials, military officers, metropolitan merchant-bankers and/or their agents. There was also a coterie of lesser and, rarely, greater nobility thrown in, as the merchant slavocracy of Nantes and other ports extended themselves physically into

---

[36]Moreau, *Description,* II, 1400. J. Saintoyant, *La Colonisation française pendant la Révolution,* 2 vols. (Paris, 1930), I, 280-290.

[37]Frostin, *Les Révoltes,* pp. 282-292, shows how absenteeism, military conscription and a brisk contraband trade with North America all fomented a spirit of "Americanism."

their western holdings for short periods of the year. Though these
grands blancs represented royal authority and garnered surplus
charisma through pre-revolutionary privileges, it is difficult
to assess their political status. The picture is complicated by
the fact of a slave-driven export economy at the infrastructure,
and a liberalizing, but Catholic, absolute monarchy at the
superstructure.[38] For *affranchis* the meaning of "citizenship"
was equally ambiguous and potentially destabilizing in such a
context.[39]

An exploration of the Creole "mind" is a tempting but
perilous endeavor, first because the extant published literature
rarely probes beyond a superficial reference to travellers'
accounts, and second, because the society's heterogeneous
make-up and large proportion of French-born residents cause
its surviving literature to seem a mere extension of European
trends. Actually, the findings of Geggus,[40] Barthélémy, Frostin,
Fouchard and others provide the outlines of a distinctive Creole
consciousness. It is evident that the native-born farmers and
planters nursed a collective, nationalistic picture of their
grievances, and that the large mixed-race population, among
whom were many accomplished individuals, of necessity could
look only to themselves, to their uniquely American origins
and Creole language, for political inspiration. Their role in
precipitating the revolution is *prima facie* evidence of a certain
"Americanism," as many realized that their fortunes were in
their hands alone.[41]

[38]A skillful recent study of a family enterprise during the last years of Saint-Domingue is Jacques Cauna, *Au temps des iles à sucre* (Paris, 1985).

[39]Laurent, *Contribution*, pp. 45-69. A sophisticated exploration of the complex ambivalence of French liberalism in the period of abolition is in Robin Blackburn, *The Overthrow of Colonial Slavery* (London, 1988). A rare glimpse of local society, very disparaging of the free colored, but caustic, revealing, and informed is Roger Norman Buckley, ed., and intro., *The Haitian Journal of Lieutenant Howard, York Hussars, 1796-1798* (Knoxville, Tenn., 1985), pp. 100-110.

[40]Geggus, "Racial Equality, Slavery, and Colonial Secession;" Anthony Gerard Barthélémy, *Le pays en dehors* (Port-au-Prince, 1990).

[41]A.N. Isnard, *Observations sur le principe qui a produit les révolutions de France, de Genève, et de l'Amérique dans le 18ème siècle* (Evreux, 1789).

Given the rapid growth of this tropical entrepôt on the maritime frontiers of the Old World and the inherent instability of institutions in a context of social and technical flux, the Creole mind was not particularly pious nor was it besieged by "intimations of immortality." It was, however, imbued with the conflicting heritage of popular French spiritism and superstition on one hand, and the fashionable mode of enlightened skepticism on the other. The largest sector of the population, the Africans, contributed yet another dimension to the religious ideography of the colony, one that penetrated the spiritual cosmos of white society at least to the level of folklore. In a pre-industrial situation, the political dimensions of popular spirituality ought not be underestimated. The religious vision of the slaves in Saint-Domingue has been ascribed a significant if not key role in the popular revolt that spawned a revolution.[42] Contemporaries did not fail to remark the eccentricities and mystic calamities they perceived as attending the reconstituted religious practices of recently transported Africans. C. Malenfant, among others, allows both vodun (animistic folk belief) and Catholicism a central place in the unfolding of events after 1789.[43] In a contrary, modern view, Eugene Genovese assigns religious messianism only a "fleeting role" in Haiti's revolution—an assumption somewhat removed from the findings of the country's ethnographic literature.[44] Robert Rotberg discloses that *houngans* (voodoo priests) mobilized resistance among some 40,000 slaves in the northern plain, sustaining the revolt until suppressed under Toussaint and

---

[42]Carolyn Fick, *The Making of Haiti: The Saint Domingue Revolution from Below* (Knoxville, Tenn., 1990), pp. 53-71, brings a fresh perspective but emphasises assention over evidence. The key source is Michel Etienne Bescourtilz, *Voyages d'un naturaliste*, 3 vols. (Paris, 1809).

[43]C. Malenfant, *Des colonies et particulièrement de celle de Saint-Domingue* (Paris, 1814), Ch. X. Useful in this connection is Hanns-Albert Steger, *El trasfondo revolucionario del sincretismo criollo* (Cuernavaca, 1972), pp. 38-56; Ivan Debbash, *Couleur et liberté*, 2 vols. (Paris, 1967), I, 113-131.

[44]The essential contemporary work on slave ethnography remains Decourtilz (1829); Eugene D. Genovese, *Roll, Jordan, Roll: The World the Slaves Made* (New York, 1974), p. 28; Eugene D. Genovese, *From Rebellion to Revolution: Afro-American Slave Revolts in the Making of the Modern World* (Baton Rouge, 1979), pp. 55-70, *passim*.

Dessalines.[45] Leslie Manigat explores the conflicting interpretations of the role of voodoos and maroons in the construction of a revolutionary consciousness among the slave masses.[46]

The contemporary, collective psychology of resistance to change from outside imposition is seen by one recent scholar as rooted both in African philosophy and in the highly politicized pattern of slave emancipation in the first decade of the last century.[47] As Alejo Carpentier[48] conveys in his short epic "inside" account of the Revolution, Saint-Domingue was a dynamic, cosmopolitan society, fully open to the currents of the world beyond the Caribbean, having one foot in an African grave and the other in political quicksand.[49]

The *grands blancs* and wealthier Creole planters soon developed a network of interests and needs at variance with those of the monarchy and its monopolistic agents at Le Cap.[50] They paid exorbitant prices to refiners of their *muscovado* (raw brown sugar) at Marseilles and Bordeaux. The Nantes slavers

[45]Robert Rotberg, "Vodun and Politics in Haiti," in Marion Kilson and Robert Rotberg, eds., *The African Diaspora: Interpretive Essays* (Cambridge, Mass., 1975), pp. 434-435. More germane is a series of essays by Henock Trouillot that explores the role of voudou in the revolution in *Revista de historia de América*, No. 67-68 (1969), 103-131; No. 72 (1971), 259-327; No. 73-74 (1972), 75-130.

[46]Leslie Manigat, "The Relationship Between Marronage and Slave Revolts and Revolution in Saint-Domingue/Haiti," in Vera Rubin and Arthur Tuden, eds., *Comparative Perspectives on Slavery in New World Plantation Societies* (New York, 1977), pp. 420-438. The most comprehensive study to date is Jean Fouchard, *Les Marrons de la liberté*(Paris, 1972), especially pp. 453-463.

[47]Barthélémy, *Le pays en dehors*, Ch. 2.

[48]Alejo Carpentier, *El reino de este mundo* (Barcelona, 1967).

[49]Alexander von Humboldt noted that Jamaica possessed a social structure with roughly the same proportions of the three castes as did Saint-Domingue in 1788: 520,000 inhabitants—40,000 whites; 28,000 free coloreds; 452,000 slaves (or eighty-six percent slave). Jamaica in 1787 was ten percent white, four percent free colored, and eighty-six percent slave. *Ensayo Político sobre el reino de la Nueva España* (Paris, 1822), I, 116. But Jamaica did not experience the French Revolution.

[50]Philip Curtin, *The Rise and Fall of the Plantation Complex: Essays in Atlantic History* (Cambridge, 1990), pp. 33-56.

charged them for Africans far in excess of prices paid in neighboring colonies. With succeeding increments to their prosperity, state parasitism and metropolitan extortion intensified. Whether the white revolts of the mid-century or the *coup de grâce* delivered by the French Revolution should be ascribed to Creole nationalism or simple class interest cannot be sorted out here. No Charles Beard has emerged to make the case very strongly, and two authorities—Manigat[51] and Nicholls[52]—disagree. Frostin[53] seems to corroborate Nicholls[54] while Fouchard[55] is ambiguous on this point. The published record, though scant, and largely restricted to the pens of Creole exiles refugeed in Jamaica, Cuba, Louisiana, and the eastern American cities, says little for nostalgia.[56] The few extant diaries, newspapers or other firsthand commentaries hardly suggest a warm attachment or sense of national loss. In contrast, the Spanish American Jesuits exiled in Modena after 1767 virtually created a nationalist historiography and in a number of cases articulated an ideology of Creole nationalism. These clergy generally originated among the *grands blancs* of their respective societies—a curious contrast. Even Moreau de Saint-Méry, a quintessential Creole savant, displayed little affection for his native land, though his encyclopedic knowledge of it implied a certain nationalist perspective.

In the manner of exile Cubans 150 years later, the Saint-Domingue refugees in the United States were constrained to elicit maximum sympathy with dramatic accounts of their ill

---

[51]Leslie Manigat, *Ethnicité, nationalisme, et politique: le cas d'Haïti* (New York, 1976).

[52]David Nicholls, *From Dessalines to Duvalier: Race, Color, and National Independence in Haiti* (Cambridge, 1979), pp. 331-350.

[53]Frostin, *Les Révoltes*, pp. 336-340.

[54]Nicholls, *From Dessalines*, pp. 258-270.

[55]Fouchard, *Les Marrons*, pp. 358-362; Winthrop D. Jordan, *White Over Black: American Attitudes Toward the Negro, 1550-1812* (Chapel Hill, 1968), p . 435.

[56]Gabriel Debien, *Esprit colon et ésprit d'autonomie à Saint-Domingue aux XVIIIe siècle* (Larose, 1954), pp. 22-30.

treatment at the hands of insurrectionists. Both refugee groups effectively sounded the taproots of American ideology and paranoid political style. The former played to the horrors of dismantling the Southern slave regime, while the latter rode the wave of postwar anti-communism. The exiled Jesuits were deft at grinding the anti-colonial axe, fuelled by resentment at bureaucratic-monarchist high-handedness that had abruptly sundered them from their extended families and privileges. Nostalgia for Saint-Domingue was forcibly drowned in a sea of bitterness at the slaves having overturned the relations of power. Whether and how refugees identified with the island is a matter long shrouded in the complexities of their origins, social status at the outbreak of hostilities, and experiences in exile.

Among the refugees were many French-born as well as Creoles of all castes. The accounts of Parham,[57] Domingnon de Brettés,[58] De Vaissière,[59] Cornevin,[60] and Debien[61] to mention only a few, suggest the development of a sort of nativism, nationalism, or Americanism.[62] In the process of forced migration, attitudes toward island society and inter-caste sentiment both underwent change, in a positive direction. But proto-nationalism was generalized throughout the hemisphere's bourgeoisies by the end of the American Revolution. Still, Nicholls, following Frostin and perhaps Bryan Edwards,[63] portrays Creole society as transient, superficially connected to the island through commerce, even isolated from the local social

[57]Althea de Peuch Parham, ed. and trans., *My Odyssey: Experiences of a Young Refugee from Two Revolutions, by a Creole of Saint-Domingue* (Baton Rouge, 1959), pp. 17-19.

[58]Domignon de Brettés, unpublished manuscript, pp. 77-80.

[59]De Vaissière, *Saint-Domingue*, pp. 124-127.

[60]Cornevin, *Le Théâtre*, p. 32.

[61]Debien, *Esprit colon*, pp. 40-50.

[62]David Brion Davis, *The Problem of Slavery in the Age of Revolution, 1770-1823* ((New York, 1975), pp. 184-212.

[63]Bryan Edwards, *A Historical Survey of the French Colony in the Island of St. Domingo* (1797; reprint ed., London, 1801), pp. 177-179.

reality.[64]   The ideological content of Creole nationalism is difficult to assess.   Large numbers of the revolution's refugees (a majority in New Orleans—the single largest grouping by 1810) were native Creoles.   More research will show whether the French-born refugees repatriated in larger proportion than did Creoles.[65]

A brief introductory remark cannot deal coherently with the complex makeup and political tendencies of the caste groups in pre-revolutionary Haiti.   Students of mass movements seek to know what forces account for the hegemony of dominant groups and the manner in which interclass fissures open the way for opposition from below.   Much of French officialdom by 1789 and after struck Creole elites as drenched in liberality, latitudinarian maxims, and sacrilegious nonconformism.   Once in the throes of the colonial situation, the vast majority of French officials, merchants and planters—regardless of status—drifted to the reactionism of group preservation.   Various officials exculpated themselves for laxity in applying the law in conformity with royal intent by reference to the "extraordinary" conditions.   The law met dedicated self-interest at every turn: M. Monnereau's manual on "How to Manage New Negroes" (1765) observed that "I have criticized the Negroes' vices, not because I think they have no virtues, but because I am writing to inform my clients on how to get them to perform the most work."[66]   Despite the weight of evidence brought against the planter Lejeune in 1788 for the torture deaths of several slaves, the sitting magistrate found him impossible to convict.   A sense of the powder keg permeates the intendants' reports after 1776.

Elites, bureaucrats and soldiers knew a good thing when they saw it, but recognized the transitory nature of "el reino de este mundo."   They registered a chilling uneasiness born of antagonistic forces within white society.   Gabriel Debien's

[64]See also François Girod, *La vie quotidienne de la société créole: Saint Domingue au XVIIIe siècle* ((Paris, 1972), pp. 54-67.

[65]This is the impression of Jacques Cauna, in "l'Habitation Clerisse: A Great Estate on Eve of the Haitian Revolution" (unpublished manuscript).

[66]M. Monnereau, *Comment on doit gouverner les nègres nouveaux* (Paris, 1765), pp. v-viii; on slave treatment, pp. 96-98; on coffee, pp. 140-143.

meticulous documentation charts the acquisition and development of many medium and small holdings by *petits blancs* and free colored farmers in the lower Artibonite and rugged south toward the last quarter of the century.[67] Doubtless the enormous personal and family efforts that went into the creation of these well-managed freeholds—the digging of wells, raising of dwellings, and nurturing of a range of delicate plants—by small groups of whites, colored and slaves, generated communities and relations of production at some variance with the industrialized plantation "factories" of the north, with their armies of anonymous slaves and class of grasping, ambitious managers, accountants and overseers.[68]

Saint-Domingue's revolution was an international event. Leaders of the slave revolt had come from all over the island, as well as from Jamaica and the Windward Islands.[69] Though much remains to be done in English to sort out the processes of the succeeding decade, even scarcer are accounts of *la vie quotidienne* from the perspective of the *petits blancs* refugeed in the United States (or in France), as literacy was not their strong suit. The accounts of how Saint-Domingue was swept into the maelstrom of the French Revolution, how civil war debilitated the country, now vulnerable to Spanish and especially British invasion and occupation; how partisans of slavery sought to restore that institution; and how Toussaint's successors forged the first black republic, the second independent American nation, are variously related with selective emphases on contemporary events and world circumstances. Writers such as James,[70]

---

[67]Gabriel Debien, *Etudes antillaises: XVIIIe siècle* (Paris, 1956), pp. 32-55.

[68]A picture of these tensions emerges from reports in Blanche Maurel, ed., *Cahiers des doleances de la colonie de Saint-Domingue pour les états généreaux de 1789* (Paris, 1933).

[69]Eric E. Williams, *Capitalism and Slavery* (New York, 1966), pp. 147, 247; Gabriel Debien, *Plantations et esclaves à Saint-Domingue* (Dakar, 1962), pp. 66-70.

[70]C. L. R. James, *The Black Jacobins: Toussaint L'Ouverture and the San Domingo Revolution* (New York, 1963), pp. 221-230.

Ardouin,[71] Brutus,[72] and Geggus[73] illustrate the multivalent character of the Revolution's historiography—so long silent on the fate of the refugees.

The establishment of a black government in 1804 did not of itself necessitate the emigration of all whites. Toussaint hoped they would remain to forestall economic collapse, and ably coaxed a good number to return. Their efforts at property settlement and indemnifications are fragmentarily preserved in the entirely neglected *Archive de la Greffe* in Cap-Haïtien.

Nearly all whites did eventually choose exile, the majority during the years 1798-1803. They fled in every direction: a few moved eastward to Santo Domingo (the Dominican Republic); others indirectly made their way back to France; others shipped for Savannah, Charleston, Norfolk, Baltimore, Philadelphia and New York. Brillat-Savarin, world renowned advocate and gastronome (1755-1826), encountered Creoles in Manhattan and recalled, "I sat next to a Creole one day at dinner, who had lived two years in New York, and still did not know enough English to be able to ask for bread. I expressed my astonishment at this; 'Bah,' he replied, shrugging his shoulders, 'do you suppose I would ever trouble to learn the language of so dull a race?'"[74] Moreau de Saint-Méry and his brother-in-law, the negrophobe physician Baudry des Lozières, travelled from France to Philadelphia to produce *la Description* . . . among other books. A large group retreated with the British expeditionary force to

[71]Beaubrun Ardouin, *Etudes sur l'histoire d'Haïti,* 2 vols. (Paris, 1853-1860), I, 231.

[72]Edner Brutus, *Révolution dans Saint-Domingue,* 2 vols. (Brussels, n.d.), I, 188-190, 220-270. Some interesting data are presented in Shelby T. McCloy, *The Negro in the French West Indies* (Lexington, Ky., 1966), pp. 51-52, 63-123; the author claims some 4,000-5,000 blacks, mostly West Indians, were in France during the Revolution.

[73]David P. Geggus, *Slavery, War, and Revolution: The British Occupation of Saint-Domingue, 1793-1798* (Oxford, 1982).

[74]Jean-Anthelme Brillat-Savarin, *The Physiology of Taste, or Meditations on Transcendental Gastronomy,* trans. Mary Frances Kennedy Fisher (New York, 1949), p. 67. *Ibid.,* trans. Peter Davies (1925; reprint ed., New York, 1960), p. 291, fn. 1. There is no systematic study of this dispersal on the East Coast. For an example see Hannah Farnham Lee, ed., *Memoir of Pierre Toussaint, Born a Slave in St. Domingo* (Boston, 1854).

Jamaica in 1798, and later found themselves in New Orleans.[75] The largest contingent departed following Leclerc's defeat in 1803 and made for the closest point of refuge across the Windward Passage at Baracoa and Santiago de Cuba, where over 25,000 had settled by 1808.[76] The refugees made a strong impact on the agriculture and artisanry of Cuba's Oriente. They introduced model coffee production units and vastly extended the cultivation of citrus, indigo, tobacco, cacao, cotton, and other crops. Even the later modernization of the sugar industry was due in good part to the technical skill of the refugees.[77] The fall of Saint-Domingue planterdom served to relocate a previously booming commerce in sugar to languishing Cuba. Pérez de la Riva[78] and Jérez Villareal[79] have identified Saint-Dominguais at the center of commercial agricultural expansion in nineteenth-century Oriente.

Their reception was ambivalent at best, though the whites, perhaps a third of the immigrants, were welcomed by officials for their color, skills and capital. Their rapid adaptation and productivity also bred resentment and, despite their political conservatism, many Cubans thought them sympathetic to the excesses of the Revolution. Nor were they completely defenseless; many had served long in the various factional armies and some had fought in the American Revolution. Some,

[75]Philip Wright and Gabriel Debien, *Les Colons de Saint-Domingue passés à la Jamaïca (1792-1835)* (Basse-terre, 1975). Moreau de Saint-Méry's account of "escape" to Philadelphia via Norfolk and Baltimore, with other refugees, sounds less than frantic. Kenneth and Donna Roberts, *Moreau de St. Méry's America Journey (1793-1798)* (Garden City, N.Y., 1947).

[76]Domingnon de Brettés, unpublished manuscript, p. 66; Reynaldo Gonzales and Luc Chessex, "La tumba francesa," *La Révolution et culture*, No. 4 (1966), 26-45, on musical influences of the refugees in eastern Cuba; Moreau, *Description*, I, 44-51, on music and dancing.

[77]Gabriel Debien, "Les Colons de Saint-Domingue réfugiés à Cuba, 1793-1815," *Revista de Indias*, XII (1953), 559-605; XIV (1954), 11-36.

[78]Francisco Pérez de la Riva, *El café: historia de su cultivo y explotación en Cuba* (Havana, 1944), pp. 26-29, 30-42, 91-94; Hipolito Piron, *L'ile de Cuba* (Paris, 1876), pp. 54-56.

[79]Juan Pérez Villareal, *Oriente: Biografía de una provincia* (Havana, 1960), pp. 87-90; Calixto Masó Vásquez, *Historia de Cuba* (Miami, 1976), pp. 109-116, 155.

like the frères Lafitte, took up profitable careers in smuggling and privateering. Spanish-Cuban fear of them seems justified when we consider their deadly siege of British forces at Chalmette, Louisiana, in 1815. Alain Yacou[80] has traced the refugees' sojourn in Cuba and their rude expulsion by the Spanish military in 1808—a direct effect of Napoleon's deposition of Ferdinand VII and Spanish fears of French territorial or other ambitions from the refugees stronghold at Santiago.

From May 1809 to January 1810, shiploads of Saint-Dominguais began arriving from eastern Cuba at New Orleans. The mayor counted 9,059 refugees in all, including 2,731 whites, 3,110 free colored, and 3,226 slaves.[81] Refugees had been entering the territory piecemeal since the onset of troubles in 1791. The total influx doubled the city's population, and most sought immediately to find work or rural properties to resume economic activity. The number who located in the rural south and center of Louisiana cannot be determined without further research, but their presence is indicated in all the sugar parishes and as far out as Natchitoches. Saint Louis received several dozens of refugee families, as did the Gulf Coast. West's Atlas indicates that Saint-Domingue surnames are distributed rather evenly, with no regional concentration.[82] Yet the frequency of spoken Creole in St. Martinville, Napoleonville, Henderson, and other areas may indicate aggregations of refugees.[83] Even today, Creole surnames exceed those of any

[80]Alain Yacou, "L'emigration à Cuba des colons françaises de Saint-Domingue au course de la révolution" (thèse de doctorat, 3e cycle, Université de Bordeaux III, 1975); Anne Perotin-Dumon, "Deux situations révolutionnaires en pays coloniale: la Guadeloupe (1793), Cuba (1809)," *Proceedings of the International Congress of Americanists*, 41st (Mexico City, Mexico, 1976).

[81]Lachance, "The 1809 Immigration," 136-137; Gabriel Debien and René Le Gardeur, "Les Colons de Saint-Domingue réfugiés à la Louisiane (1792-1804)," *Revue de Louisiane*, X, No. 1 (1981), 11-49.

[82]Robert West, *An Atlas of Louisiana Surnames of French and Spanish Origin* (Baton Rouge, 1986).

[83]Ingrid Neumann, "Le créole des blancs en Louisiane," *Etudes Creoles*, VI, No. 2, (1984), 63-78.

other group of French origin in the state. Moreover, one authority finds that *"la langue maternelle des Créoles de Louisiane n'est pas, au XIXe siècle, le français mais le créole."*[84]

The refugees' manner and customs are unforgettably portrayed in Carpentier's classic.[85] These include distinctive music and dances such as the *passepied* and *contredanse*—accompanied by small orchestras whose techniques, most notably those of the early Cuban *danza and danzon,* are direct forerunners of styles and melodies popularized by Jelly Roll Morton [Ferdinand laMenthe Mouton, a grandson of refugees].[86] Slave dances—the *bomba* and *tumba*—informed many of the later popular dance styles, essentially the *calenda*—a slave version of *contredanse* that evolved into the conga, *charanga, mambo,* etc., and in Louisiana into *counjaille* and *bamboula.* The latter evidently inspired the young prodigy, Louis Moreau Gottschalk, the son of a refugee.[87]

Significant proportions of refugees came from Jacmel Parish in the south and Jean Rabel Parish near Port-de-Paix in the northwest, suggesting *petit blanc* status. Marriage contracts involving refugees to 1835 indicate slightly lower average incomes than those of local Creoles. Those with urban "professions" such as hotelier, baker, silversmith, cabinetmaker, hairdresser, fencing master, musician, barber, or actor easily found employment. Physicians, lawyers, engineers, builders, surveyors and publisher-printers remained in and around the Louisiana capital.

The overall impact of this large migration to the new

---

[84]Patrick Griolet, *Cadjins et Creoles en Louisiane* (Paris, 1986), "Les noirs francophones," pp. 69-71.

[85]Francisco Pérez de la Riva, *La habitación rural en Cuba* (Havana, 1952), pp. 78-81; Carpentier, *El reino,* p. 45; Emilio Bacardí y Moreau, *Crónicas de Santiago de Cuba,* 3 vols. (Barcelona, n.d.), II, 40-56; Harold Palmer Davis, *Black Democracy: The Story of Haiti* (New York, 1929), including map, p. 22.

[86]Ernest Borneman, "Jazz and the Creole Tradition," *Jazzforschung,* I (1969); Thomas Fiehrer, "From Quadrille to Stomp: The Creole Origins of Early Jazz," *Popular Music,* X (1991), 21-38.

[87]Louis Moreau Gottschalk, *Notes of a Pianist,* ed. Jeanne Behrend (New York, 1964), pp. 42-46; Vernon Loggins, *Where the Word Ends: The Life of Louis Moreau Gottschalk* (Baton Rouge, 1958), pp. 17-18, 172.

American state has yet to be appreciated, as it was diffuse and quickly absorbed.[88] That it was profound was not lost on Barbé-Marbois, who observed that "Louisiana has been enriched by the disasters of St. Domingo, and the industry that formerly gave so much value to that island, now fertilizes the Valley of the Mississippi."[89] The francophone population, once in fear of economic competition from the wave of American migration into Orleans Territory, avidly received the newcomers, and intermarriage was frequent. Local institutions like newspapers, opera, theaters, pharmacies, music schools and the book trade all flourished for the first time,[90] and Creole political ascendancy, or at least group preservation, seemed assured until the Civil War. The caste systems and civil law of Louisiana and Saint-Domingue were identical, and all racial groups, especially free colored females, were augmented by the refugees. Saint-Domingue slaves represented almost a third of the 1810 slave population of New Orleans and its precincts (10,824) and 10 percent of the slaves of Orleans Territory (34,660).[91]

In ethos and class structure, local society already bore great resemblance to the tri-caste model of the refugees' past,[92] but local creative and commercial potential was catalyzed when

---

[88]Hunt, "Haiti's Influence."

[89]François Barbé-Marbois, *The History of Louisiana, Particularly of the Cession of That Colony to the United States of America* (1830; reprint ed., Baton Rouge, 1977), p. 354. Jacques Houdaille and Maurice Lubin found it useful to consult cemetery headstones in Haiti and Louisiana, to establish continuities. Lubin, "Les exilés antillais dans les cimetières St. Louis," *Revue de Louisiane*, III (1974), 83-88, lists names common to both: Lafargue, Latour, Aubourg, Viau, Legendre, Eyma, Devezin, Poujol, Leblanc, Rey, Blanchard, Fortin, Larrieu, Dejan, Balland, Goutier, Guillot, Peralto, Dupuy, Justin, Montplaisir, Duplessis, Durocher, Labadie, Chenet, and Delland are a few examples.

[90]René J. Le Gardeur, *The First New Orleans Theatre, 1792-1803* (New Orleans, 1963).

[91]Paul Lachance, "The Politics of Fear: French Louisianians and the Slave Trade, 1786-1809," *Plantation Society*, I (1979), 189.

[92]Elizabeth Shown Mills, "Mézières, Grappe, Trichel: A Study of a Tri-Caste Lineage in the Old South," *The Genealogist*, VI (1985), 4-84; Gabriel Debien, "The Acadians in Saint-Domingue," in Glenn R. Conrad, ed., *The Cajuns: Essays on Their History and Culture*, 3rd ed. (Lafayette, La., 1983), pp. 19-78.

faced with bold American competition and when reinforced with
the gifts of the newcomers. Refugees of all three castes had
experienced the exodus and exile together. They were drawn
close by ties of blood, affinity and economic interdependence.
They shared a lengthy, tumultuous experience and a common
Creole sub-culture. Pressed close together by the spatial
limits of New Orleans, forced upon each other by the shores
of the lake and river, they congregated in the "back of town"
and in Faubourg Marigny, where their building traditions
are everywhere in evidence.[93] Households in these areas were
frequently shared by all three castes, as several of the federal
censuses illustrate. Though all levels of island society appeared
in Louisiana, elites are obviously most conspicuous. Any list of
mid-nineteenth-century notables confirms the point: the chess
genius Paul Morphy, the piano virtuoso/composer Gottschalk,
the distinguished legists Moreau-Lislet and Etienne Mazureau,
the black composer/director Edmond Dédé—were among
refugees and their children. So also the fiery publisher Louis
Roudanez, the historian R. L. Desdunes, the poet Armand
Lanusse, the public spirited nun Henriette de Lisle—all were
offspring of *affranchis.* Colored refugee descendants led the
struggle for black political participation during Reconstruction,
which for them doubtless extended the principles of the French
Revolution.[94] Their most enduring legacy was the creation of a
number of musical genres that converged after the Civil War
to form "primitive" or pre-recorded jazz (from *jaser* meaning
to chatter), ultimately America's most potent contribution to
world pop culture. The influence of refugee descendants in the
prosopography of early jazz is unmistakable.[95]

In the Glen Pitre-directed film, *Belizaire the Cajun,* the
protagonist, a *traiteur,* refers to *gri-gri* he acquired from a
Saint-Domingue slave woman, a stock character in regional
folklore in the past century. The implications of popular

[93]John Michael Vlach, "Haitian Origin of the Shotgun House." *International Review of African American Art.*

[94]David Rankin, "The Politics of Caste: Free Colored Leadership in New Orleans During the Civil War," in Robert R. Macdonald, et al., eds., *Louisiana's Black Heritage* (New Orleans, 1979), pp. 107-146.

[95]Fiehrer, "From Quadrille to Stomp," 21-38.

medicine and religious sensibility brought with the migration have yet to be taken up in mainstream literature. The standard "classic" histories of the region, works of Creole scholars like Charles Gayarré,[96] Alcée Fortier,[97] or François-Xavier Martin,[98] mention or discuss but do not realistically explore the effects of the refugee presence. The popular dimensions of the phenomenon escape detection altogether. The racial politics of Reconstruction and afterward explain this lapse among Creole historians. Still, the movement of ten to eleven thousand Caribbean people to this peripheral enclave of North America at such a crucial juncture in its social formation commends our attention.

Refugee descendants cherish a prototypical tale rooted in the circumstances of their ancestral island exodus. Gottschalk brooded over it in his *Notes*. The *émigré* ancestor, as it goes, was slipped out of the turmoil of burning Cap-Français as a babe in a basket borne by a faithful slave. The myth is formative in the residual lore of the Haitian Revolution. Families across the expanses of Louisiana and up the Mississippi Valley still recount this tale, which represents the inverse image of the "savage" slave—pillaging, burning, murdering—left behind to his devices by the exodus. Though refugee and American press accounts uniformly portrayed the flight of white planters as a nightmare retreat from slaughter, there is little evidence of alleged butchery.[99] The collective work of the redoubtable Gabriel Debien may suggest a contrary interpretation. In his vast sampling of colonial correspondence and planter accounts, the incidence of violence between slaves and Europeans is miniscule. The white retreat was not a precipitous dodge of the

---

[96]Charles E. A. Gayarré, *Histoire de la Louisiane*, 2 vols. (New Orleans, 1846-1847).

[97]Alcée Fortier, *A History of Louisiana*, 4 vols. (New York, 1904); and *Louisiana: Comprising Sketches of Parishes, Towns, Events, Institutions and Persons, Arranged in Cyclopedic Form*, 3 vols. (Madison, Wis., 1914), II, 146, acknowledges only 4,000 refugees.

[98]François-Xavier Martin, *The History of Louisiana from the Earliest Period*, 2 vols. (New Orleans, 1882).

[99]See Fick, chs. on violence of slaves.

blood-drenched machete of legend, but was a gradual process
extending from 1790 to 1804. During those years the refugees
were in motion, to Jamaica, thence to Cuba, and later the United
States.[100] Marriage records indicate that many children were
born during the protracted exile. From Castonnet des Fosses,[101]
Hilliard d'Aubertuil,[102] and others, we know that some 25,000
whites were enumerated in 1780 and upwards of 40,000 in 1790,
including many French *arrivistes* who returned home at the
outbreak of hostilities. Irene Wright[103] and Emilio Bacardí y
Moreau[104] relate the figure of 27,000 refugees in Oriente, Cuba,
in 1803. The figures from the greater Antilles and Louisiana
account roughly for most refugees, excluding those bound back
to France or residing on the East Coast, throwing doubt on the
long-accepted tale of mass homicides. Even C. L. R. James, the
most partisan historian of the slave revolt, assumes the validity
of the myth, reporting a "massacre" for which there is scant data.
Still, practically all whites left in 1803, suggesting at the least
an unbearable level of tension.

Treatment of the slave revolt in the antebellum press is
thoroughly invested with a "Manichean allegory," portrayed
by the idealized faithful slave and her inverted mirror, the
cannibal insurgent bondsman. Such an allegory infuses the
"deep structure" of colonial texts generally.[105] In the social
history of the circum-Caribbean the model assumes a set
of relations—slavery/colonialism—that embraces an entire
society, one constructed upon a European fragment, and whose

---

[100]Wright and Debien, *Les Colons.*

[101]Henri Louis Castonette des Fossses, *Le Perte d'une colonie: la révolte de Saint-Domingue* (Paris, 1893).

[102]Michel René Hilliard d'Auberteuil, *Considérations sur l'état présent de la colonie française de Saint-Domingue* (Paris, 1779).

[103]Irene Wright, *Cuba* (New York, 1910), p. 361.

[104]Bacardí y Moreau, *Crónicas de Santiago,* II, 361.

[105]Abdul R. JanMohammed, "The Economy of Manichean Allegory: The Function of Racial Difference in Colonialist Literature," *Critical Inquiry,* XII (1985), 69, 83; also Stelio Cro, *The Noble Savage: Allegory of Freedom* (Waterloo, Ontario, 1990), ch. 3.

expansive character has, since the Renaissance, pitted it adamantly against a demonic "other"—the native.[106] Caliban is a "noble savage" if properly domesticated or extirpated: the North American Indian, the shiftless Mexican snoozing beneath his sombrero, the faithful slave with her pregnant basket. But Caliban becomes a menacing brute once the relations of power are challenged, as in Saint-Domingue.[107]

During that formative eighteenth century, Louisiana and Saint-Domingue were interdependent, sharing everything but the island's mountain vistas. Consequently, a very large percentage of South Louisianians (and other Americans along the eastern seaboard) descend to some degree from those refugees—white, colored, and black—who departed the civil conflict and eventually settled in our midst. The examination of regional census data alone paves the way to clarifying who the refugees were and how they survived being uprooted not once, but at least twice in two decades, many having completely rebuilt their fortunes in Cuba.

But records alone do not a history write. Ultimately there are only interpretations. The one that has governed the treatment of the Saint-Domingue refugees in local historiography is a product of Reconstruction; of the diplomatic propaganda that isolated and besmirched nineteenth-century Haiti; of the many prejudices that capture even inquiring minds. Recent analyses of censuses and genealogical investigation provide concrete data on the material and ethnic constitution, demographic distribution, and family composition of Louisiana's sister (and early parent) colony.[108]

The demographic perspective allows us, however modestly, to retrieve the past from the expansionist agenda of the American state which, having arbitrarily acquired the Louisiana territory

---

[106]Fernando Coronil, "Mastery by Signs, Signs of Mastery," *Plantation Society in the Americas*, II (1986), 201-207.

[107]On the vicissitudes of injecting "political correctness" into research on past atrocities and demographic disasters, consider Thomas Fiehrer, "Tropical Civilization and Its Discontents," *Race and Class*, XXXIII (1991), 93-101.

[108]These include Geggus, Cauna, and Jacques Houdaille's various works, including "Quelques données sur la population de Saint-Domingue au XVIIe siècle," *Population*, no. 45 (1973), 859-872.

(among others), then omitted and misrepresented its past through "official" accounts. To resurrect and reappropriate local history in that context, we often must begin from scratch. The answer to the question of who actually created the society, whether native Americans, Europeans, Africans, or the racially mixed population (whose accomplishments are even further submerged than those of Creoles in general), still in large measure eludes us. Identifying the creators of local architecture, medicine, legal scholarship, music, cuisine, folklore, sugar technology, and art (Clementine Hunter and Georges Rodrigue come to mind) is an ongoing project.

Since the international context of the colonial society, i.e. its place in the systemic global process of accumulation, has been studiously ignored, official versions of Louisiana's past are not inclined to map the earlier connections between the Gulf Coast and the adjacent islands or the common populations, cultures, traditions—the civilization they share. Louisiana's history awaits a general reinterpretation that transcends the confines of national boundaries, metropolitan diplomacy, and the program of American imperialism in the Caribbean. There is a past to be uncovered, a lost reality awaiting discovery. History, until recently, was the precinct of the politically privileged, and as such it imprisoned and negated local reality and homogenized the past through fabrication and omission. History has now entered the popular arena and may serve as a tool of creative reconstruction.

We share much with our Caribbean neighbors, once despite history, now because of it.

The Saint-Domingue Refugees in Cuba, 1793-1815

by Gabriel Debien

translated by David Cheramie

Part I

The scattering throughout America and the destruction of what had been the society, the world, and the culture of the colonists of Saint-Domingue is one of the most exciting episodes in the history of the French Revolution in the colonies. Without doubt, these dramatic events mark the conclusion of struggle between the whites, their former slaves, and the people of color; also the refugees' memories of these departures and flights present the persistent images of a great upheaval and a bitter failure, and, in many hearts, a long and pernicious thirst for revenge. This is the story of a vanquished people.

The story is difficult to reconstruct because of a succession of minor events, the fates of individuals, a multiplicity of dates, and the scattered places where the refugees were given sanctuary. The interrelationship of causational factors reveals itself day after day through the juxtaposition of lives, [through] genealogy, partly through fragments, [partly] through fortuitous discoveries. It is not always possible to arrive at a clear unfolding of the facts. In such a case, history is like a man who seeks and observes other men and who requires names, many names, petty or great, significant or not. By this means it is possible to examine the misery, [see] the [refugees'] intentions in a better light, and maybe then patient reconstruction of the facts will engender a less distorted synthesis, one which, despite the intervening years, places, and random events, penetrates to the heart of the essential themes and events.

The colonists from Saint-Domingue sought refuge nearly everywhere in the Antilles. On the continent, some went to Louisiana, Georgia, Virginia, and the large ports of New

England. Crushed by the slave uprising, embittered against a France which they considered responsible for the colonial disaster, they forsook the remaining French lands, Guadeloupe and Guyana, as being too far away and where, they thought, they might have to confront either the same social menace or the same reversal of their fortunes.

The most important reception centers were initially the closest foreign lands having the easiest access: the Spanish part of Saint-Domingue,[1] Jamaica, Cuba, and finally Louisiana. The small English, Dutch, or Danish Antilles received few refugees. Saint-Christophe, Saint-Croix, Saint-Eustace, Saint-Thomas, Grenada, and Barbados had had for a long time a mixed population, part French, part Dutch or part English and served as a shelter or as a way station in the Protestants' flight from the French islands in the seventeenth century. Jamaica became the haven for all who considered England and its fleet as the best protection from the political regime and the society which was collapsing in Saint-Domingue. The refugees in Jamaica and Louisiana will form the basis of a future discussion. This article will concern those who headed for Cuba.

Contrary to the situation in most of the English Antilles, where a significant Huguenot population existed, the Spanish colonies before the Revolution contained no large concentration of French-speaking people. Even in the Spanish part of Saint-Domingue which lived, to a certain extent, in symbiosis with the French coffee and sugar plantations, furnishing animals for labor and meat, there were few French-speaking inhabitants. The flow of trade did not create a parallel movement of people. The [island's] colonial experience of the seventeenth-century consisted, for both the Spanish and the French, of a long period of war and reciprocal pillages and massacres. The eighteenth century was a century of grudging coexistence and incessant disputes over a chronically disregarded border.

Following the evacuation of Saint-Domingue, small colonies

[1]The island of Hispañola was split in the eighteenth century between France and Spain: to the west, French Saint-Domingue, to the east, the more extensive Spanish part, called Santo Domingo, which was supposed to go to France in 1795 under the Treaty of Basel.

of French planters established themselves in Cuba and Santo Domingo. In Cuba, they became the ancestors of most of the well-known French families, still very numerous, found around Havana and especially in the Eastern provinces of the island. And if, after 1815, the political turmoil of the Restoration and the lure of riches from Cuban coffee, and then sugar plantations, attracted many Frenchmen, it was nevertheless the refugees from Saint-Domingue who formed the initial French participation in the Cuban prosperity.

They stayed primarily because they found there something better than shelter; they found a chance to build a new colonial homeland. Most of the colonists who went to the United States considered their stay there to be only a stopover before continuing on to the metropole. On the other hand, New Orleans and even Savannah and Charleston were places from which they could longingly look back to their abandoned plantations. France, for these refugees, meant little more than distant cousins, a difficult life in a cold climate, and customs which were already strange.

In the beginning, most refugees regarded Cuba as little more than an outpost for waiting and observation. Access to the island was as easy as to the northern coast of the Spanish part of Saint-Domingue.[2] It was refugees from the North who first arrived in Cuba. Those from Cap-Français (present-day Cap-Haitien) tried hard to believe that the problem was only a passing crisis. They sought a tranquil place, a wharf almost in sight of their sugar and coffee plantations whence they would be able to return to their homeland during a lull in the violence. They regarded Cuba as a roof to shelter their faithful domestics, commodities, and the papers of their plantations.

As the war dragged on, as the neutrality of ships was violated, and as the Revolution in the islands became a racial war, new attitudes surfaced among the refugees. Some returned to Saint-Domingue; others went to France; the largest group of refugees, those who were in Jamaica or in Santo Domingo, went to Cuba, solid ground for white resistance, a way station for those who

---

[2]Annotator's note: The islands of Cuba and Hispañola are separated by the Windward Passage, a strait approximately sixty miles wide.

watched and waited hopefully to return to their homeland.

The individual comings and goings of the refugees and the deportees which were at first obscure evolved into massive and controlled movements, within which we can distinguish phases and more precisely delineate intentions.

I.—THE FIRST REFUGEES (1793-1798)

Isolated departures began in 1792, but increased in frequency in 1793, after Spain declared war on the French Republic. Entire families were sometimes involved, but more often it was a case of women accompanied by children. The men remained, after retreating to the cities, where, by choice or necessity, they rendered undistinguished service in the militia. Diverse reasons—not always fear—guided these [departing] families toward Cuba. Business relations and familial ties do not appear to have been considerations. Some [refugees] had lost confidence, having always considered Saint-Domingue to be a land affording merely profit and speculation. This was all that interested them. They were going to pitch their tent elsewhere, without looking back over their shoulder. They left business ventures moribund. The plantations which they were trying to sell no longer found any buyers, or more accurately, any payers. But the more adept [speculators] left more or less at the time of their choosing, "with all the cash" it was then possible to raise. Their farms remained under the watchful eye of a manager or a steward, honest, if at all possible. The departure of others, involved in political life, in the disputes and passions of the parochial assemblies, was a matter of spite, resistance, and protestation against the mother country's decrees that accorded, then retracted, then finally rendered equality to the people of color that the colonists spurned. Those involved in administration were beaten or were going to be. Prudence dictated heading for cover.

As early as 1793, many of the colonists who were officers or who were from military families chose to take refuge in Cuba as a matter of honor, being driven there by festering Anglophobia. To confront the people of color and the slaves, they willingly called upon the Spanish and, invoking the cooperative spirit imposed by the Family Pact and by the establishment of mutual borders in 1776, they requested a massive "social police action" emanating from Santo Domingo. They consciously upheld the views of the political regime they served. They had on their side the comte de Provence. Almost all [of the refugees], before reaching Cuba, offered their sword to the Spaniards of Santo Domingo. It was no longer a matter of individual departures, but the beginning of organized immigration after negotiations, largely undocumented, with the authorities of Santo Domingo and Cuba. Among these soldiers, we can identify Baron de la Valtière, who had been a royal lieutenant in Môle-Saint-Nicolas from 1770 to 1789[3] and also interim second-in-command of the North. He had taken refuge in the United States in 1792, but had returned in March of 1793, only to head for Havana shortly thereafter.[4] He was accompanied by other colonists from the Jean-Rabel sector, planters like himself, by people from Môle-Saint-Nicolas, and by garrison officers such as Carles, the regimental adjutant.[5]

The same was true for the Marquis D'Espinville, colonial coffee grower from the Mirebalais sector in the West, who helped the Spanish for two years, permitting them to take back the Verrettes from Toussaint L'Ouverture.[6] He [D'Espinville] commanded this recently developed country until he retired to

---

[3]Moreau de Saint-Méry, *Description de la partie française de Saint-Domingue*, 2 vols. (Philadelphia, 1796-1797), I, 281; II, 20, 39.

[4]Garran-Coulon, *Rapport sur les troubles de Saint-Domingue*, 4 vols. (Paris, years V-VII [1796-1798]), III, 379; IV, 145.

[5]*Ibid.*, IV, 144-146.

[6]Annotator's note: Pierre Dominique Toussaint L'Ouverture (1743-1803) was the liberator of present-day Haiti. Following emancipation of the colony's slaves in 1793, Toussaint L'Ouverture joined the Spanish in Santo Domingo as commander of a force of 600 former bondsmen. By the spring of 1794, his force had grown to 4,000. During the summer of 1794, he abruptly abandoned the Spanish and returned to Saint-Domingue to help fight British invaders. His army forced the British to evacuate the colony in 1798. Toussaint L'Ouverture then consolidated his power in Saint-Domingue by defeating Rigaud, leader of the island's large mulatto population. By 1801, Toussaint L'Ouverture had gained undisputed control over the colony. He opposed the French attempt to regain control over the colony and to reimpose slavery upon the black population. Toussaint L'Ouverture was captured by French forces, charged with conspiracy, and sent to France, where he died in prison.

Cuba in late 1795.[7]

The spontaneity of the movement of military personnel was encouraged by the Spanish authorities who spread a proclamation across the French half of the island. They called on the "honest colonists" to join in a common effort to fight the blacks and the revolution. This proclamation reached Europe and was distributed among the immigrants after the collapse of the Princes' army. The English were not the only ones looking for new recruits. Some refugees joined the colonial regiments organized in Saint-Domingue by the English to assist them in their occupation of Saint-Domingue and their defense of the old order. Others preferred to serve the Spanish, as advised the "regent" who disavowed the procedure of Venault de Charmilly and Cadusch, colonists of Martinique, who plotted with Pitt[8] and Dundas[9] to obtain a commitment of British protection.

Sailors were especially attentive to the Spanish appeals. The marquis de Messemé, son-in-law to one Mme Hux from Bayeux in the Morin sector, a naval lieutenant, and, in 1791, colonel in the national guard in Loudun, was one of those who left the Princes' army in late 1792 to go to Havana. He hoped to patch together a few odds and ends from what was left of his wife's interests in the Bayeux sugar mills in the northern sector. His efforts were more or less unsuccessful, and in 1794, in order to survive, he solicited employment in the Spanish Antilles squadron.[10] Louis-Pierre de Morteaux, brother of the priest in Sainte-Marie, Martinique, also went into the Spanish service, in Cuba, around the same time.[11] The marquis Duquesne, naval officer and planter in the Gonaïves, had commanded in 1792-

---

[7]Archives Nationales T. 1087; Agoult Papers, letter dated February 23, 1795.

[8]Annotator's note: William Pitt the Younger (1759-1806), prime minister of Great Britain.

[9]Annotator's note: Henry Dundas, Viscount Melville and Baron Dunira (1742-1811). Dundas served as the British secretary of war from 1794 to 1801 and as treasurer of the British navy from 1784 to 1800.

[10]G. Debien, "Joseph-Désiré de Messmé (1751-1821), son émigration, la vente, et le rachat de ses biens," *Bull. Soc. Antig. Ouest*, (1942), p. 84-86, 89-91.

[11]J. Renard, *La Martinique. Historique des paroisses. Des origines à la Séparation* (Thonon-les-Bains, 1951), p. 171.

1793 a free corps in his sector, then, under English occupation, he was promoted to the rank of lieutenant-colonel in the British Royal Legion of Saint-Marc. Shortly before the Treaty of Basel,[12] he joined the Spanish navy.[13]

The Chappotin family also moved to Cuba. François-Aimable de Chappotin, a Creole from the Cul-de-Sac sector [and] a former naval office, retired to Limbé, entered the Spanish army, and in 1799, at the birth of one of his children in San Felipe y Santiago de Bejucal, he was named "sergeant-major in the Legion of Carlos IV." He already had a small plantation. Similarly, Paul Gleizes from Maisoncelle, went to Havana at approximately the same time and became a soldier and planter, and Eustache Leroy de la Vérouilère and his wife Jeanne-Gertrude de Chappotin, owners of the sugar-mill in Passage à la Croix-des-Bouquets, lived in Havana with their brother François-Aimable.[14]

With regard to the other refugees who suddenly fled the incendiaries and the threat of death, one must consider the speed of a crossing aboard a coastal vessel hastily freighted, haphazardly arranged, a thousand circumstances peculiar to panic. Besides, whatever the departure dates for Cuba were before 1798, they were then much less numerous than those for the continent or for Jamaica. We record with difficulty throughout this first period of flight and immigration a few names, almost all members of the military.

It seems that these officers quickly made a place for themselves in Cuba. They were centered in Havana. Military service was probably not a sinecure, especially at sea. The crossings are long. The *piastres* of His Catholic Majesty did not always have the courtesy of arriving on time, but between shipments "one [found] the means to live honestly." However modestly and irregularly paid they were, salaries did procure some credit for them. Messemé thus acquired as early as 1795

[12]Annotator's note: The Treaty of Basel (Basle), concluded on July 22, 1795, gave France full title to the former Spanish colony of Santo-Domingo.

[13]G. Debien, "Messmé," 96.

[14]Letter from Col. Le Marois, April 5, 1952.

a "small place" near Havana. His goal was to establish a coffee plantation there. He went into association with D'Espinville to increase its value. Messemé provided the land, some money, and slaves, certainly not very many, though. D'Espinville provided some men and his expertise in coffee farming in Saint-Domingue. He directed the operation.

The marquis Duquesne married before 1798 Doña Maria Estrada, from a family of Havana planters. François-Madeleine de Chappotin, having come with his brother François-Aimable, married Michoele Seydel. Their descendents still live in Cuba. Their son Leroy de la Vérouillère wed in Havana "a very pretty woman, the governor's niece."

Duquesne, François-Madeleine de Chappotin, the young Leroy de la Vérouillère, were already three Cuban settlers.

II.—THE EVACUATION OF SAINT-DOMINGUE (1798-1802)

In 1798, when the English evacuated the last sectors they occupied in Saint-Domingue, the French in their service did not follow them to Jamaica. Expressing confidence in the policy of amnesty and assembly announced by Toussaint L'Ouverture, some colonist-officers preferred to stay. Those who had not served under the English but who did not accept Toussaint's regime withdrew to Cuba in great number in Nivôse of year VII.[15] From Cuba they would wait to see what Toussaint L'Ouverture and Hédouville,[16] the Directory's agent, would do about the colonists who, during the English occupation, had accepted positions with the administration, the police, or the judiciary and also they would wait to see how well Toussaint would succeed in organizing the workers on the plantations.

---

[15]"Précis historique des Annales de la Colonie française de Saint-Domingue depuis 1789 à l'année 99," 2 vols., Archives de la Vienne, Depot 102, II, 41.

[16]Annotator's note: General T. Hédouville lacked sufficient military force to sustain the authority delegated to him by the Directory. He consequently pitted Rigaud against Toussaint L'Ouverture in an unsuccessful effort to keep the latter from gaining control over the French-speaking portion of Hispañola.

The departures in 1798 and early 1799 had all the characteristics of a well-planned retreat. We know some names: Jean-Baptiste-Louis Mongin, lieutenant in the *sénéchaussée* of Saint-Louis then Port-au-Prince, native of Nantes, owner of a coffee plantation in Platons de Torbeck, representative from Saint-Louis du Sud to the colonial assembly of Saint-Marc, and one of the most ardent of the Léopardins;[17] Villejouin; Chancerel, farmer from Léogane and Cul-de-Sac; Henri de David, viscount of Lastours, former captain of the Port-au-Prince light cavalry, who had commanded a company in the Hussars of the British Legion;[18] Cornalet; Etienvrain; Fiard; and the adjutant Duportail, landowner in the Saint-Jean à la Croix-des-Bouquets sector.[19] All of these colonists came from the western sectors: from Port-au-Prince, from all of Cul-de-Sac, or from Jérémie.

"I received a letter from Jérémie," wrote Silvain d'Abnour from Cap-Français on Vendémiaire 7, year IX (late September 1800),[20]

by Mr. Bertrand, a businessman from this area,[21] who tells me that my mother has left the island on Brumaire 14, year VIII (November of 1799) for Santiago de Cuba by a boat which, upon leaving Jérémie, was seized by barges coming out of a cove above the city. They underwent at the hands of these monsters the most atrocious treatment. Seven men who were aboard were murdered and the women stripped of their belongings. An hour after this action, the barge itself was captured by an American cruiser and taken to Havana, on the same island of Cuba, with their spoils and their

[17]Moreau de Saint-Méry, *Description de la partie française de Saint-Domingue,* 2 vols. (Philadelphia, 1796-1797), II, 648. "Précis historique," II, 28, 37, 201; State of indemnities . . . 1831, Vanssay papers. Smith and des Rouandières; M. Launet, *Erreurs et vérités dans de Haïti* (Port-au-Prince, 1945), p. 95.

[18]Archives Nationales. Colonies, E 259.

[19]*Ibid.,* E 161.

[20]Mlles. Richard de Tussac, then in Poitiers, sisters of the author of *La flore des Antilles,* [to Silvain d'Abnour]. This letter was obligingly communicated [to him] by Mme Vignès d'Abnour.

[21]Probably Pierre Bertrand-Laville, wholesaler and important planter.

unfortunate victims.

At that time, my mother gave testimony of her life amongst all this immorality . . . For the last eleven months, she has not given any news of her whereabouts nor of her well-being to anyone.

Mme d'Abnour soon let it be known that she was in Havana. One of her neighbors from Jérémie, Eténaud, refugee in Santiago, wrote to her on February 14, 1800, that he was not one of those who was happy to have landed in Cuba:

I am very happy to learn that you and your child, as well as the ladies and the other children who were with you, are still alive, for the rumor up till now was that you had all been murdered . . . You have forgotten to write me the names of the ladies and children saved with you and the other refugees that you had on board. I well fear for the poor souls who were put on board the Rigaud[22] boat. None has appeared up till now. . . . At Grande Rivière, eighteen landowners have just been murdered. . . . You wish to know if the land has resources. No, Madame, the majority of the many Frenchmen here have trouble making a living. Several have come to the end of their means and have been obliged to embark with the corsairs.[23]

In July and August 1800, upon Rigaud's departure for France, after Toussaint L'Ouverture's triumph in the South, the vanquished people of color embarked for Cuba,[24] an exodus of over 700 officers and soldiers. They went away just far enough to be able to wait conveniently for the first occasion to return. This migration of military personnel had no lasting impact upon Cuban history. They joined with other groups of men of color,

[22]Annotator's note: André Rigaud was the leader of the mulatto faction in Saint-Domingue. In January 1800, Rigaud's army was defeated by Toussaint L'Ouverture's superior forces, and the mulatto leader was forced into exile.

[23]Annotator's note: To sail with the pirates of the West Indies.

[24]Castonnet des Fossé, *La Révolution de Saint-Domingue* (Paris, 1893), p. 211.

an action which gave rise to suspicions.[25] Upon the arrival of Leclerc's expedition, four hundred of these officers and soldiers returned to the colony, to which Rigaud had also gone.[26] The Santiago that these soldiers knew was the one Descourtilz described for us when he went there in early 1799. But he paid more attention to the morals and the ogling of the Spanish Creoles and the city's general poverty than the settlement of his compatriots who were already quite numerous.[27]

III.—THE GREAT EXODUS (1803)

The great migration to Cuba, however, occurred in 1803, when the colony and the expeditionary corps were cut off from France by the resumption of the war with England. Troops, administrators, colonists, and merchants left when the ship [of state] began to sink. This was the year of massive evacuations.

In this exodus, military personnel had a higher profile because they left in convoys. Not the troops in the northern parts, of course, who were blockaded by the English cruisers and who had no means of evacuation, but the ones from the West and the extreme South.

The evacuation of the troops began at Jérémie. On Thermidor 15 (July 3), General Fressinet,[28] the local commander, embarked there for Cuba with a few men. He was later captured at sea by the English and conducted to Jamaica.[29] He left behind

---

[25]Testimony of the Cabildo solemnized at the town hall of the city of Havana, December 16, 1796, which treats, among other matters, the conspiracy of the French and the people of color. Bol. Arch. Nac. 1949. Edict of the Governor of Santiago de Cuba so that all foreigners and nationals may present themselves, 1799. *Ibid.*

[26]Castonnet des Fossés, *Révolution*, p. 260.

[27]*Voyages d'un naturaliste et ses observations faites . . . à Saint-Yago de Cuba . . .*, 3 vols. (Paris, 1809).

[28]Annotator's note: Philibert, baron Fressinet (1769-1821). Fressinet departed France in 1802 with the expedition sent to subjugate the island colony. He disapproved of the arrest of Toussaint L'Ouverture. This dissension resulted in his exile upon his return to France. After five years of disgrace, he was rehabilitated. In 1812 Fressinet was appointed commander of the Fourteenth Army Corps.

[29]F. Kundall, ed., *Lady Nugent's Journal* (London, 1939), pp. 233-235.

elements of the 90th Half-brigade under the orders of battalion commander Heurtand, whose escape to Cuba would have a happier ending [than that of Fressinet].[30]

Port-au-Prince was evacuated in October. Hardvilliers, a Cap-Français businessman, wrote to his French associate, Stanislas Foäche, on November 10:[31] "A sailboat from Santiago de Cuba arrived despite the vigilance of the English and carried dispatches from General Lavallette[32] who evacuated Port-au-Prince. He is in Santiago with 2,000 troopers who, they say, do not want to go back to Saint-Domingue."

Lavallette probably had his reasons for not desiring to return to Port-au-Prince. A colonial magistrate, Couët de Montarand, refugee in Cuba, suggested as much to General Rochambeau[33] in a sort of report dated from Santiago the day after his arrival:

Brumaire 18, year XII.

---

[30]M. Laurent, *Révolution*, p. 260. Annotator's note: This reference apparently refers to François Laurent, *La Revolution française*, 2 vols. (Paris, 1967).

[31]M. Bégoauen-Demeaux, *Mémorial d'une famille du Havre, Stanislas Foäche* (Paris, 1951), p. 233.

[32]Annotator's note: Prior to his withdrawal from Saint-Domingue, Lavallette, commander of the French forces at Port-au-Prince, had dispatched a detachment to drive black insurgents from Petit Goave. The ensuing defeat of this detachment gave the black revolutionaries undisputed control over the interior in the southern portion of Saint-Domingue. Assisted by forces from Dessalines' army, the southern insurgents laid siege to Port-au-Prince, and, with the assistance of the British navy, destroyed several supply vessels bound for the colonial port. Cut off from all assistance by land or by sea, confronted with the prospect of famine, and facing unrelenting pressure from the Dessalines-led insurgents who were erecting batteries on the heights surrounding the city, Lavallette was compelled to sue for peace. He was given eight days to evacuate the town, provided the French did not attempt to destroy the city's fortifications. James Brown's *The History and Present Condition of St. Domingo*, 2 vols. (Philadelphia, 1837), II, 134-137.

[33]Donatien-Marie-Joseph de Vimeur, vicomte de Rochambeau (1750-1813) was the son of the French admiral who assisted Washington at the Battle of Yorktown The younger Rochambeau was named colonel in the Régiment d'Auvergne in 1779. He was promoted to field marshal on June 31, 1791, and was promoted again to lieutenant general on July 9, 1792. He functioned in the latter capacity as commander of the French Windward Islands.

The evacuation of Port-Républicain[34] must have caused
you, Citizen General, as much surprise as indignation. The
infamous General La Vallette had a few days before convoked
two war councils to prove the necessity of the evacuation. I do
not know why I was summoned to it. I dare assure you that
it was stopped . . . with Dessalines['s[35] arrival]. General La
Vallette had been dealing with the rogues for the last three
weeks. It had become indispensable, all of the out-posts had
been ambushed, the fort lacked both commodities and war
munitions.

It is quite true that he had betrayed the city before
the convocation of the two war councils. On the eve of the
evacuation, General Dessalines demanded, by virtue of
General La Vallette's terms of surrender, the clerk of court's
registers and minutes as well as the Negroes who had
been embarked; a man named Bonnet, mulatto, adjutant-
commander of the Negroes' army came to demand the papers
from the scribe; he was accompanied by Citizen Marchand,
aide-de-camp to General La Vallette. These papers could not
be unloaded.

A Negro named Quiambois (Creole for *quille en bois,* a
wooden keel), Dessalines' aide-de-camp, who, accompanied
by the local adjutant, Desilles, went to get all the Negro men
and women, who debarked . . .

Finally, the infamous Citizen General La Vallette sold
weapons and munitions to the rogues: He had nonetheless
assured us that the whole lot would be destroyed or shipped
away. I could give you many details which would prove the
innumerable heinous crimes committed by La Vallette, but
the time which has passed since the evacuation of Port-
Républicain makes me think that they must now be known
to you. Moreover, I urge you to summon me so that I may

[34]The name of Port-au-Prince since 1793.

[35]Annotator's note: Jean-Jacques Dessalines was perhaps Toussaint L'Ouverture's most
aggressive and capable lieutenant.　　On January 1, 1804, Dessalines proclaimed the
independence of the former French colony and renamed it Haiti.　In 1805 Dessalines
had himself crowned emperor of Haiti in emulation of Napoleon.　He was assassinated
on October 17, 1806.

provide all the information you may require and thus prove to you my devotion to the Republic.[36]

Couët de Montaran and his brother-in-law, Terrefort de Gorsse, had obtained, through "the goodness" of General Rochambeau, permission to evacuate their wives and children to Santiago de Cuba. "Seeing that a voyage under these conditions was quite perilous," Gorsse, then comptroller of customs in Port-au-Prince, requested and obtained a leave of absence to accompany them, promising to return to his post as quickly as possible. The colonial prefect granted this leave request on Prairial 26, year XI (June 14, 1803). It does not appear that Gorsse was able to return.

Montaran shared the fate of numerous other refugees from Port-au-Prince. Sailing upon the *Sophie* which fell into British hands, he was sent to Jamaica. After two weeks, he received permission to join his family at Santiago de Cuba, where he arrived on Brumaire 17.

General de Noailles[37] was able to escape from Môle-Saint-Nicolas with some of his people. "He conveyed his plans to a black man from Cap-Français,[38] who did not attempt to block his departure. . . . He [Noailles] is in Havana and makes as light of this fact as Mr. de Lavallette."[39]

How many colonists and families were nearby? "Our unfortunate city," wrote Morange to Stanislas Foäche from Cap-Français on August 9, 1803, "becomes more depopulated every day. They go to America, to Havana, or to the Spanish half [of Hispañola]."[40] Hardivilliers, Foäche's other associate, wrote on

---

[36]Regnault de Beaucaron, *Souvenirs de famille. Voyages, Agriculture. (1775[?]-1832)* (Paris, 1912), p. 144.

[37]Annotator'snote: Louis-Marie, vicomte de Noailles (1756-1804) was assigned to Saint-Domingue with the rank of *général de brigade*. He capably commanded the Môle-Saint-Nicolas defenses against an assault by British invaders. Noailles subsequently managed to escape with his soldiers, eventually leading them to Cuba. He was killed on January 9, 1804, when his ship was attacked by a British vessel while en route to Havana, Cuba.

[38]Dessalines.

[39]Regnault de Beaucaron, *Souvenirs*, II, 241; February 4, 1804.

[40]Regnault de Beaucaron, *Souvenirs*, II, 221; and Vanssy papers (Dupessis Correspon-

November 1:

> The embargo has just been lifted and tomorrow at least
> 300 individuals will leave Cap-Français to scatter themselves
> out in all directions, some to Baracoa,[41] others to Santiago
> de Cuba, these to New England, those to Puerto Plata,[42]
> Samaná,[43] Saint Thomas,[44] no matter where, provided that
> one could flee from the claws of the Ogre.[45]

Joseph-Louis-Simon Le Gardeur de Tilly and his wife arrived
from the Nippes sector in June of 1803.[46]

One must make distinctions by month. In August, in the
days following the split with England, General Rochambeau,
commander-in-chief, still only accorded the departure of women
for Santiago de Cuba. The men were needed for defense purposes.
An American woman, Mary Hassel, sister-in-law to a Creole
colonist from Saint-Domingue going by the name of Saint-Louis,
recalled the difficulties pertaining to her departure in a letter
sent from Cap-Français in July or August:

> [Clara] asked the general for a passport for Santiago
> de Cuba. He answered her that he only accorded them to
> old and ugly women and that not fitting into this category,
> he was obliged to refuse her request. However, after many
> solicitations, she obtained one for herself, for me, and for six
> domestics. We shall leave in a few days. They allow all the
> women to leave but not one man can obtain a passport. A few

---

dence, Bordeaux, January 14, 1804). The Spanish half had been ceded to France by the
Treaty of Basel.

[41]Small port on the northeast coast of Cuba.

[42]Port on the northern coast of the Spanish part of Saint-Domingue.

[43]A province of northeastern Santo Domingo.

[44]Danish island.

[45]Probably Dessalines. Bégouën-Demeaux, *Mémorial*, II, 232.

[46]René Le Gardeur Papers in New Orleans, Louisiana.

succeed in escaping through disguise, and they are fortunate, for it is much to be feared that those who remain will be sacrificed.

All ships leaving here are taken and pillaged by the English. But since we are American women, maybe we will be able to go. Our intention is to remain in Santiago until Saint-Louis is able to join us. . . . [47]

These American women traveled without too much trouble. Saint-Louis was able to follow them.

He understood that it was time for him to steal away from the danger threatening him. Having learned that a ship was about to leave, he convinced a fisherman to take him out of the port and to wait until the vessel came out, the captain not having dared board him in the harbor itself. On the appointed day, Saint-Louis disguised as a fisherman, got in the dinghy, and rowing hard, they were soon beyond the fort.

The ship arriving shortly thereafter, Saint-Louis embarked and had thought himself out of danger. But once we were within the reach of the English vessels, the ship was stopped, pillaged, and sent to Baracoa. Saint-Louis had neither trunk nor clothing, but carried hidden upon himself a large sum of money in gold. . . . He spoke of buying a plantation and of settling here. . . . [48] Many farmers from Cap-Français came here after losing all they own. A large number remained. [49]

The hard-headed Creoles wished to leave the burnt land of Saint-Domingue only when it turned into hot coals beneath their feet. They were fixtures on the landscape, [bound to their homeland] as much by attachment to the climate, the cuisine, and the comforts of their colonial palaces as by business interests.

[47]H.P. Sannon, *Le Cap vue* [sic] *par une Américaine* (Port-au-Prince, 1936), p. 112. Mr. Sannon's translation.

[48]*Ibid.*, pp. 114, 116. Letter XIX written at Santiago de Cuba.

[49]*Ibid.*, letter XXI, p. 118.

"They only feel at home in America,"[50] and in America, nowhere better than in Saint-Domingue. Naturally, they were on their guard, in a state of alert. Their bags were packed. Those from amongst their people who would leave with them had been chosen. They would not wait, so they said to one another, until the last minute, the moment when it became "every-man-for-himself." But they remained working daily to accumulate laboriously a few more *francs*. They would only leave when misfortune came upon them.

The presence in Cuba of the largest concentration of refugees attracted, as if by suction, parts of the groups, both large and small, who went to Jamaica, the United States, Louisiana, or Saint Thomas. They quickly discovered that their compatriots were most numerous in the eastern portion of Cuba, and that immense tracts of land ideal for coffee-growing were available. With a bit of credit, one could obtain a concession. Everywhere exiles attracted exiles, cousins attracted cousins. The strange environment fostered solidarity, temporarily erasing economic and social differences. They went to Cuba from everywhere. From Jamaica, where good tracts of land were hard to find for the refugees, or from Martinique or the south of Saint-Domingue—the Chadiracs, the Vézien des Ombrages, Richard d'Abnour,[51] Baron de Léaumont,[52] Pierre-Antoine Sauvalle[53] from Jean-Rabel; it must be noted that they were all accustomed to the half-solitary, austere life of the hills. They had gained, but lost, comfort and wealth through coffee farming. They were lured by the promise of new lands, hoping to return to the coffee-groves where their experience and their past led them.

Some of the refugees who went to the United States or to Louisiana and married young American brides went to Cuba to

---

[50]Bégouën-Demeaux, *Mémorial,* II, 255.

[51]G. Debien, "Les sources de l'histoire coloniale aux Archives de la Vienne," *Revue des bibliothèques,* (1934,) 40-44.

[52]Laurent-Marie de Léaumont, "Précis historique," II, 241, 297.

[53]Bégouën-Demeaux, *Mémorial,* II, 254; colonial coffee-planter who had made some attempts at planting.

be near their brothers and to return to the crops they knew before leaving Saint-Domingue. For example, Pierre-Léon de Chappotin, a Creole and a brother to those already mentioned, married in Boston and then settled in Cuba, where his children were born and where he died in 1823. Denis Gaston, from Saint-Léonard in the Limousin, went to seek his fortune in Saint-Domingue around 1780. He first worked as the manager of a plantation, then opened a store, and then found the good life with a beautiful mulatress. He fled with his friend to Louisiana in 1793. In 1803, he went to Cuba, where, with his friend, he rebuilt his fortune.

Casimir Delavigne's uncle, a coffee planter, took refuge in Cuba; R. Delrieu, a veterinarian, and Mr. and Mrs. Guriot, also in 1803.[54] They all lived on coffee plantations.

In Saint-Domingue, the small coffee planters were among the last to leave. The sugar-colonist was often a non-resident, absentee capitalist. The coffee plantations were the work of the owners themselves. They had long lived on their concessions in isolated areas, close to their slaves, heading small workshops run like a family enterprise. They knew the countryside better than anyone; they were a part of the country. Coffee had promoted them to the high rank of planter. The chances of a future with this crop and the knowledge of the general situation of the market, sent them to Cuba, to the hills in the east, around Santiago. A Creole civilization persisted, wishing to survive as close as possible to its place of origin.

IV.—IN SANTIAGO DE CUBA WITH THE REFUGEES

Santiago de Cuba was the city where so many colonists from Saint-Domingue would disembark. Two of them described it as they saw it, one in September of 1798, the other in 1803.

---

[54]Information graciously communicated by Mr. René Le Gardeur of New Orleans (1952). We can also cite the names of Sarrazin (Archives de la Vienne, Eu 553), and of Antoine Leclerc, in Havana in 1803 ([Jean-Baptiste] Lemonnier-Delafosse, *Seconde campagne de Saint-Domingue, du 1er décembre 1803 au 15 juillet 1809* . . . [Le Havre, 1846], p. 102; Duranton, *Memorial*, II, 249).

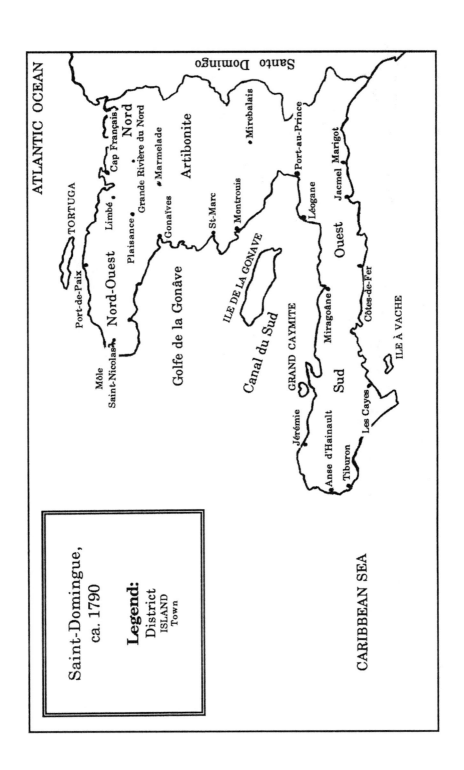

ATLANTIC OCEAN

Santo Domingo

Saint-Domingue,
ca. 1790

Legend:
District
ISLAND
Town

TORTUGA

Port-de-Paix

Nord-Ouest

Môle
Saint-Nicolas

Cap Français
Limbé
Grande Rivière du Nord
Plaisance
Marmelade

Nord

Artibonite

Gonaïves

St-Marc

Montrouis

Mirebalais

Golfe de la Gonâve

ILE DE LA GONAVE

Canal du Sud

Port-au-Prince

Léogane

Jacmel Marigot

Ouest

Côtes-de-Fer

GRAND CAYMITE

Jérémie

Anse d'Hainault

Tiburon

Miragoâne

Sud

Les Cayes

ILE À VACHE

CARIBBEAN SEA

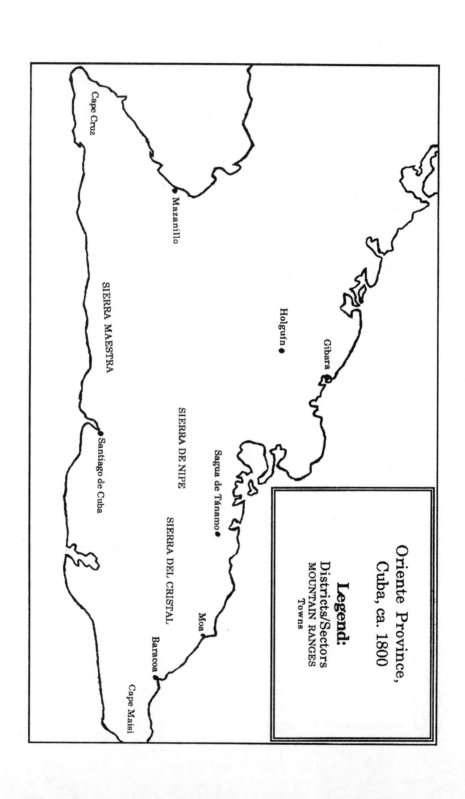

Oriente Province,
Cuba, ca. 1800

Legend:
Districts/Sectors
MOUNTAIN RANGES
Towns

Cape Cruz

Mazanillo

SIERRA MAESTRA

Holguin

Gibara

SIERRA DE NIPE

Santiago de Cuba

Sagua de Tánamo

SIERRA DEL CRISTAL

Moa

Baracoa

Cape Maisi

The next day, we arrived in Saint-Jacques [Santiago] de Cuba. This city . . . is situated on the river of the same name, two leagues inland, on the south side.

The mouth of the river is defended by a fort constructed from and carved out of a high rock . . . at a height of between 250 to 300 feet and whose access is very difficult because of its steepness. One can only get there by some small trails along the mountainside. It could be considered unconquerable if it had fresh water. It is impossible to penetrate the river without encountering the guards posted at the bottom of the fort.

After that first visit, we also suffered one of the five or six customs-boats so troublesome that no matter how in order your papers could be, there was nothing better to get rid of them than to give them a few *gourdes*.[55]

All formalities taken care of, we went upriver. Its banks presented a most pleasing aspect. No matter which direction the eyes may travel, they always fall upon delicious sites. Over there are the small hills where pineapples grow without being cultivated, further on, fig-trees and banana-trees. On the opposite bank, orchards of small areca trees or plains covered with melons of all kinds and colors! Ah! If nature has done everything on the enchanting banks of the Ozanna, here art has come to second it in order to give to its riches more brilliance and magnificence. The whole countryside which rises slightly on the right and on the left is crowned by groves of acacias, lemon-trees, orange-trees, and arecas arranged in such a picturesque manner that the eye, after seeing them, can no longer formulate any sort of desire. Some cabins, constructed with taste and almost all surrounded by columns supporting nice porches, look like so many small temples consecrated to the pastoral gods, and finishing the painting, make this place the most beautiful place in the universe.

. . . This city . . . is situated two leagues inland; but one can

[55]The money of Saint-Domingue, the *piastre grosse* (*gordo* in Spanish, big or heavy in English) whose value, depending on the exchange rate, varied from 5:1 to 8:1, 10 *sols*. The Spanish particularly surveyed the southern coast facing Saint-Domingue and its rebellious slaves.

say that the meanderings of the river hardly permit seeing it
before one is near arriving there. It was built at the very spot
where the river turns suddenly to the left; it rises in the form
of an amphitheater extending from the port, and is almost
entirely surrounded by trees, which renders a very romantic
setting; but the pleasing impression one gets is destroyed
upon entry. It is not very big and poorly constructed, and
even if the streets are wide and in a straight line, they are
not paved; some have sidewalks. With the exception of a few
edifices, such as the cathedral and the episcopal palace, which
would not get any attention anywhere else, the governor's
mansion, and about fifty other individual homes, the rest
is not worth any attention . . . I am not talking about the
convents in this city; as in all Spanish towns, they are rather
numerous, but few are noteworthy. The population may be
as high as 6,000, two-thirds of whom are blacks or men of
color . . .

In peacetime, this port is gloomy and deserted; and before
the migrations from the French colony of Saint-Domingue, this
country, although surrounded by European establishments,
afforded only overpowering solitude almost unknown in
the rest of the universe. The small amount of commerce
conducted here consisted of livestock, and still this commerce
was illegal, conducted with the ease the coast allowed. As for
the trade of colonial goods, it goes without saying that they
are non-existent; sugar produced in the area of Santiago is
used almost entirely to make jam out of pineapples, lemons,
and especially guavas, which are excellent and are said to be
the best in all of the Spanish colonies. However, the colonists
only farm for their own needs, and to attain a certain [level
of] material comfort, they only have to be willing to make an
effort.

This city, upon my arrival, had attained its highest
degree of prosperity. The disasters of . . . Saint-Domingue
had deposited here a large number of French fugitives who
had been joined by a few industrious immigrants from the
United States. They all speculated in the outfitting [of ships]
then underway, and in less than three months, the coast of
Jamaica had been covered by a swarm of corsairs who would

have certainly ruined the commerce of this colony if the Spanish governors had not, by their accord with the English, paralyzed and often neutralized the efforts of the ship-fitters and the audacity of the French sailors.[56]

Another refugee, arriving in Santiago hidden in the hold of a sailboat loaded with non-combatants, found:

A small town encumbered by 15 to 20,000 French— colonists, farmers, merchants. . . .

What a sight! What misery awaited us there! . . . I have come to add my misery to that of so many others. I had nothing more than the few rags covering me.

French industriousness there was, nevertheless, the same that it is everywhere. They created a second city on land designated by the Spanish government; it was called the French Quarters. Stones will eventually replace the wood of the primitive constructions, and, if Santiago is today bigger, [and] more heavily populated, it is a result of Saint-Domingue's misfortune.

In spite of the misery that weighed heavily upon everyone, the French temperament did not change, and [though] deprived of the basic necessities, they did not forget about pleasure. . . . In Santiago, where the misery was killing us, or so we thought, we built a Tivoli. We made a ballroom and a delightful garden which soon attracted the admiration of the Spaniards.[57]

[56]Dorvo-Solastre, *Voyage par terre de Santo-Domingo, capitale de Saint-Domingue, au Cap-Français, capitale de la partie française de la même isle, entrepris et éxécuté au mois de germinal, an VI, par les ordres du général du division Hédouville*] . . . (Paris, 1809), pp. 105-106, 115-119.

[57]We have an echo of this admiration provoked by this fashionable café/dance hall in a description by José María Callejas in his *Historia de Santiago de Cuba* (Havana, 1911): "High above Loma Hueca, protected by boards with a majestic frontispiece obeying one of the rules of architecture, they made their figures and seeded the land as it should be done and in the background they constructed Tejamán roofs with linen ceilings that covered from three to four hundred people and lined the walls with the same material, the whole thing painted in the best of taste, to which the name Tivoli was given. Moreover, they built two huts in the best manner and where all sorts of food and drink were served, excellent musicians and a few young French ladies led the whole French population there for the price of admission of one *duro* per individual, and within two months, they had paid off the immense cost of their work, and had a lot

Building a temple of pleasure upon a land of exile watered by our tears, a land where sorrow and misery successively claimed victims who had escaped the Negroes' knives! Dancing upon the ruins soaked in blood! What greater proof of national frivolity is it possible to give? The French Tivoli gained favor; French and Spanish ladies hastened there, trying to out do one another in accoutrement. This admirably designed garden, to which the tropical vegetation did not take long in giving refreshing umbrage, became the meeting point of all of the social groups. *Tertulias,* a great rotunda, was the ballroom; in a word, they did not neglect a single thing of all the pleasures such a place could reunite. We were miserable but we danced! And the entrepreneur did a marvelous business.

Luminous insects came to embellish still further these *soirées.* The ladies used them as ornaments; they attached them to their hair, their dresses, and their accessories and they then looked like Sylphides covered with brilliant emeralds. . . .

But alas! As everywhere, these recreations, these pleasures were shared among the rich, and there were even those among them who had fled Saint-Domingue; some had been able to save their money. As for the unfortunate, they were helped as much as possible. However, this relief had to come to an end and the misery was a deep hole impossible to fill. Charity itself was cooling off.

When I arrived amidst this colony, I had neither friends nor acquaintances; and yet I had to eat. A Creole named Courjol,[58] reduced to selling bread in a market for a baker, receiving one for every dozen sold; with his meager earnings, he fed his wife and sister; his beneficial generosity admitted me to the sharing of this bread with his family. But I had to put an end to this burden. A ship

---

left over to undertake other speculations."

[58]Probably François Courrjolle *dit* Corréjolles the younger, surgeon and colonist at Vallière and a home owner in Fort Dauphin.

equipped for privateering, commanded by French navy officers, led by frigate captain Boucher, had left New Orleans. A fine sailing ship, she had already made a few good hauls and was supposed to continue privateering for three months; I presented myself and was accepted as aspiring volunteer.[59]

Thus, according to the accounts of Dorvo-Soulastre[60] and [Jean-Baptiste] Lemonnier-Delafosse,[61] part of Santiago and its refugee population derived a living from, and speculated in, privateering. Soldiers transformed themselves into sailors, while even the smallest boats collaborated to watch Caribbean-bound shipping and to pounce upon slow and poorly defended vessels.

"The French corsairs fit out in Cuba."[62] "There is danger in going past the Tortugas; a French corsair has made several attacks there; he takes them to Baracoa where General Noailles has established his headquarters and has already judged the Americans to be easy pickings. This is enough to disgust any expedition for this region," Morange wrote to Stanislas Foäche speaking of the American merchandise much in need in Cap-Français.[63] In Santiago, the agent acting as provisional consul, Peyrussel, simultaneously served as receiver of the French government's duties arising from the sale of captured goods.[64] As with Trabuc, our consul in Havana,[65] Noailles was soon thereafter killed while coming alongside an English corsair.[66]

---

[59]Lemonnier-Delafosse, *Seconde campagne de Saint-Domingue* (Le Havre, 1846), p. 102.

[60]Annotator's note: See Dorvo-Soulastre, *Voyage par terre.*

[61]Annotator's note: See Lemonnier-Delafosse, *Seconde campagne.*

[62]Bégouën-Demeaux, *Mémorial,* II, p. 242 (early 1804).

[63]*Ibid.,* II, 243, February 18, 1804.

[64]Dorvo-Soulastre, *Voyage par terre,* p. 126.

[65]*Ibid.,* p. 407.

[66]Bégouën-Demeaux, *Mémorial,* II, 246. Annotator's note: Noailles was sailing to Ha-

Thus, Cuba was overflowing with Frenchmen at this time. This congregation of colonists and troops was to be short-lived. Lavallette's troops returned to Santo Domingo as soon as the English blockade was lifted.[67] General Ferrand,[68] former commander of the Spanish part [of Hispañola], soon assembled all of the debris from the Leclerc expedition which had escaped the capitulation of Cap-Français. A proclamation posted on the walls of Santiago invited the colonist-refugees to return to Saint-Domingue. Lemonnier-Delafosse, who had returned to Santiago after having been captured by the English, responded to this call, as well as "two hundred [others] of all ranks, officers, administrators, employees."[69]

A spontaneous sorting occurred as follows: The military elements, overwhelmingly strangers to Saint Domingue with its Creole mores and viewpoint, moved away, leaving the former colonists who were accustomed to the climate, to the means of production, to the country's way of life, ready for a new beginning which was the survival of a society, a return to a lost world, and the re-establishment of the values and the classes they thought had disappeared.

This installation in the east of Cuba, this conquest of the hills by the coffee growers thus becomes the very history of the refugees. All we have to do now is to open the works of the Cuban historians and to sum up first of all the one by Mr. Pérez de la Riva.[70]

vana at the time of his death.

[67]*Ibid.,* 250, May 7, 1804.

[68]Annotator's note: Marie-Louis Ferrand (1753-1808). Ferrand was commissioned lieutenant in the French army in 1792. He was promoted to squadron chief the following year. After a brief period of detention as a political prisoner, he became commandant of the Pas-de-Calais region. In 1802, Ferrand participated in the Leclerc expedition to Saint-Domingue. Following Leclerc's death, Ferrand became commander-in-chief of the French forces in the French-speaking portion of Hispañola. Following the capture of Cap Français by black insurgents under Dessalines, Ferrand and his army withdrew to Spanish-speaking Santo Domingo, where he assumed control of the defenses for the eastern portion of the island. On March 3, 1803, Ferrand's forces defeated Dessalines' 22,000-man invading army. Ferrand remained commander-in-chief of the eastern half of Hispañola until his death.

[69]Lemieu-Delafosse, *Campagne,* p. 167.

[70]*El café, historia de su cultivo y explotación en Cuba* (Havana, 1944), p.383.

V.—COFFEE IN CUBA BEFORE 1800

One cannot say that it was the successful beginnings of the Spanish coffee growers in Cuba that encouraged the refugees to come to the neighboring island. The exploitation of coffee groves was just getting underway.[71]

Not everyone agrees upon the date when the first attempts were made [to grow coffee in Cuba]. The first seeds seem to have been planted around 1748. They could have been brought by Don José Gelabert who founded a small plantation on a corner of his property around the present-day village of Wajay in the province of Havana. They did not seek to obtain seeds to grow roasting beans but rather the kind used to make alcohol.[72] One must also consider the fact that the introduction of coffee trees for dried beans did not take place until 1768, when beans were brought from Puerto Rico.[73]

The success of the French coffee groves in Martinique and Saint-Domingue encouraged these experiments. In Europe, the consumption of coffee increased annually. The example of Don José Gelabert, not much followed in the beginning, was commented upon and imitated a little more actively when the royal decree of 1779 authorized commerce with almost all the ports of mainland France. But even in 1789, no comparison whatsoever was possible between the 3,117 coffee groves of Saint-Domingue producing 662,000 quintals[74] and the four or five Cuban plantations. Only 1,850 quintals[75] were produced in Cuba

---

[71]This chapter and many of the following chapters owe much to the book by Mr. Francisco Pérez de la Riva, *El café* (Havana, 1944). They are often nothing more than a summary.

[72]José M. de la Torre, *Lo que fuimos y lo que somos o La Havana antigua y moderna.*

[73]José Antonio Saco, Collección de papeles científicos, históricos, políticos y de otros ramos sobre la isla de Cuba. Paris, 1858-1859, t. I

[74]Rd. P. Cabon, *Histoire d'Haïti*, 4 vols. (Port-au-Prince, s. d.), II, 515.

[75]7,400 local *arrobes.*

during 1790, and the results of the first expeditions were hardly encouraging. Poorly prepared and poorly presented, the Cuban coffees were not highly prized. Havana obtained the coffee it traditionally liked from San Juan, Puerto Rico. But a change was about to take place.

The independence of the continental English colonies had the same consequences for the closest Spanish islands as for the French Antilles. Coffee, a Franco-American product, began to supplant English tea in New England, and in return, American flour came to compete more intensely in Cap-Français and in Port-au-Prince with the Aquitaine flour, the distribution of which was monopolized by Bordeaux. The American world was growing increasingly interdependent. An increase in coffee and sugar prices resulted and stimulated coffee growing in Cuba as well as in Saint-Domingue.

A modification of the fiscal system, outlined as early as 1768, also sought to direct the Cuban colonists towards coffee production.[76] Most official aid came from another direction. Cuba had not received the hundreds of thousands of slaves that Saint-Domingue had. Unlike Saint-Domingue, they had not been gripped by the fever to make a fortune at all costs. The creation of a few plantations quickly depleted the available supply of manual labor. There was a greater need for slaves in Cuba than in Saint-Domingue. A royal decree of February 28, 1789, conceded the free entry of slaves from foreign markets to Cuba, Puerto Rico, Santo Domingo, and in the province of Caracas.[77] Over the next eighteen months, 4,000 blacks were introduced into Cuba, more than half of them by the English company of Barker and Dawson.[78] But the port of Santiago, restricted to Spanish commerce, had not received any workers to

[76]F. Pérez de la Riva, *El café,* pp. 12-13.

[77]*Ibid.* p. 10.

[78]*Ibid.* p. 12: "England had always had great interest in the slave trade with Cuba. It would be particularly observant after this commerce was banned in 1815." E. Williams. "The Negro Slave Trade in Anglo-Spanish Relations," *Caribbean Historical Review,* I (1950), 22-45.

speak of. Cuban coffee groves are not developed on this end but rather around Havana, near Wajay, in the Arcos de Canasi sector, in the neighborhood of Guanajay, and in the vicinity of Macaguabo. They moved toward Santa Lucia Yayabo and Banao, but without noticably affecting the countryside. Again, it is not always easy to date the beginnings of these plantations many of which do not appear to have been established before 1793.

The troubles in Saint-Domingue immediately diminished French production and upset the general conditions of the market. The rise or drop in coffee and sugar prices was of such widespread international interest that the beginnings of the Revolution in the Antilles and the slave uprising in August 1791 were for all of the big international market places subjects of anxiety or competition and for everyone a matter to watch and ponder.

Here the action of the *Société patriotique des amis du pays*,[79] an organization patterned after the multiple-section academies common to the eighteenth century which had been founded in Santiago, then moved to Havana in 1793, was timely. Its agriculture and rural economy section did some good work locally. Its delegate to the royal court, Francisco de Arango y Perraño, very quickly saw how Spain could turn the insurrection in Saint-Domingue to its advantage. He immediately conceived a plan for Cuba to fill the void in the European market created by the loss of French commerce. With this goal in mind, mainland Spain had to pay special attention to renewing agriculture on the big island. Arango obtained financial exemptions for Cuban coffee and the appointment of a commission which, after a fact-finding mission, would issue a comparative study of the English, Dutch, and French colonists if at all possible.[80] Arango and the Count of Casa Montalvo took part in this commission which did not leave until 1794 and ran into every sort of problem imaginable. Montalvo made a lengthy sojourn in Jamaica and left for Havana only to die

---

[79]Translator's note: Patriotic Society of the Friends of the Country.

[80]Spain had been at war with France since early 1793.

there. Most of the planters assembled for this mission were
lost in a shipwreck near Cuba. But in Kingston, the commission
was able to persuade several experienced colonists from Saint-
Domingue to relocate in Cuba. These refugees arrived with
Arango.[81]

We do not have the names of the first Frenchmen who came
with the precise intention of attempting to cultivate coffee in
Cuba. But one may speculate that they had done some serious
research beforehand and that they had armed themselves
with some capital and good [business] connections. It is also
probable that those who came from Jamaica were able to bring
with them some slaves and that these slaves were accustomed
to the cultivation and preparation of coffee. These newcomers
settled around Havana or Matanzas, next to those who had
already set the stage for small-scale operations. These coffee
farms had from fifteen to thirty slaves and the largest counted
51,000 coffee trees. The *El Moca* coffee farm with sixteen slaves
exploited 16,000 trees; *Bellavista* with twenty-eight slaves,
35,000 trees; *Los Placeres* in Ubajay with twelve slaves and
11,125 trees; *El Limones,* thirty-one slaves and 51,000 trees; *Las
Verdudes*, twelve slaves and 17,000 trees. Marquis Duquesne's
plantation was already established in 1766.[82] It was located in
the Candelaria sector and had been called the Union, maybe to
indicate that, originally, it was part of an association.

In 1795, the price of a quintal of coffee in Havana was at
fourteen *piastres* and in 1798 the colony exported 4,641 quintals.
In spite of the early official encouragements, Cuban production
was not yet in full swing. Exportation to Louisiana and the
United States was increasing, but the European market was
looking more toward Asia for its coffee.

The Treaty of Basel (1795) and the Treaty of San Ildefonso
(1796)[83] made former enemies Spain and France collaborators in
the fight against the English navy. Though the attitude of the

[81]*El café*, p. 16.

[82]*Ibid.*, p. 18.

[83]Annotator's note: The first Treaty of San Ildefonso, concluded on August 19, 1796, established "in perpetuity an offensive and defensive alliance between the French Republic
and His Catholic Majesty." Article 18 of the treaty, however, obliged Spain to become
involved directly in open warfare only if England were a party to the hostilities.

Spanish colonist toward the revolutionary assemblies' decrees hardly changed, the borders of the Spanish holdings were more easily opened to the refugees. Many who had sought asylum in Jamaica considered arranging for themselves, through a stay on allied soil, a return to France where they had been registered on the rolls of *émigrés*.

VI.—THE LAND PROBLEM

Just what lands did the refugees find? Nowhere, it seems, had Cuban soil yet borne any true intensive agriculture. Rural real estate had been divided up by the town councils into concessions, to increase settlement. These lots were used as corrals for raising large and small livestock.[84] They had contented themselves with watching over the herds that grazed in the savanna. Cuba was, like the Spanish part of Saint-Domingue, primarily a pastoral country. A concession was less of a farming permit than a means of preventing the installation of neighboring ranchers. Don Buenaventura Pascual y Ferrer and the French refugees describe to us what they found in 1798: an abandoned, almost desert-like countryside.

Land prices had risen slightly toward the end of the eighteenth century but its added value was only perceptible in the Havana area. Even there, land was much cheaper than in the French Antilles. Bryan Edwards in the 1780s speaks of the difficulties of acquiring good Jamaican land near the sea and accessible to a wharf. All land more than ten miles inland, unwanted by the sugarcane growers, went for £10 per acre.[85] The average cost of a *carreau* (1.26 hectares),[86] within the normal price range of the common small planter growing coffee or other crops, remained

[84]*Ibid.*, p. 25.

[85]*Ibid.* p. 28.

[86]Rd. P. Cabon, *Histoire d'Haïti*, I, p. 62. *Peuchet, Dictionaire de la France commerçante* (Paris, year VII), p. 201, says that the *carreau* in Saint-Domingue measured 1 hectare (2.47 acres).

much more expensive in the hills of Saint-Domingue than in Cuba. But it was no longer a question of returning to the newer settlements in the French part [of Saint-Domingue].

At the outset, the problem of property and its subdivision had to be resolved, as did the the eternal confrontation between the unlanded laborer and the huge uncultivated domaines. Up until the end of the eighteenth century, *accensement*[87] had been the customary basis for allocating Cuban lands and the principle method of improving them. Since capital was lacking, one could not imagine a better way to utilize the fallow lands. Potential takers, who could not previously consider acquisition of real estate, preferred this technique. This tradition began giving way to short-term leases, especially for the coffee fields. The East was still untouched by these innovations.

To determine the disposition of arable lands or to own them outright, colonists used diverse schemes depending upon the local and regional circumstances.

It seems that they initially used, particularly in the West, the old form of association of city capital with country men, such as it was practiced in Saint-Domingue. An owner or lender of funds—usually Spanish—and slaves made an agreement with a refugee and confided to him the management of his land and his manual labor for part of the profits. The refugee sometimes brought a few of his own slaves into the venture, and sometimes the capital or a part of it. Such was the case in the arrangement between Joseph de Messemé and D'Espinville and in the case of François-Aimable de Chappotin, who would not have his own coffee plantation with 100,000 trees and a house until 1806.[88]

In other instances, associations remained strictly family businesses. Land, slaves, "establishments" for the drying and sorting of the coffee beans remained undivided for a long time because it was imperative that each brother, each father and his children draw together what little [money] they could save and, above all, consolidate their efforts.

---

[87]Annotator's note: a system in which tenants who hold a hereditary right to rent specific tracts of land.

[88]Chappotin Papers, Col. Marois, Le Lude, by Saint Sauveur le Vicomte, Manche, 1952.

Royal lands were also divided up and ceded at fixed monetary rates, five percent of the land's value,[89] as in the case of the properties around Nipe Bay on the northern shore of the eastern half. They immediately attracted the colonists taking refuge in Santiago. The same phenomenon was observed in the Dos Bocas mountain range and its surrounding hills and in the Sierra Madre. The fertile grounds of the East also had much in common with the soil of Saint-Domingue. On the coast, coffee plantations were able to go up in the districts of La Guira, Guánica, Candelaria del Aguacate, Santa Rosa de Lima, El Cuseo, San Blas, Carajiraca, El Rosario, and a part of Rangal where they parcelled out the largest private domaines through individual contract sales. Sierra Maestra, Limones, Zacatecas, Suetos, Canto Jiguani, Holguin, Sagua, and Mayari were mostly royal possessions.[90] These allotments were of great help in the refugees early efforts.

Not all of these concessions were handled directly. The royal domain was alienated into vast tracts of land. Intermediaries intervened, as well as speculators. A businessman from Santiago, Prudencio Casamayor (Prudent Grandmaison?), related to several refugees, bought from the royal domain and from individuals the Limones lands in the Sierra Maestra, unexploited hill-land that one had reason to consider fertile. Casamayor divided it up into lots of 100 *carreaux*; rather small judging by American standards. He had them tenant farmed or sold them to refugees who planted coffee trees and also some cotton. For a very long time, Casamayor acted as the general agent, businessman, advisor, and probably banker to most of the French colonists.[91]

In certain cases, the immensity of the properties being acquired imposed [the creation of] a new form of stockholding company. Several refugees had to unite to buy a large tract, not

---

[89]Information directly given by Mr. Pérez de la Riva who is preparing a study on the origins of rural property in Cuba.

[90]*El café*, p. 27.

[91]B. Maurel, "L'habitation d'un Bayonnais à Saint-Domingue (1784-1804)," *Bulletin Soc. des Sc. Bayonne* (1935), 354; Debien, *Les Sources . . .*, p. 43.

only to divide it up amongst themselves but also to put some of it back for sale in large sections. In this manner a large group of investors united around Louis de Bellegarde, former lieutenant in the regiment at Cap-Français,[92] which included: Lambert, colonist in Dondon who came to Cuba after having taken refuge in the Spanish part of Saint-Domingue;[93] Savon, refugee from Baradères on the southern coast; Thomas; Duran; and Moreau, from Dondon, right next to the Spanish border where he ran a coffee plantation;[94] the viscount d'Alzon who had commanded, under English occupation, the York colonial corps;[95] and Jean Depaigne.[96] With them, and perhaps backing them, was Don Prudencio Casamayor; all these French colonists were already running their own small coffee plantations around Santiago. They bought from Don Manuel Justiz the Santa Catalina tract to organize a general settlement, which would become the setting for a French village.[97]

It was located in Ticoabo parish, Guantánamo province, one of those immense half-wooded, half-pastoral regions. Its approximate surface was 16,000 Saint-Domingue *carreaux* (about 17,500 hectares). The sea was only three or four leagues away; four or five rivers[98] watered this plain still covered in large part by cedar and gaianicum forests.

The company's capital was divided into sixteen parts or

[92]Louis-Joseph Laforgue, chevalier de Bellegarde. AN Colonies E, 25.

[93]J. G. Hopkirk, *An Account of the Insurrection in St. Domingue . . .* (Edinburgh, 1833), p. 24.

[94]Two Moreaus were coffee-colonists in Dondon, Jacob-Vincent and his wife Elisabeth Torel in Mare à la Roche (*Etat des indeminities*, 1831; hereafter cited as *Etat*) and Antoine, a colonist in Haut du Trou (*Etat*, 1830). See also S. Hazard, *San-Domingo: Past and Present* (London, n.d.), p. 504.

[95]A. Michel, *La mission d'Hédouville*, p. 185; [Charles] Chalmers, [*Remarks on the Late War in St. Domingo, with Observations on the Relative Situation of Jamaice* (London, 1903)], pp. 32, 56. *Précis historique des annales*, I, 283; *History of San Domingo*, pp. 141-142.

[96]Co-owners of houses in Cap-Français. *Etat des indemnities*, 1831.

[97]*El café*, p. 25.

[98]In the island's lingo, a river was considered to be any flowing water on a more or less permanent basis.

shares, of which Bellegarde owned three. Each associate carved out of this great expanse a 200-*carreaux* lot, and the rest, undivided, offered the foundation for eighty more plantations of about 200 *carreaux* each. Bellegarde and Casamayor had begun building in the middle of this immense spread a corral for about 500 mules, horses, and cattle destined to be used as a source of beasts of burden and as meat for the first pioneers.

Three principal advantages could be drawn from these concessions, according to Bellegarde who acted as spokesman for the partnership:[99] first of all, wood to be used in boat building and other construction work that one could one day send to a unwooded Saint-Domingue; the flatness of the land and the abundance of water invited the planting of sugarcane fields that need consistent humidity; and under the trees near the clearings, coffee could be planted.

> The proximity of this terrain to the coasts of Saint-Domingue and the United States of America is also a consideration not to be neglected and whose influence is such that the expenses of a settlement upon a territory just as advantageously situated would not make up one-sixteenth of those we were obligated to incur in Saint-Domingue.

No one amongst the refugees had yet lost hope of returning.

> On the island of Cuba and more particularly in the region of Santa Catalina, pigs are very common and of a large species, which represents a major object of speculation and consumption by the inhabitants.
>
> Honey bees are also very common . . . All of the grounds of this concession can be easily watered and with almost no expense; there is a multiplicity of rivers which offer easy access due to the fact that the land gently slopes from the foot of the mountain to the sea; this could be a great resource for the sugar mills and even for any sort of mechanical construction that one could only operate in a most expensive

[99]*El café*, Appendix no. 3, p. 317-321; summary of the Bellegarde plan according to the Archives du Port de Toulon, SRI, no. 20.

66   *The Saint-Domingue Refugees*

manner due to the use of animals . . .

By way of comparison, land on the coast of Havana went
for up to 2,000 *gourdes* plus the horse-corral which comes out
to around 200 *gourdes* per *carreau*.[100] The French population
and industry alone have caused such a considerable rise
in prices and yet they were still far below the land rates in
Saint-Domingue where sugarcane fields are sold for up to
1,200 *gourdes* per *carreau* and coffee as much as 600.

Who knows if this is not what is in store for Santa-
Catalina real estate?

Moreover, in the establishment in question, Mr. de
Bellegarde undertook to obtain at this time the quantity of
land that one might want at less than 4 or 5 *gourdes* per
carreau or 50 *gourdes* per horse-corral. . . .

Once peace is made, we should be able to count more on
these farms being established in this fertile country than on
any of those we might establish in Saint-Domingue. . . .

Certainly, in this grand project there was a speculation
scheme, and a rather bold one at that. It was nevertheless
a wise one. But it was also risky, for, though this land was
deep and fertile, Negroes were scarce everywhere in Cuba and
thus very expensive, especially in the sectors just opening to
agriculture. The state of the French and Spanish navies left
little hope for a positive change over a short period of time.
Installing the types of immense sugar mills built at great
expense over generations in northern Saint-Domingue was out
of the question. The tendency was to establish "little sites" with
a few slaves for the routine of tilling the soil, planting the cane,
and trimming it. Extra hands were hired during the periods of
more intense activity such as the harvest, the grinding of the
cane, and the fabrication of sugar. Or better yet, they would use
a sort of sugar-mill "co-op" run with rented slaves. This practice
greatly reduced each sugar plantation's operating expenses. In
addition, the high yield of the sugarcane with so little manual
labor fostered great hopes. Rotation in Cuba was different from

[100]One *carreau* equals 1.26 hectares or about 1,000 pounds per square or 800 *francs* per
hectare.

the one practiced on the plantations of northern Saint-Domingue where the fields were replanted after the fourth or fifth season, whereas in Cuba, "once planted they [served] for a whole generation." The slaves had to turn the soil less often, plant less often.

What a French colonist would find hard to believe is that there is a sugar-mill near Santa Catalina where there are only two Negroes and that usually when grinding time comes around, there are only ten or twelve in all.

In spite of its grand pretensions, the association mostly served as a support group for the small *habitations* or farms. One of the first to be established in Santa Catalina appears to have been Morel de Guiramand, lawyer before the *parlement*,[101] who experienced his hour of glory at Port-au-Prince in December of 1789, when he organized a sort of corporation to support [financially] the colony's government and administration when they were attacked by Baron de la Chevalerie's men and the provincial committees. His nomination, under the English, to the position of civil and criminal lieutenant in Saint Mark, had forced him to seek exile in 1798.[102]

These plantations were thus reminiscent, in more than one respect, of the ones on the high hills of Saint-Domingue where "colored people" were so numerous. The framework is narrow. The family is helped by a few blacks—ten, fifteen, or twenty at the most. These establishments were in no way speculative in nature. There was no capital available to acquire new land, clear and till it and then resell it in order to buy elsewhere. One worked to live. The beginning of co-operative farming was the new addition, something one had never seen before in Saint-Domingue; individual sugarcane fields arranging themselves around an animal-driven sugarmill jointly managed; first

---

[101]Annotator's note: Quasi-legislative and judicial bodies in *ancien régime* France.

[102]Not to be confused with another Morel, much younger, who was a long time refugee in Santiago de Saint-Domingue and who was Bishop Mauviel's interpreter in 1801. Rd. P. Cabon, *Notes*, p. 75.

figuration of the centrals that appear in the second half of the century.

VII.—THE ORIGINS OF FRENCH COFFEE FARMS

The development of French properties in Cuba occurred in 1806-1807, at a time when the refugee population was most likely at its highest point. In fact, it is so high at that time that the rumor amongst the colonists was that Spain was going to exchange the eastern part of Cuba for the formerly Spanish part of Saint-Domingue ceded to France by the Treaty of Basel. The western part [of Cuba] contained the sugar mills and Havana.

In June of 1807, General Turreau,[103] agent of the imperial government to the United States, sent to his minister, Tallyrand,[104] a long report which reveals the role Napoleon foresaw for this core of Frenchmen in the reconquering of Saint-Domingue.

Since my arrival in America, I have received several reports, all confirming the prosperous state that the island of Cuba has attained ever since a few refugees from Saint-Domingue have activated the existing agriculture and enriched it with several new crops.

This growth of Cuban products, as a result of its commercial relations, is the work of approximately 18,000 individuals composed of former colonists from Saint-Domingue and a few black or mulatto slaves who followed them.

The nucleus of the French settlement, centered primarily in Santiago, will become very precious, whatever the future outcome for Cuba might be. I ventured my opinion to this effect in an old memo[105] . . . and everyday experience confirms

[103]Annotator's note: Louis-Marie, baron Turreau de Linières (1756-1816), was s the French ambassador to the United States from 1804 to 1811. He entered the French diplomatic service after a long military career, during which he had served as commander of the military forces along the Spanish border (1793).

[104]Annotator's note: Charles Maurice de Talleyrand-Perigord (1754-1838) served as the French minister of Foreign Affairs from 1797 to 1807.

[105]Other memoirs of Turreau are to be found in the Archives of Foreign Affairs, United States political correspondence, volumes 58 to 67.

to me its accuracy.

Cuban soil is just as good if not better than the Saint-Domingue variety and yet what kind of progress has been made in the last century? Coffee-growing was unheard of before the arrival of the French refugees. Still their first attempts were delayed because the locals would uproot the burgeoning plants, because this innovation seemed so dangerous.

While waiting for Spain to become sufficiently enlightened about the advantages of abandoning an insular colony that it cannot adequately protect, and indeed which other circumstances, other factors force it to cede, it seems to me, without claiming an insight into its views regarding Cuba, that it is in the best interest of the government to protect and feed this nucleus of Saint-Domingue *émigré*-colonists, to increase its influence, and to foster its development. It would appear to me especially advisable not to leave to their own devices these Frenchmen, who have been cast upon a strange island by misfortune. Effervescent but embittered, these Creoles find themselves without direction [and] without support.[106] Yet they themselves could still find the will to combat these problems, were they not forced to struggle against this country's prejudices; the hate, ignorance, and superstitions of its people; the partiality of its laws; and the tyranny of its magistrates.

This assemblage of French Creoles in Cuba in any case would be a very important advantage for us,[107] especially if the [French] government sought to acquire Saint-Domingue[108] after abandoning Saint-Domingue, whose ruin will be completed by recent events and the ensuing bloody struggle. We cannot hide from the fact that the only remaining resource available to revitalize this colony is the

[106]An allusion, it seems, to a few divisons amongst the colonists.

[107]Annotator's note: France.

[108]Slip of the pen for Cuba.

few blacks who live there, and this resource has already been altered by the internal war and the licentious life of these hooligans. It must be observed that, whatever the means used in retaking Saint-Domingue, we will probably be forced to sacrifice a rather large number of them in order to crush all resistance. *Marronage*[109] of long duration after the reconquest of the colony will also divert many more [black laborers] from farming. Upon returning to Saint-Domingue everything would have to be started over again, and if, as is commonly known, all the rich land-owners of this colony were completely ruined, when and how will Saint-Domingue return to its former state of prosperity?

But without anticipating the policy the government should adopt, I would judge it convenient to establish in Cuba, with a residence in Santiago, a French agent with the title of consul general. His commission, his official and patented instructions, would only deal with commercial affaires. These particular instructions could have another meaning. There already has been, and there will be again, in Cuba, agents or commissioners sent by our captains-general. But these commissioners did not have enough authority and their mission has always been nearly useless because of either a lack of power or personal finances. . . .[110]

Bellegarde, who seems to have been an agent of the Guadeloupe commandant, must be counted amongst these commissioners. In 1805, Couët de Montaran had been named agent for the French government in Santiago by General Ferrand, Rochambeau's successor. His first task was to aid the French refugees. His instructions from General Ferrand have been preserved, as well as a portion of his correspondence and his account books.[111] He occasionally travelled to Saint-Domingue to visit the general-captain. He went there in 1806 and in 1807 upon the sloop *L'Impérial*. His principal duty soon became the collection

[109]Annotator's note: A term applied to the uncertain status of runaway slaves.

[110]*Revue de la Revolution*, (September 1886), 65-70. Letter about Cuba.

[111]Beauregard papers, with Mme. de Beauregard in St. Omer (1939).

of duties for the prizes taken by French corsairs in the Antilles. Most of it [the revenues] paid the army's expenses in Saint-Domingue. Collection of this tax was hindered by great difficulties; and in his own words, if he had pursued only to his own interests, the immediate ones at least, he would have settled near Santiago as a coffee planter, or better yet, in one of the sections of Santo Domingo still protected by French divisions. They enjoyed a seemingly perfect tranquility when compared to the thousand annoying details whose origin the refugees in Cuba blamed on the Spanish administration's ill will.

Rear Admiral Wuillaumez, who commanded the naval division in Havana, wrote to him on November 29, 1806:

> I am afraid that the French agents will be forced to endure [these problems] with the patience they have shown until now in all areas within the jurisdiction of the Marquis [de Somernalos]; but the day will come they will be [avenged] by the exemplary punishment that our powerful sovereign will surely demand for those who will have mistreated his subjects . . .

Montaran disregarded those who painted an enchanting portrait of the plantations in the formerly Spanish part [of Hispañola]. He remained in Santiago. He kept alive his hopes for Saint-Domingue, and he wrote incessantly to his brother-in-law who had remained in France and who had acquired land there that gave him nothing but trouble:

> Santiago, October 17, 1807.—I would have liked very much, my dear Degorsse, to acknowledge receipt of a few letters from you or from my dear sister; but since the one you wrote on December 20, we have received nothing from you. Such a long time! . . . Remember that of four letters [mailed to me], I am very fortunate if one reaches its destination. My wife is sorry not to be able to relieve her sister's suffering. . . . We would then forget the wrongs we have endured; I am far, however, from complaining about my situation. I am not needy, thanks to my worthy and very good General Ferrand. He ended my misery . . .

I have just lost 400 *gourdes* . . . The ill-fated Leris had
just borrowed the sum from me last September 16 with the
promise to return it to me within a month's time, when,
on the twenty-ninth, he put a bullet through his head. . . .
He was the Frenchman most well-liked by his compatriots
and by the Spanish and would have found the resources for
work.

If peace causes land to regain much of its former value,
you would do well to sell yours [in France]. Saint-Domingue
is where you can re-establish your fortune and make one for
your family. It will be many years in the making; you must
give up France![112]

The 18,000 Frenchmen proposed by Turreau in all likelihood
must have been exaggerated. Mr. Pérez de la Riva estimates
the figure at 10,000 colonists, whites and coloreds, who arrived
in Cuba between 1801 and 1806.[113]   Such an immigration, so
clearly concentrated, must have significantly raised prices for
colonial goods and created an important demand for virgin land
by stimulating the old sugarcane industry around Santiago. In
the sugar and coffee sections, land prices quintupled between
1800 and 1806.

Their value attained unbelievable heights, even for the
worst of them that were used to cultivate coffee. The driest,
the worst exposed, the lands least adapted to this crop were
bought and tilled without anyone worrying about its real
profitability or about a possible future reduction in the price of
coffee. Speculation came into play, as is always the case when
new lands are involved. A *chevalée*[114] of forest land upon divided
property and capable of sustaining coffee cultivation went for
as much as 5,000 *piastres*. In all of the land sales announced
in the newspapers, one reads the same refrain: "excellent land
for growing coffee." The merchants wanted to have at hand
this coveted grain and coffee served as a means of exchange;

[112]Regnault de Beaucaron, I, p. 146.

[113]*El café,* p. 27.

[114]Thirteen hectares.

houses,[115] plantations,[116] slaves,[117] are up for sale, always payable in coffee.

The rise of coffee production also has its tacit eloquence. Before the arrival of the refugees, the harvest had never reached 8,000 *arrobes* (2,000 quintals). As early as 1805, it went to 80,000 *arrobes,* 300,000 the following years.

In the province of Santiago, the attitude of the local governor, Kindelan, helped develop this wealth. One of the reports to the royal consulat in Havana juxtaposes the eight coffee farms hardly worth mentioning in 1803[118] with the 54 which were established in the single year of 1804, comprising over 500,000 plants. In Dos Bocas, the most important coffee district, before 1803, there were only 73,000 plants. In 1804, 305,000 were planted, 362,000 in 1805, 289,000 in 1806, 162,000 in 1807. In 1803 there were 12,000 plants in the Guia district. To these were added 12,000 in 1804, 61,000 in 1805, 96,000 in 1806, 112,000 in 1807. In the Guanian district, the 10,000 coffee trees of 1803 increased to 83,000 in 1804, to 270,000 in 1805, to 441,000 in 1806, 538,000 in 1807. The same progression occurred in Candelario; from 10,000 to 121,000, to 350,000, to 526,000, to 652,000. Elsewhere the departure was longer in coming. Sierra Maestra was not planted until 1807 (60,000 plants), the Canto, the Tinguabo, and the Sueltos not before 1806; but as early as 1804 in the Limones and the Sacateca whose coffee farms comport 568,000 and 146,000 plants respectively in 1807.[119]

All of this new cultivation would not be in full production for several seasons. Kindelan calculated nontheless that in his province 10,000 quintals were harvested in 1807, 20,000 in 1808, at least 30,000 in 1809, and 40,000 were expected in 1810.

These results were the work of a few enterprising and energetic men, each heading up a small number of slaves. In

[115]El aviso de la Havana, no. 94 (1809). Cited by Mr. Pérez de la Riva.

[116]*Ibid.,* no. 82 (1809).

[117]*Ibid.,* no. 434 (1811).

[118]Just as a comparison, in 1800 there were only sixty coffee plantations on the whole island of Cuba.

[119]*El café,* p. 28-29.

the province of Oriente, Kindelan counted 192 coffee colonists in 1807. There are only forty-nine of them with 336 workers in Dos Bocas exploiting 1,148,000 plants, only twenty-six with ninety-nine men in La Guira for 293,000 plants, just ten colonists with 257 blacks for 625,000 plants. Moreau de Saint-Méry[120] in Saint-Domingue praises the Bonseigneur plantation in Port-de-Paix, on the Moka heights, which, in 1784 with twenty-five blacks, harvested ninety *milliers*[121] of coffee, which represents approximately 120,000 plants of all ages, and over 4,000 per worker. But these figures are exceptional;[122] all points to the fact that the average slave yielded on these new lands, under the supervision of his master and grouped into small teams, more here than in Saint-Domingue. The proportion of the number of slaves per thousand coffee trees is much less in Cuba than in Dutch Guyana where Pinckard counted two blacks for every acre and 450 trees per acre.[123]

The colonists complained of a lack of available manpower in the face of such a success. Slaves remained rare, especially in the eastern provinces. Kindelan reports that it was only possible to buy 250 of them when paying cash. They had been introduced by a French corsair who had taken them from an English slave-trader.

In Santiago, the emigrants, and by extention coffee growers, had the support of Don Gréag, "canon of the cathedral church . . . one of the richest landowners in this part of the island, a highly

---

[120]Annotator's note: Médéric Louis Elie Moreau de Saint-Méry (1750-1819) had been a prominent attorney in Saint-Domingue before the black revolution. He was a founder and president of the Museum of Paris. Active in the French Revolution, he was forced to flee to the United States in 1794. He established and operated a publishing house in Philadelphia between 1794 and 1798, when he returned to France. Moreau de Saint-Méry served as an administrator in French-occupied Italy from 1802 to 1806.

[121]One *millier* equals one thousand pounds in weight.

[122]Moreau de Saint-Méry, *Description de la partie française de Saint-Domingue*, 2 vols. (Philadephia, 1796-1797). See also in the La Rochelle Library the Boutin papers, Ms. 85, Letter of September 30, 1788. One black produced 3,600 pounds of coffee.

[123]*Notes on the West Indies during the Expedition of Sir R. Abercromby . . .*, 3 vols. (London, 1806), III, 404.

educated man, friend and protector of the French."[124] Near Havana, they received encouragement from Don Gabriel María de Cárdenas, second marquis of Montehermoso, very rich landowner, who founded on his estate the city of San Antonio de los Baños, an important coffee center. He established for himself a large coffee plantation. Coffee trees reached sections of Alquizar, San Juan, and Artemias. Alquizar had as many as 84 plantations and produced 80,000 *arrobes* (20,000 quintals)[125].

We have a general list of the Cuban coffee farms in 1807,[126] and here are the names of the French planters one can find in it:

In the district of Dos Bocas:

Mathurin	who owned	30	slaves.
Crombett?	" "	30	"
Dufouard & Company	" "	40	"
Dauvergne	" "	3	"
Foucher[127]	" "	20	"
Drouillet[128]	" "	40	"
Martin[129]	" "	5	"
Lefèvre[130]	" "	15	"
Rey, the elder[131]	" "	3	"
Georgette	" "	5	"
Cauchois[132]	" "	15	"

[124]Dorvo-Solastre, *Voyage par terre,* p. 107, note.

[125]*El café,* p. 29.

[126]Published by Mr. Pérez de la Riva, p. 143-145, according to the National Archives of Cuba. Leg. 92 no. 3,929.

[127]Most likely Jean Faucher, owner of a coffee plantation in Port-Margot (*Etat des indemnities,* 1829).

[128]There were Drouillets in Cayes and a Bernard Druillet, coffee grower in Nippes (*Etat,* 1829).

[129]Louis Martin, colonial coffee grower in Montaña Terible, in Mirebalais (*Etat,* 1832).

[130]The coffee-growing Lefèvres were too numerous in Saint-Domingue to be able to identify this particular one.

[131]J. Rey, from Jérémie.

[132]Thomas Cauchoix, coffee grower in Jérémie (*Etat,* 1832).

Marillet[133]	"	"	10	"

District of La Guira

Frit	who owned		6	slaves.
Sterlin[134]	"	"	45	"
Goyo	"	"	3	"
Beurier	"	"	10	"
Delza	"	"	18	"
Jabuteau	"	"	2	"
Deniaut	"	"	10	"
Cholet[135]	"	"	22	"
Henri[136]	"	"	5	"
Dupré	"	"	5	"
Isnard[137]	"	"	5	"
Lépine[138]	"	"	12	"
Santaraille	"	"	4	"
Lombard[139]	"	"	12	"
Fourtetot	"	"	2	"
Malbernac	"	"	2	"
Montégut[140]	"	"	20	"
Despaigne & Company	"	"	80	
Mallet[141]	"	"	10	"

[133]From Saintes, former manager of the Daubonneau coffee plantation returning from Philadelphia where he had taken refuge in 1793 (Arch. Nat. DXXV. 84, 817).

[134]Etienne Sterlin, coffee grower from Matador, Dondon section (*Etat,* 1831).

[135]François-Claude Cholet?—a coffee grower in Nippes (l'Anse-à-veau) (*Etat,* 1831).

[136]J. B. Henri, coffee grower in Cahos, Little River section (*Etat,* 1832).

[137]Planter in Irois, at the point of the southern peninsula.

[138]Two Lépine brothers owned a coffee plantation in Limonde (Fonds Bleaus). (*Etat,* 1830).

[139]Maybe J. B. François Lombard from Terrier-Rouge.

[140]Pierre Montégut, coffee grower in Grand Vicent, Jérémie section (*Etat,* 1832).

[141]Maybe the René Mallet who was forced to flee Port-au-Prince after the Cocarde affair in October of 1789, going through the Spanish half, then to Santiago de Cuba where he

Rainbeau[142]	"	"	75	"
Vigneron	"	"	6	"
Lassus[143]	"	"	20	"
Chapduc	"	"	40	"
A. Chapduc	"	"	21	"
R. Congocamp	"	"	90	"
Lapray?	"	"	4	"
Monneron[144]	"	"	6	"
Lambert[145]	"	"	25	"
Mairepoux	"	"	60	"
Langes and Julienne[146]	"	"	90	"
Jauffrein	"	"	30	"
Chrétien[147]	"	"	15	"
Lombart	"	"	19	"
Châtelain[148]	"	"	9	"
Fondin[149]	"	"	25	"

District of Candelaria

Salembert	who owned		25	slaves.
Frenteteau	"	"	50	"
Cheradam, brothers	"	"	20	"
Hugon[150]	"	"	100	"

died in 1843; See *De Saint-Pierre de Maillé à Santiago de Cuba* in "Nouvelle République du Centre-Ouest," XVI (1950).

[142]A Jean Raimbeau was a coffee grower in Platons de Torbeck (*Etat*, 1830).

[143]Maybe one of the Lassuses from the northern plain.

[144]Antoine-Joseph Monneron owned three plantations in l'Anse-à-Veau.

[145]Coffee grower in Dondon, originally a refugee in Santo-Domingo.

[146]There were Juliennes in Fort-Dauphin.

[147]Jacques Chrétien, colonial coffee grower in Abricots (*Etat, 1*832).

[148]One René Châtelain had a cotton and indigo farm in Artibonite (*Etat*, 1830).

[149]Julien Fondin, coffee planter in Cap-Dame-Marie (*Etat*, 1831).

[150]Jean-François Hugon, *dit* Desdemaines, coffee grower from La Rivière à Mahot à Jérémie.

Landeau[151]	"	"	110	"
Saindos?	"	"	5	"
J. Rey[152]	"	"	18	"
G. Préval[153]	"	"	40	"
Ch. Préval & Cie.	"	"	22	"
Sariol and Durand	"	"	50	"
P. L. Lay[154]	"	"	52	"
Bourgeois[155]	"	"	30	"
de Ronseray & Company[156]	"	"	25	"
Chavenet	"	"	5	"
Goignard	"	"	10	"
Barreau	"	"	25	"
Cornet[157]	"	"	12	"
Julien[158]	"	"	5	"
Foucauld	"	"	4	"
Falandrin	"	"	3	"
Vavasseur	"	"	4	"
Brossard[159]	"	"	12	"
Noailles[160]	"	"	12	"

[151]Louis Landeau, coffee grower at the Hermitage in Roseaux à Jérémie (*Etat,* 1829, 1832).

[152]From Jérémie.

[153]Jean-Louis or Simon-Charles Gallien de Préval, indigo and cotton planters in Artibonite.

[154]Jean-Pierre Lay and Madeleine Faure, his wife, coffee growers in Dondon.

[155]Louis Bourgeois, Paul Boyer's associate in running the Bellevista coffee farm which had 36,000 plants in 1808.

[156]There were at least two Ronseray brothers in Cayes and in Port-au-Prince; the friend of Rigaud will remain in St.-Domingue until 1802.

[157]Pierre Cornet, coffee grower in St.-Louis (*Etat,* 1830).

[158]Probably Jacques Julien from l'Anse à Veau where he was a coffee planter (*Etat,* 1832).

[159]Maybe Antoine Brossard, coffee grower in Grand-Rivière (*Etat,* 1831).

[160]The widow of Louis-Marie, viscount de Noailles, Lafayette's brother-in-law, who, upon returning from immigration, had gone back into military service as a brigadier general and died from his wounds in a naval battle near Santiago. Mme de Noailles was able to save some movables from her plantation in Croix des Bouquets.

District of Sacateca

Lamanon	who owned	15	slaves.
Gigaud	" "	32	"
Marchais	" "	16	"
Lange	" "	6	"
Desbois	" "	2	"
Bustaret	" "	8	"
F. Laplante	" "	7	"

District of Canto y Vicina

Biery[161]	who owned	6	slaves.
L. Cassou	" "	60	"
S. F. Doutre	" "	4	"
Faure[162]	" "	8	"
Erovard	" "	7	"

District of Guanicú

Hénault[163] who owned	6 slaves.		
Dupré	" "	25	"
Cobian	" "	80	"
Paty[164]	" "	45	"
Dugas[165]	" "	26	"
Hubert[166]	" "	45	"
Mandé	" "	50	"
Labau	" "	50	"
Causse	" "	20	"
Debordes[167]	" "	30	"

[161] See Archives Nationales, Colonies, E, 31.

[162] It was a Faure who had introduced coffee in Torbeck in 1781. But there were also coffee-growing Faures in Port-de-Paix and in Fond-Baptiste.

[163] André Hénault, coffee grower in Pilats.

[164] Possibly a De Paty or a Mercier du Paty?

[165] The Dugas were very numerous in Saint-Domingue.

[166] Jean Hubert *dit* Saintonge had two coffee farms in Plaisance (*Etat*, 1828).

[167] Maybe Pierre Debordes, surveyor.

Imitié	"	"	8	"
Brouet[168]	"	"	5	"
Blangue	"	"	80	"

District of Sierra Maestra

Erhel	who owned	12	slaves.
Durand	"	"	15	"
Michel	"	"	12	"
Garau & Company	"	"	11	"
Roy[169]	"	"	6	"
Girard[170]	"	"	8	"
Thomas[171]	"	"	2	"
Larroque[172]	"	"	6	"
Lahouze	"	"	2	"

District of Limones

Cordier[173]	who owned	45	slaves
Lepot	"	"	8	"
F. Brun	"	"	80	"
Bonne & Company	"	"	90	"
P. Casamayor[174]	"	"	100	"
Maraud & Company[175]	"	"	120	"
Bonne & Company	"	"	10	"

District of Tinguabo

[168]From Grand-Fond.

[169]The Roys were very numerous in St-Domingue.

[170]In Petit-Goave, there was a Girard coffee farm, *L'Espérance,* in the Palmes sector (*Etat,* 1832).

[171]A Jean-Gabriel Thomas was a coffee farmer in Léogane (*Etat,* 1829).

[172]Laroques were to be found in Plaisance, Limonade, and Cap-Français.

[173]There were Cordeliers living in Cayes and Port-de-Paix.

[174]This is not Prudencio Casamayor, but Paul Casamayor, the man who made the use of baskets in coffee picking popular. See *Casamayor, Famille de Casamayor. Un peu d'histoire, sa noblesse, ses alliances et son expansion* (Paris, 1905).

[175]Maybe some Marauds from the Grottos of Torbeck.

Savon who owned 30 slaves.

A. Fournier[176]	"	"	10	"
Muzard[177]	"	"	15	"
Sagneau	"	"	10	"
Planche	"	"	25	"
Mallet	"	"	22	"
Ivonet	"	"	25	"
Charon[178]	"	"	30	"
Jarossert & Company[179]	"	"	35	"
Javier	"	"	30	"
Lasille	"	"	20	"
Ramont	"	"	28	"
Campagne	"	"	3	"
Dut	"	"	1	"
Mus	"	"	3	"
Michel[180]	"	"	4	"
Dulau	"	"	30	"
Lescabes[181]	"	"	60	"
Carmagnole[182]	"	"	2	"
Delmas	"	"	6	"
Destures	"	"	25	"
Charpentier[183]	"	"	4	"

[176]Maybe Antoine Fournier from the Hermitage, coffee grower in Baynet (*Etat*, 1831).

[177]A Michel Muzard had a large coffee farm in Cavaillon (*Etat*, 1832).

[178]A Charon de Bris had two coffee farms, one in Marmelade, the other in Acul. *Ibid.*

[179]Most likely one of the Jarossays, sugarmen in Vases, coffeemen in Boucassin (*Etat*, 1820).

[180]The Michels were very numerous in Saint-Domingue.

[181]Two Jean Lescabes had established two coffee farms in New Plymouth, Jérémie (*Etat*, 1830).

[182]Elisabeth-Victoire Carmagnole owned a house in Port-au-Prince (*Etat*, 1829).

[183]In Jérémie (cantons of Cayemites and Plymouth) two Charpentier brothers had two coffee farms (*Etat*, 1830).

Person[184]	"	"	2	"
Fourcauld[185]	"	"	5	"
Blanchard[186]	"	"	15	"
Gautier[187]	"	"	2	"
Mutel	"	"	5	"

The foregoing individuals are only some of the colonists who managed to establish new coffee farms. The list includes only the principle names. Here are a few more identified in various readings I happened upon.

In 1818, upon his return from a trip to Haiti where he painted Boyer's portrait, Charles-François Liot, former supply clerk in Port-au-Prince, stopped at Santiago de Cuba. He wanted to see the former managers of his wife's and his own plantations, J.B. Lelièvre and J. S. Monnier, to determine whether or not they had been able to salvage something by going to Cuba. He found both of them in charge of a coffee farm. Lelièvre got his started all alone, but Monnier "had enjoyed the rights to Mme Liot's properties in Saint-Domingue while she and her family were absent from Saint-Domingue."[188]

Laurent Martel, with the help of Jorge Fanelio Manson, commissioner of the royal armada, established in Alquizar a very beautiful coffee farm at Dos Amigos.[189]

François-Joseph and Jean Degut owned in Canasi the El Moka coffee farm with 29,000 plants.[190]

---

[184]Maybe a wholesaler from Port-au-Prince.

[185]There were four Foucaulds, coffee growers in Saint-Domingue, all established in Jérémie (*Etats*, 1828, 1829, 1832).

[186]A J. B. and a Pierre Blanchard owned coffee farms in Cayes (*Etat*, 1832).

[187]Gautiers are to be found in Jean-Rabel, Petit-Trou, and Vazeux.

[188]Maxime Trigant, *Les Tringant: Souvenirs de famille* (Bergerac, 1895-1896), p. 120. Mme. Liot, *née* Méhul, was the widow of Antoine Lorquet, general administrator of the post office in Saint-Domingue.

[189]Pérez de la Riva, *El café*, p. 133.

[190]*Ibid.*, p. 132.

Alexandre Kenscoff, former counsellor to the seneschalsy in Port-au-Prince and owner of a coffee farm in Grand-Fond in the mountains above that city which gave its name to a high altitude station.[191]

Mahy de Chevenelles was a former militia commander in Saint-Louis parish.[192]

The Marquis de la Rochejaquelein, wounded by corsairs upon his return from Saint-Domingue, found the money necessary to keep up his customary lifestyle by calling upon a former colonist from Saint-Domingue, René Joseph, coffee grower in Grande Ravine, Cap-Dame-Marie.[193]

François-Nicolas de la Guillaumie was a land owner in Cuba and lived in Havana in 1805.[194]

Michel Ponse, from Saint-Sever (Pyrénées-Atlantique) and his wife, *née* Claverie, from Mirebalais, had one child, Joseph, born in Santiago in 1804.[195]

Claude-François Jean Bellanger des Boullets, indigo planter in Verrettes, established a Cuban coffee farm by going into partnership with a Spaniard and becoming naturalized.[196]

Mme de Bocazel, *née* Le Mean, from Plaine-du-Nord,[197] died at her daughter's home, Mme de Courréjolle, in Cuba in 1814.[198]

Jean-Pierre Bauduy was first a refugee in the United States where he went into partnership with E. I. Dupont to establish a

---

[191]*Ibid.*, p. 166 and "Précis historique," II, 103, and the La Barre papers. Vienne Archives, 1968.

[192]Pérez de la Riva, *El café*, p. 133, note 19. And the National Archives, colonies E. 80.

[193]Ch. de Beaucorps. "La famille de la Rochejaquelein aux Antilles. Souvenirs d'émigration," *Revue historique des Antilles*, (1932), 26; *Etat, 1832*.

[194]Archives du Ministère de la France d'Outre-Mer. The indemnity dossiers, Joubert Grasset.

[195]Loire-Inférieure Archives, E, 691.

[196]Delahaye-Le-Bouis papers in Bourges. Note dated June 8, 1818 (Communication from Mr. R. Richard) (*Etats*, 1830 and 1831).

[197]Born December 19, 1735.

[198]Viscount Odon du Mantais, *Une famille bretonne à Saint-Domingue*, p. 241, note.

powder mill in Wilmington. He then went to Cuba, where he invested in a sugar mill and spent the rest of his life.[199]

Marie-Jeanne Bouché, wife of René-Jean-Pierre Leroy de Chavigni, a former colonist, died at Santiago in 1803.[200] And a certain Mme V. from Cap-Français settled in 1803 at Cobre, near Santiago, where she bought a small plantation.[201] Then there was this Manet who Descourtilz met in 1799 amidst corsairs based in Santiago.[202]

Among these adventurers, who do not all deserve the label of corsair, a few Frenchmen found their way into these ranks, including Saint-Mars the younger from Languedoc, who had just participated in the sieges of Toulon, Quiberon [Bay], and Charleston.[203]

Finally, there were those who only stopped for a short time in Cuba, whether to catch their breath while looking for a better place to stay, or to rest a while before continuing their journeys. Joubert and his nephew Jacques Hector Joubert de la Muraille remained in Cuba several months before travelling on to Baltimore. Count de Montaraë, former counselor in Cap-Français, deputy to the Assembly of Saint-Marc, took refuge in Santiago after 1800. There he became the agent of the French government. He stayed there until October 1808, when he was called to a besieged Santo Domingo.[204]

The story of Pierre Collette, important coffee grower, from Jean-Rabel, was told to us in a very amusing way by M. G. with the help of his family papers.[205] Collette, who had been waiting

---

[199]Miss F. S. Childs, *French Refugee Life in the United States, 1790-1800* (Baltimore, 1940), p. 47.

[200]Letter from the Baron Durie de Beauregard, August 1, 1946.

[201]P. Sannon, *Le Cap vu par une Américaine*, p. 129.

[202]Descoutilz, *Voyage d'un naturaliste*, p. 12.

[203]Dorvo-Soulastre, *Voyage par terre*, p. 187.

[204]Couët de Montatran papers, with Mme. de Beauregard, in Saint-Omer, 1939.

[205]"Etude sur la colonisation française en Haïti. Origines et développement des propriétés Collette," *Revue d'histoire d'Haïti*, (1938-1939); "Un colon de Saint-Domingue pendant la Révolution, Pierre Collette," *Revue d'histoire d'Haïti*, (1939-1941).

a few months for the opportunity to leave Saint-Domingue, had bought near Puerto Plata in the Spanish part, a few *carreaux* in order to raise coffee (October 1803). But he was unable to go there[206] and only against his will did he go to Santiago de Cuba.

At New Orleans, November 16, 1804, to Stanislas Foäche.[207]

Having left Cap-Français for some time now, my respectable friend, long enough to have avoided being a victim of the cannibalistic masters of Saint-Domingue, I was taken away, against my will, to Santiago de Cuba, for my intention, in leaving Cap-Français, was to go to Santo Domingo. The poor condition of the sailing vessel in which I embarked did not permit us to remain under sail and it was necessary to backtrack in order to reach Cuba. My nine-month stay on this island only confirmed the repugnance that I had about going to the Spanish possessions; besides all the problems they try to give to the French, there is the regime and the Spanish subject you have to give in to; add to that superstition and the lowest form of ignorance possible and you will have a good idea of my plight; some say that the colony is too isolated to have any culture. The French are establishing coffee farms there; if Saint-Domingue ever re-establishes itself, they will not last very long . . . The lands in general are far inferior to those in Saint-Domingue, the island is poorly watered, there are no alluvian plains which make the richness of Saint-Domingue.

Thrown upon Cuba with only a few domestics as my only resource,[208] uncertain that I would keep them, seeing how easily Negroes here leave their masters, the cost of living, as miserable as it seems, is very expensive. Rent is sky-high due to the number of refugees. In a word, everything here leads me to look at other counties to find a more convenient place to live. I thought I saw in Louisiana the place that would offer the most advantages to a poor colonist forced to

---

[206]Bégouën Demeaux, *Mémorial* II, 233, 234, 242, 247, 249.

[207]*Ibid.*, 267.

[208]He was able to take along twelve domestics with him.

flee, because, first of all, they [Louisianians] speak the same
language. What's left of our Negroes is worth a lot more
money, and they are more easily rented [there]. Moreover,
one finds there the same habits, as well as Frenchmen who
know more or less who you are, either personally or by
reputation, and who share more or less the same culture.
Finally, its climate is not unlike our own. I was not mistaken;
if I had found that out earlier, I would not be experiencing
my present troubles.

VIII.— THE REFUGEES' TECHNICAL EXPERIENCE

The refugees' great strength was their vast experience with
a topography much more difficult and complex than the one in
Cuba and with a less predictable climate. Their agricultural
knowledge was learned by trial and error, by long struggles with
a variety of conditions: soil quality, slopes, altitude, orientation,
and humidity. It reflected many different individual failures, the
price paid in Saint-Domingue to learn how to make the best
coffee at the least cost.

We have seen that the colonist represented a select social
group who had survived the difficulty of pioneer life and the
isolation of the Saint-Domingue hills. The rich did not make
their homes here. Too distant from life's material comforts,
their homes made no pretence at opulence. They were the
resource of those industrious and active men who "in spite
of their humble beginnings, still hope to make a fortune."[209]
Hilliart d'Auberteuil, who did not have any particular affection
for these new colonists, agreed that coffee growing required
men of strong, frankly American character. [They were] the
foundation of a new wave of immigration.[210] This recent form
of colonization, beginning with the French Revolution and the
evacuation of the hills of Saint-Domingue, led them to natural

[209]Girod-Chantrans, *Voyage d'un Suisse dans différentes colonies d'Amérique* (Neufchâ-
tel, 1785), p. 295.

[210]*Considérations sur l'Etat présente la colonie française de Saint-Domingue*, 2 vols.
(Paris, 1776), I, 186.

settlement sites comparable to the ones they had just turned into prosperous coffee farms. Standardized coffee-growing techniques came into being on the smaller coffee plantations, where the planters were less intent upon making a quick profit and more reluctant to engage in speculation—after all, they made a living as planters.

The colonists who disembarked at Cuba cleared the land. They had that special instinct of those who love to "work the land," even when it is located in a forsaken area or is hard to reach. Among the first 192 French colonists to reach Cuba, one saw few of the planters who had worked on coffee farms that were appendages of sugar plantations or were associated with them, near the large "*habitations*" where mutual assistance and sometimes supplementary man-power existed. They [the foregoing planters] were more the back-woods type when one looked upon them from the plains; they were the front runners when one worked beside them.

They knew the optimal surface that can be worked by a team of five, ten, or twenty slaves, the proportion of the farmstead that can be used for coffee cultivation, the amount of pasturage that must offset it [the area under cultivation], how much of it has to be reserved to the blacks, and how much "standing wood" [forest land] one should have to replenish the land as the crops deplete it, where the bunk house and the slave quarters should be located, and the slave quarters, how many crops should be planted at the beginning of land-clearing to feed lumberjacks and carpenters and to serve as your food source until the first revenues come in where it was preferable to plant the green vegetables, and where to plant the tubers: potatoes, manioc, etc. . . .[211] These root plants could act as intercalary plants. A smart colonist knew how to distribute them in such a way that neither the peas nor the potatoes need a special field, because manpower was in short supply.[212] Corn stalks and banana trees provided the necessary

[211]G. Debien, "Le plan et les débuts d'une caféière à Saint-Domingue. La plantation la Merveillèreaux Anses-à-Pitre, (1789-1792)," *Revue d'histoire d'Haïti*, (October, 1943).

[212]Ducoeurjolly, *Manuel des habitants de Saint-Domingue*, 2 vols. (Paris, 1802), II, 7; *Moreau de Saint-Méry*, I, 131.

shade for the young coffee plants.

The refugees in Cuba sowed their own seeds in fertilized plots or in crates filled with good earth, just as Father Labat had recommended in the past.[213] In Saint-Domingue, everyone did not follow this method, for the plantations devoted much time to this choice of plants.[214] In Cuba, there was no alternative. The red seeds were sown in tight rows. The first clearings were finished and the bushes were transplanted at eighteen months under the awaiting shade.

Once the coffee trees were planted, the colonists could not agree as to when was the best time to trim the plants. Some prefered an annual trim, while others liked to wait two or three years between cuts. All agreed upon its importance. Few dared to graft. When a storm or strong wind blew over a coffee tree, the colonists from Saint-Domingue knew better than to raise it back up. Experience had taught them that this was the best way to destroy the remaining roots. They limited themselves to covering up the exposed roots as soon as possible. This practice was certainly not defensible in every instance, but the scarcity of labor was the official excuse for it.

The new colonists did not harvest the crop in a hurry, from August to October. They took the whole second half of the year, carefully selecting only the finest beans.

The need to hoe, the necessity of watching [the beans], and the need for soil conservation dictated the planting of trees in straight rows. They knew that even the best land would be worn out in about twenty years. They sought a short reprieve by spreading out the plants. The density of the plantation would be diminished but the plants grew more vigorously.

The colonists paid close attention to the milling, cleaning, drying, and glazing operations. There were strict rules establishing the best means of exposing the grains to sunlight and of protecting them from the dangers of fog, cold, and wind.

They had already sustained enough losses through diseases—especially lime disease—insects, and weeds to know at least

---

[213]*Nouveau voyage aux îles d'Amériques* (Paris, 1742).

[214]Girod-Chantrans, *Voyage,* p. 280.

how to limit the damage.

All of this agronomical science had just been summed up in 1798 by a planter from Saint-Domingue, Laborie.[215] To be used by the Jamaican colonists, it had codified the best practices of the coffee growers of the southern peninsula. But the people of Jamaica were not the ones to profit most from this guide. The development of their coffee farms had little in common with that of the Cuban plantations. Laborie's work soon became the "Bible" of the Cuban coffee grower; so much so that in 1809 it became necessary to translate from English into Spanish this book that had never been published in the language Laborie wrote it in.[216] The *Junta de Fomentación* contributed to the printing costs and had a prospectus widely distributed that summarized the theme and the intentions of the book. Laborie had taken care to add his own experiences as a colonist in Saint-Domingue, as well as all that his correspondence with the refugees in Santiago had taught him about farming conditions in the new Cuban settlements.

IX.— THE SPANISH WAR CRISIS (1808-1815)[217]

This prosperity that grew daily was nearly destroyed by a crisis which lasted several years. This crisis was caused by the Spanish War and the continental embargo. Following the fall of the Spanish Bourbons and their replacement by Joseph Bonaparte, the American colonies remained faithful to Ferdinand VII and severed relations with France.

In Cuba, the [favorable] immigration policy, which closely supervised but tolerated, and even encouraged, agriculture, that Governor Kindelan applied to the French [refugees] was counteracted by the influence of the archbishop of Santiago, Don

---

[215]*The Coffee Planter of Santo Domingo with an appendix containing a view of the Constitution, Government, Laws, and State of that Colony . . .* (London, 1798), p. 193.

[216]Juan Laborie, *Cultivo y beneficio del Café*, trans. by Pablo Boloix (Havana, 1809).

[217]This chapter is for the most part a summary of several pages of *El café.*

Joaquín de Oses de Aluza,[218] who waged a personal war against the French. Overnight, the French became equated with Huguenots and were amusingly defined as "Jews baptized with rotten swamp water." They were publicly called "Godoy Spaniards," the worst insult at that time.

Kindelan was forced to stop giving out naturalization papers; and it became difficult to sail for Cuba. A large number of refugees left Cuba for New Orleans, like the Guirots, or for New York, like Delavigne.[219] Once again, there was a dispersal following a concentration [of refugees]. About a hundred people set sail for the Spanish[-speaking] part of Saint-Domingue, the closest French land—theoretically—they could reach. The Spanish ship which transported them presented itself as a cartel ship at the port of Santo Domingo. This act was interpreted as a declaration of war. General Ferrand, the commanding officer in Santo Domingo,[220] vainly tried to prevent the debarkation of the refugees. This incident sheds some light onto the political situation of the Antilles at that time.[221]

General Ferrand, short of men, summoned the French refugees of Cuba. Civil servants and French agents, such as Couët de Montaran, rushed to Santo Domingo (October 1808).[222]

In Cuba, they [Spaniards] feared a revival of the movements of 1799. A republican legion, organized by Dehogues and including more than 250 French volunteers, was viewed as a fifth column with poorly defined intentions. These legionnaires were deported. All of the refugees who remained French citizens were also expelled. Those who had been naturalized and were

[218]Dorvo-Soulastre (*Voyage par terre*, p. 127), shows us that in 1803 this predence on the contrary, was openly francophile, great admirer of Corneille, Voltaire—Voltaire the tragedian most likely, Racine, and even l'Abbé Grégoire.

[219]Information provided by René Le Gardeur; and F. Schoell, "L'Agonie du français en Louisiane," *Revue de Paris*, February 15, 1925.

[220]C. Le Four, *De Besançon à Saint-Domingue. Le général J. L. Ferrand (1758-1808)* (Besançon, 1938), pp. 54-80; and Miguel Artola, "La Guerra de reconquista de Santo Domingo (1808-1809)," *Revista de Indias*, XI (1951), 441-484.

[221]See the December 14, 1808 edition of *l'Aurora* cited in *El café*.

[222]Couët de Montaran papers, at Mme. de Beauregard's house, in Saint Omer, 1939, and Regnault de Beaucaron, I, 148.

not involved in politics were able to remain, like those who did not become Spanish but held public positions or served in the [Spanish] fleet.

The captain-general had to decide some very delicate cases. Also, in order to avoid gross errors and injustices, he established so-called vigilance committees composed of administrative and judicial authorities. They reviewed individual cases, ordering deportation for some, but permitting persons who had contributed to the country's prosperity to remain.

The situation deteriorated when one learned of the defeats suffered in Spain during the campaigns of 1808-1809. Tempers flared, and hatred was unleashed. Public opinion demanded more stringent measures [against the refugees] in the province of Santiago. Kindelan did not dare block these demands for fear of appearing to be too weak and francophile.

Fires of mysterious origin broke out on French plantations. In order to avoid greater disorder, the refugees' departure was hurried along. But there was some delay because of the large number [of refugees] and because of their difficulty in disposing of property that many of them had acquired, the debts for which usually remained oustanding. There were simulated sales. Still it was necessary to find Spanish friends upon which one could rely. Others had to sell at less than market value the coffee farms they had so much trouble getting started. The anguish of the first years of the Revolution in Saint-Domingue reappeared, with the difference being that if hate was still an important factor for all parties concerned, the struggle was no longer a racial one. The men were especially persecuted. Several, in order to avoid being molested or struck, sought refuge in the forts. The women who were left alone were not bothered. Coffee plantations abandoned through the hasty departure of the owners were auctioned off.

"We have been threatened for over a year now," writes the Marquis Duquesne to his friend Messemé,[223]

---

[223]Havana, December 17, 1816, Messemé papers, in the Château de la Motte de Messemé (Vienne), with the Count de la Boullerie.

French belongings are confiscated, sold, and pillaged. Mine were not touched because I was in the king's service, but I have nonetheless been pillaged; even my coffee has been taken this year. In town, I was respected and nothing was done to me. And during war time the price of coffee was from four to five *gourdes* per quintal, which overwhelmed and ruined us all. . . .

During the revolution[224] I was denounced for holding some of your money and for not denouncing that fact myself and putting the money in the royal treasury. I always maintained that you were in Spain serving in the army and General Don Juan Errera, my friend, furnished me with the papers necessary to get me out of this embarrasing situation and I was able to save your money.

If Duquesne, who had served Ferdinand VII and who had married a Cuban woman, had been the center of so much controversy, one can guess[225] how much execration was in store for those who had no political connections. In less than three months, over 6,600 Frenchmen, including slaves and free men of color, left for New Orleans from the ports of Santiago, Baracoa, and Havana. Their number has been rather precisely established by two reports submitted by James Mather,[226] then mayor of New Orleans, to W. C. C. Claiborne,[227] governor of the Orleans territory. These two reports, dated July 18 and August 7, 1809, provide the names of forty ships, thirty-five from Santiago,

---

[224]That is to say, during the Cuban crisis of 1809-1810.

[225]L. G. Chausson, *Précis historique de la Révolution de Saint-Domingue* (Paris, 1819), p. 120.

[226]Annotator's note: James J. Mather, a native of Coupland, England, emigrated to America around 1776. He was appointed to the Louisiana legislative council in 1804 and again in 1805. He served as mayor of New Orleans from 1807 to 1812.

[227]Annotator's note: William Charles Cole Claiborne (1775-1817) served in the Tennessee constitutional convention of 1796. He was elected to Congress from Tennessee the following year. Claiborne was appointed governor of the Territory of Mississippi on May 25, 1801, and served in that capacity until his appointment, in 1803, as governor of the Territory of Orleans. He was elected governor of Louisiana in 1812 and United States senator from Louisiana shortly before his death in 1817.

four from Baracoa, and one from Havana, with the following number of refugees aboard:

	Men	Women	Children Under 15	TOTAL
Whites	989	455	443	1,887
Free men of color	282	926	852	2,060
Slaves	603	905	605	2,113
TOTAL	1,874	2,286	1,900	6,060

Mather further declared, in his report of August 7th, that three more vessels had entered the port of New Orleans after his earlier report had been completed: one from Baracoa and two from Santiago, upon which there were about 604 passengers, all classes put together. It is very possible also that after this date other ships arrived, but their names and the number of their passengers had not been preserved.

In any case, according to the reports submitted by Mather, it appears that between May 19 and August 7, 1809, around 6,660 refugees arrived in New Orleans from Cuba, transported on the forty-three vessels he cites. This considerable influx of immigrants, concentrated in a period of less than three months, brought a large increase in the population of the city, something in the neighborhood of thirty to forty percent.

The entry of slaves, as well as free men of color over fifteen years of age, was forbidden in Louisiana. Claiborne, having taken pity upon the refugees, bent the rules concerning the slaves by accepting surety bonds provided by their masters: they were supposed to give their people to whomever asked for them first. This request was never made, and before all was said and done, the entry of slaves into the U. S. was legalized by a special act of Congress. As for the free men of color, a few of them were forced to move on, but most were allowed to stay with the cooperation of the authorities.

One of the most important of these documents is the petition submitted to James Madison, president of the United States, dated September 5, 1809, by fifty-seven refugees in New Orleans and which solicited their repatriation to France. Here is the text of this petition; the original is conserved in the National Archives in Washington:

James Madisson [*sic*], president of the U. S. of America

We Subscribers, refugees and sufferers of the late political occurences which have taken place in the Island of Cuba, being in the necessity to go to France, humbly beg that the vessel should be cleared from this port, under a flag a truce [*sic*] for Nantz [*sic*] or Bordeaux, in order that we may be transported there with our family and baggage only. Our number cannot be properly ascertained at present, by the continual emigration of other fellow sufferers from Cuba to this place, and for the degree of sickness now prevailing among them; it is by that reason impossible to fix on the size of a particular vessel, which then may be left to the discretion of the Collector of this port, when the permission is granted, and the necessary papers obtained for the free navigation of the vessel in question.

With due respect for your person we beg the acceptance of our sincere wishes for the prosperity of your administration.

New Orleans 5.th Sept.r 1809

Fifty-seven signatures follow, some unreadable; but the following names can be identified with some degree of certainty:

Charles Lejeune Malherbe,   *père*, Saint-Domingue, [Charles Lejeune Malherbe], *fils,* Saint-Domingue, Pierre Petit, Paty, Jean Dagnon, Joseph Gerbeau, G. Corréjolles, Besset, Fleury, P. Subrat, E. Cardinaud, Bigot, Charles Mérieult, Bellanger, *jeune*, Soufflot, Pierre Despainge, Brierre, Chatry, *fils*, Lachataignerais, Mr. de Conny and his son, Barbet, Joseph Montamat, A. Faltel, P. A. Lay, F. Dupuis, J. J. Toussaint, Le Roy, R. d'Abnour, Lambert, L. G. Hiligsberg, Dunay, Murotte, A. Lafargue, Philippe de Neubourg, Delmas, Ballon des Ravines, Miltenberger, J. C. Mairot, Durre, Nicholas Marchant, Honoré, Chambert,

Mongrue *jeune,* François Fournier.

It is to be believed that they did not obtain the ship they requested, for many of these names can be found at a later date in New Orleans and the surrounding area.

The guarantees provided by the slave owners all seem to have disappeared. However, two or three declarations made by passengers or by the captains of the vessels which give us several names do exist:

Jean-Jacques Boisfeuillet, arrived from Santiago on the *Arctic,* Captain Davis, Françoise Hellison, Marie-Catherine Guérin, Claude Grare, and Mrs. Laure Edain, arrived from Santiago on the *Francis,* Captain Gardner; Gabriel Corréjolles and Pierre Bazzi, arrived from Santiago on the *Freeman Ellis,* Captain Sparrow [the spelling of several of these names is uncertain].[228]

Private papers conserved in New Orleans give us the following names:

Arrived in Balise (a port at the mouth of the Mississippi), June 21, 1809:
Mr. and Mrs. Joseph-Simon Le Gardeur de Tilly, who had left Nabittes [Nuevitas?] on May 25, also Mr. Dérence [spelling uncertain], who died the day of his arrival. Arrived on the *Fair America,* Captain Abraham Barges, Yves Le Monnier.[229]

---

[228]All of the preceding information concerning the refugees' immigration to Louisiana has been communicated to me by René Le Gardeur, from New Orleans, who transcripted them from a microfilm of the original documents which are conserved in the National Archives in Washington. Many of these documents have been published in the following books:

Dunbar Rowland, ed., *Official Letter Books of W. C. C. Claiborne,* 6 vols. (Jackson, Miss., 1917), IV, 351-418;
Clarence Edwin Carter, ed., *The Territorial Papers of the United States,* volume IX, *The Territory of Orleans, 1803-1812* (Washington, D.C., 1940), pp. 841-843, 847, 848, 850.

[229]Information provided by Mr. Le Gardeur.

"I have the honor to announce to you my recent move to this city," wrote J. P. Legros to Martin Foäche, a Le Havre businessman, from New Orleans[230] on September 24, 1809,

> seeing that all the Frenchmen of Baracoa and the other cities on the island of Cuba have been expelled. . . .
>
> I shall tell you that all of the French have been obligated to leave this country, taking nothing with them for the most part, and after having lost the price of their works [*sic*]. I cannot allow myself to tell you more. I will let you guess the rest.

The same message, in greater detail, can be read in other letters written by these new refugees which resume their situation upon arrival in Louisiana.

> New Orleans, March 28, 1811.
> If I waited so long in letting you know my current whereabouts, it was only in the hope of being able to impart to you more favorable information about my situation. But everything has conspired against that wish, particularly as this just might be the most wretched country known to man. That's all I needed, to be thrown upon such a marshy land, after having lost, through my Spanish sequestration, the dependents[231] who had remained faithful to me. Your Negro Anne and her nephew Amédée were, most unfortunately, among that group. I was allowed [to leave with] only two slaves who, because they spoke English, worked aboard the American ship which, in view of its advanced age and poor condition, miraculously transported me here. The scarcity of ships also contributed to the loss of your slaves. No matter what I did or how much I spent trying to get them to accompany me. We unfortunately ran into a French renegade who, by his smooth talking, took us to the edge of

---

[230]Bégoën-Demeaux papers in Le Havre.

[231]Annotator's note, slaves.

the cliff without our realizing the pitfall awaiting us. 'Don't hurry,' he told us in good French, 'the government wants you to leave, but it does not want to be accused of having done so at the cost of your life's savings. Await the next opportunity and then leave.' On a sailing vessel of about thirty tons, we numbered more than 200.

Upon departure, I left your people as well as mine in the hands of Don Antonio Lorés, from whom I even obtained a notarized procuration, perhaps a useless precaution, for I have learned by fairly recent news that they were all still on the same farm where I had left them in August of 1809. But many of them have been *sold,* leaving us little hope of ever seeing them again. That alone brought me here; otherwise, I would have chosen Charleston where the introduction of blacks has proved most difficult.

In recounting his second exile to Martin Foäche, Guillaume Andigé, former coffee grower at Jean-Rabel and Port-de-Paix,[232] indicates that he had started his life anew as a novice colonist in the Mississippi Delta, eight leagues from New Orleans. Only this time he was planting rice, not coffee, with his two Negroes, who were about all he was able to retrieve from Cuba, where he was permitted to board ship with only one trunk and a mattress.

The same animosity was experienced by Frenchmen in other provinces. In Havana, there was even a day of rioting. Two Frenchmen returning from their fields were arrested just outside of Tierra and interrogated by the captain of the guard and then led to the courthouse without being informed of the reason. The general population—colored for the most part—crowded around them, insulted them, threw stones at them, and began pillaging French homes. Six of them were plundered, but only one person was murdered—a goldsmith who, in protecting his boutique, had wounded one of his aggressors. Someruelos placed the garrison under arms. He scoured the city and re-

[232]He also owned an indigo farm and a cotton farm in Bas-Moustique de Jean-Rabel (228,000), *Etat* , 1831, and two coffee plantations in Haut-Moustique in Port-de-Paix (695,000), *Etat,* 1831.

established order. It all ended with the cry of "Death to the French." But since trouble was expected on the outskirts of town, the militia was sent the next day to San Antonio de los Baños, where many refugees had settled in Alquisar and Artémisa. Fortunately, peace was restored without any blood being spilled.

The rich neighborhood of Cienfuegos did not escape the uprising. Adventurer Carlos Ramos inflamed this region by spreading the rumor that the French of Jagua, who were completely apolitical, were plotting to seize control of the district. He started a peasant uprising and led attacks upon plantations. Nonetheless, the vigilant French dispersed the gangs.

Nevertheless, more than one sugar plantation and several coffee farms were ruined in different places. Once the colonists left, first the underbrush and then the forest overwhelmed the crops. Even entire plantations, fallen into the hands of incompetents or greedy speculators, went to seed.

*   *   *

Spain's legislative assembly had discussed the problem of French propertyholdings in Cuba.[233] It sought extraordinary powers to use against the [Saint-Domingue] invaders. Mejia proposed immediate sale of the properties, cash on the barrel, as a means of avoiding sequestration and maintenance costs. Jean Jaurégui, a Cuban legislator, opposed the implementation of this brutal plan. Since the law had already allowed for the naturalization of any Catholic foreigner who was either a farmer or an artisan, provided he take a solemn oath to obey Spanish laws, it was necessary to distinguish between those who had been naturalized and the others. Jaurégui reminded the assembly that the quick sale of the plantations would inevitably lower their value. Spanish-owned plantations and other immovable property would not be immune from this drop in prices. A general economic crisis would follow. The departure of the French and the sale of their plantations had already cut in

[233]*Diario de Sesiones de las Cortés generales y extraordinarias,* no. 289, p. 1,465 and no. 290, pp. 1,469-1,471.

half the appraised value [of Cuban real estate].

Jaurégui's defense of the naturalized French [Cubans] before the Spanish legislature spawned another crisis in Cuba. It became popular to find fault with everything the refugees did. The captain-general had managed to supress the movement; still, he urged the departure of as many Frenchmen as possible, even those [refugees] who had been naturalized. In a note published in the *Diario de la Habana* on September 15, 1811, the Council for Revenge explained the Regency Council's instructions dated March 22. In sum, it [the Regency Council] revoked the government's powers to issue naturalization papers. It ordered the restoration of all illegally confiscated French goods, but it also prohibited any policy of toleration [regarding the refugees].

The attacks thus continued. They had not only been directed against the French, but also against the Cortés itself. The *Censor Universal,* in its twenty-fifth issue, accused Jaurégui of having proposed that all of the French, whether they were expelled or had left of their own free will, be allowed to return to Cuba. A lively polemic followed, the *Diario de la Havana* responding to the *Censor.* The quarrel became vitriolic; the criticism against the Cortés was getting slanderous. The captain-general, to put an end to the calumny, ordered the seizure of the *Censor's* forty-second issue. But he could do nothing to counteract the songs.

Francés montuno	Wild Frenchman
Ay, ay, ay,	Aye, aye, aye,
Siempre lo he sido	Always has he been so
Ay, ay, ay,	Aye, aye, aye,
Mira mi campo	Look at my field
Ay, ay, ay,	Aye, aye, aye,
Qué florecido.	How flowery it is.

French works were regarded with derision and described as the inventions of a perverse age. Naturally, the waltz came to be known as a shameful French dance; but, alas, it also became very popular in Cuban society:

Our character had always distinguished itself by its

honest simplicity, by its absence of affectation, up until
the day the libertine French morals worked their way into
the homes of a large number of our compatriotes, greatly
damaging our traditional customs. Now that we hate with
all our might the maxims of this degenerate nation and
that we have written in stone the treason that victimized
the august person of our beloved king, Ferdinand VII (God
save him!), why should we admire the waltzes and the
counterwaltzes, those always indecent inventions that a
diabolical France has introduced here? These two dances
are completely contrary to the Christian spirit. Gestures,
lascivious movements, an unabashed immodesty are their
elements. They provoke concupiscence through the fatigue
and the heat they produce . . . [234]

The slaves themselves poked fun at their masters' marriages
in creole songs.

> Blan la yo soti en Frans, oh! jélé!
> Yo pran madam yo servi sorelle
> Pu yo carece neguès . . . ![235]

El Aviso published these civilities tailored to these
circumstances:

> Aunque me digan bribón,
> Desvergonzado, atrevido,
> Insolente, mal nacido,
> Pícaro, infame, ladrón:
> Que mis procederes son
> los de Faraón, o Fines,
> Que Lutero mi padre es,
> Y en fin lo más afrente,

[234]*El Aviso de la Habana*, September 28, 1809.

[235]A translation follows,

> The white men who come from France, oh! Jélé!
> They treat their wives like they treat sorrel horses
> To be able to caress the black women . . .

Todo me es indiferente
No llamándome 'francés'[236]

The continental blockade intensified to this social and economic crisis. The manner in which the coffee farms were developed precluded any possibility of suddenly suspending their operations. The coffee trees were growing and producing. But the blockade reduced coffee sales only slightly. As a general trend, from 1804 to 1815, the quantity of exported coffee increased. But from 1810 to 1814, perceptible decrease occurred. The prosperity generated by the pre-1810 production sustained them [the coffee growers]. The price of the quintal of coffee fell to, and remained at, four *pesos* between 1812 and 1815. This low price must be attributed to export problems, the effect of contraband, and especially the departure of the Frenchmen.

X.—RESULTS

The general peace which permitted free commercial exchanges gave Cuba the chance to ship its coffee and sugar throughout the world. The 1815 exports were twice those of 1814, and France, which had unequivocally lost Saint-Domingue, became one of Cuba's best customers. The golden age of Cuban coffee dates from 1815 to 1840. This was a time when things begin to settle down, when one could better see and understand certain power plays and measure their scope. One would like to

---

[236] A translation follows,

Even if they call me knavish,
Shameless, bold,
Insolent, low-born,
Roguish, infamous, thieving,
That my procedures are
Those of Pharo or of Fines, That Luther is my father
And finally all that outrages the most,
It's all the same to me
As long as they do not call me "French."

(*El café*, p. 36.)

locate the vestiges of the refugees' presence and gauge the impact of their way of life.

* * *

The new colonist had less leisure time than the former *hacendado*; but he did have some. He made time for himself. His cabin was not just his house out in the fields, but his home. He loved it, he decorated it because it was the setting of his family life. He ornated it with gardens, fruit trees, and shade trees. His life was surrounded by frugal comfort. Around 1820, owning a coffee plantation meant having achieved a balanced life—a new approach to the art of living. This was so widely recognized that, to achieve social panache and lifestyle [of the coffee growers], colonial sugarcane farmers and cattle ranchers added a coffee-grove to their canefields and their ranches, less for the profit they hoped to derive from it than for the upward social mobility the title "coffee planter" procured. By the time of this writer's childhood, the prestigious sign "*Planteur de Caïffa*" had not lost its social significance.

The [Spanish] Creole colonists were satisfied with simple wooden houses, roofed with palm leaves. No further thought was given to decoration. They were surprised to see the French colonists align their rows of coffee plants, trace their gardens, and build their homes while dreaming of establishing there something other than a roof or a shelter under which to sleep— [creation of] a place [in which they could create] a civilized life [and] the survival of a French culture, transplanted after a long period of colonial and Creole adaptation in Saint-Domingue.

As a barometer of improving business, the French colonists improved their creature comforts, and their social life became more varied, more radiant. Fine furniture, tapestried walls, paintings and engravings, the first ones naturally being family portraits and Italian-style historical landscapes; these were the essential luxuries that were quickly added to the primordial ones of the table. The French introduced a taste for curios. Balls became commonplace. Small concerts were given. The coffee plantations became centers of entertainment and culture.

A few plantations had libraries, Angerona for example. For some planters, a library was a collector's hobby; for others, a manifestation of their snobbery; for still others, a means of maintaining contact with a society from which they were becoming estranged. It would be interesting to determine what they liked to read, and if their libraries had more newer publications than those of the [Spanish] Creoles. In none of the foregoing categories did individuals claim to be avid readers, but books were more common in Cuba than they had been in Saint-Domingue. It is possible that in Cuba, the French tried to appear more literate than they did in Saint-Domingue, as a means of affirming their superiority and also as a means of showing their disdain for the rustic society surrounding them.

The Stiges' coffee farm, established twelve leagues away from Santiago, was one of the richest and most famous plantations built by the French refugees. Emilio Barcardi in his *Chroniques de Santiago* describes it as one of the most beautiful of all the eastern plantations. It had some very large gardens. The house was almost a palace, with a reception hall, billiard parlor, boudoir, library, and chapel. The furnishings, which were plain throughout, were enhanced by paintings. The cuisine was absolutely first-rate. The Archbishop Claret spent summers, and the governor often stopped there for brief periods. The stables were filled with the province's best horses. Every week there was a reception and in the evening, the house was transformed into a ballroom, with an orchestra on feast days. Even theatrical productions were staged.

The Délices' plantation, in the Cangrejeras sector, was another one of those beautiful properties that was talked about for miles around because of the organization of its home life and for the beauty of its plane-trees. The hurricane of October 1846 uprooted all of its trees and caused considerable damage to the buildings that had escaped from previous storms. It had been established and developed by the Marquis Duquesne[237].

In the eastern region, where the French influence was more strongly felt, the interior arrangement of the work-cabins was organized according to a colonial type, slightly different from

[237]*El café*, p. 71.

the Cuban model. In Cuba, the house looked like a patio surrounded by a vaste portico leading to the rooms. Behind [the house] was a patio for the help. The refugees' house plans were more complicated. In the center was the lobby, onto which opened a large room from which the bedrooms were joined together by passageways. In the corners, porticos communicated with the gardens. Around the house stood a porch surrounded by a wood railing and covered, not with blinds, but with a linen cloth or a flat tile called "French tile" by the Cubans. The roof of the main body was often covered with slate.

The refugees were also responsible for the improvement in [local] roads and transportation. They constructed the first back roads, according to reliable data, studying the slopes and devising a system for draining water. In the mountains to the east, these roads still exist more or less the way they were laid down. They are called "caminos de Colin," named for Colin, the engineer who designed them. But this appelation has come to mean simply mountain or hill roads. Modernization of the roadways caused a corresponding improvement in the means of transportation. The uncomfortable and dangerous Spanish coach, without suspension nor buffer-springs, with a wooden axle, gave way to the lightweight cabriolet and later to the "volantes" set upon springed axles and a belted suspension system that not only absorbed the shocks, but also assured the stability of the vehicle in the ruts.[238] Visits to the city increased because of the comfortable and rapid means of communication. [Residents of the] countryside assumed a new point of view.

*   *   *

But French customs constituted the most visible legacy of the refugees. First, the slaves had introduced their own pastimes. In the eastern provinces, the French *tumba*, originally from Saint-Domingue,[239] was one of the most popular dances. A king and a queen, elected by the slaves, presided over the festivities. They

[238]See R. T. Hill's *Cuba and Porto Rico* (London, 1898), the picture on p. 48, Afternoon Drive in Rural Cuba.

[239]*El café*, p. 130.

occupied a sort of throne before which stood the Dancemaster. The room was decorated with palmetto leaves and often French and Spanish flags. These dances seem to have been very different from those of the other Cuban slaves.

The blacks who came from Saint-Domingue brought along their Creole language. Through song and dance, this language found its way into local folklife; the refrain below was repeated for a long time:

Tabatié mué tombé,	*I dropped my tobacco pouch,*
tabatié mué tombé	*I dropped my tobacco pouch*
Tabatié mué tombé,	*I dropped my tobacco pouch,*
Mam'sel Mari	*Miss Mary picked it up*
ramasé le pu mien, oh!	*for me, oh!*
Tabatié mué tombé	*I dropped my tobacco pouch*
Mam'sel Mari	*Miss Mary picked it up*
ramasé li pu mué.	*for me, oh!*

The imitation of French fads and customs, unquestionably initiated by the export of Cuban coffee to France, enlarged, indeed doubled, the imprint made by the former refugees. [The refugees] tried to follow Parisian trends in clothing, shoes, and hats. Certain French mannerisms survived the refugees and the changes in business that began after 1815; they remained in use, even after the former colonists blended into the local population and one still remembers in Santiago the names of Coufonnier, the famous coiffeur; Mousquet, the shoe-maker for elegant women; Colette, the lithographer; and Pisany, the daguerrotypist of the early days.

Dr. Antommarchi, who had treated Napoléon on Saint Helena, came to Santiago where he died of the yellow fever he was studying. He was not from Saint-Domingue. However, Dr. Fontaine, of the University of Montpellier, was a refugee. He held the chair in Anatomy at the Havana School of Medicine .

The first Cuban [Masonic] lodges were founded by the refugees in Santiago under the names *La Concorde* and *La Persévérance*. The oldest of the lodges in Saint-Domingue had been established in Saint-Marc in 1749 under the name *La Concorde*. In Havana, the lodges *L'Amitié* and *La Concorde bienfaisante* were maintained under Spanish names after the massive expulsions of 1809. The lodge in Santiago became *Le Temple des vertus théologales*, where the meetings continued to be conducted in French.

* * *

The Cuban economy with the *hacienda* at its center was closely related to the Merovingian-villa type of exploitation by its production for local consumption, by its closed-in life-style, and by its large number of useless slaves. The rare Creole *hacendados* who had settled in the island's interior in the eighteenth century initially did not seek profits. They had little business sense and only a vague concept of what their work could achieve. They had no market for their products. They had little economic incentive to produce beyond their needs. If they coveted the large landholdings and many slaves at all, it was only because of the social status they provided, not their money-making potential. This attitude, rather common in Spanish America, was probably more pronounced in the Mexican *hacienda,* which would maintain its insular economy throughout the nineteenth century and beyond. In Cuba, Negro slavery, which was much more widespread and very different from the Mexican types of servitude, and which was sustained, to a certain extent, by the coasting trade with Anglo-Americans, imposed upon regional life a few new characteristics.

Into this quiet, sleepy, archaic milieu plunged the French colonists, spurred on by their desire to carve for themselves a new place in the colonial world. They were like yeast leavening dough. Cuban society received quite a blow. A new way of looking at the world was emerging, and, at first, they [Spanish Cubans] found it shocking. While considering the fundamental role played by loyalty to the crown during the Spanish War, one must not overlook this phenomenon, for it belies the underlying cause for all of the hostility that the French presence in Cuba provoked.

The Cuban historians have tended to attach great

significance to the English capture of Havana in 1762.[240] They regard this as a watershed event, resulting in the island's artistic and economic awakening. This claim appears to be an exaggeration. The much more sustained contact with the French refugees, with their ideas and new technics— whether they were accepted or rejected—seems to have been more decisive in introducing part of Cuban society into the mainstream of Western society.

The colonists who remained after 1815—practically all of those who had not gone to New Orleans in 1809—were already an integral part of the country. Most of them had been naturalized. Nearly twenty years of residency had integrated them into the population. Many of them had intermarried into the island's [Spanish] families and had no intention of ever returning to France. Naturalization solved many administrative problems and facilitated the process of becoming and remaining a land-owner. In this manner, they blended into the Cuban Creole world with increasing ease, yet they also ushered into [that society] a new method of living and persisting [culturally].

Along with coffee-growing, the refugees introduced into Cuba two types of men who would not be duplicated [by native Spaniards] for some time: the small planter with a family-owned coffee farm and the large coffee grower.

The [demands of] production and preparation of coffee, much less mechanized than their counterparts in the sugar industry, as well as the lack of seed-capital and manpower imposed upon the new colonists the necessity of living off their own production. This was their means of survival. Because of its scale, the work was less impersonalized, less regimented than that of large farms. The master or his children closely supervised the clearing of the land, the planting, the trimming, the weeding, and particularly the harvesting. Not that there is any slacking off or sloppy work—much to the contrary—the slave lived close to his master who was more like a boss; his humanity was recognized to a far greater extent here than on the large sugarcane farms in the West or in Saint-Domingue.

On the other hand, whenever a Creole wedding, a successful

---

[240]A. Savine, "Les Anglais dans l'île de Cuba au XVIIIe siècle," *Revue Britannique*, (1898), 162-199.

partnership, or loans permitted, the colonists established much larger coffee-farms, but with the work was organized in a very different form from that of the *hacendados'* vast sugarcane plantations. The Creole sugarcane grower generally lived in Havana, far from his plantation, just as so many planters in the North of Saint-Domingue had done. They travelled to Spain and other countries, leaving their estates in the hands of an overseer. [The Spanish sugar planter] only stayed there a few weeks per year. The large French coffee planter lived on his plantation, around which his life revolved. His slaves, the very few he was able to take along, and those he bought or rented were under his constant supervision. A cadre of slaves that he retained served as the framework of his work force. Saint-Domingue slaves were selected to lead work gangs and were entrusted with the details of discipline and maintenance of the [work] routine. The French slaves long remained marginalized vis-à-vis the Cuban black Creoles. They had other different methods, a different time schedule, and, most importantly, a much quicker pace of work. The Saint-Domingue slave had the pride of a productive worker. Underlying that pride was the ambition and the iron-fist of the colonist who wanted to get rich and attain a certain social status quickly. Such a man had known the misery of poverty and was not worried about what people would say about him in his adopted country. While it is true that the organization of the large coffee plantations in Cuba under the Saint-Domingue model permitted the island's economy to enter the mainstream of world commercial exchanges and while it enabled it [the Cuban coffee industry] to respond to the demands of annually rising European coffee consumption levels, its direct and immediate consequence was negative. The slave system became more inflexible, the physical well-being of Cuban slaves generally declined, for they were compelled by their masters to work ever harder, and to accelerate the pace to increase production, just as Saint-Domingue planters had done [before the revolution]. Although Cuba's agriculture modernized, the island became, in the early nineteenth century, heavily dependent on slave labor because of trends established by the refugees. The slave had become a source of labor even more important than in the past, [human] capital that had to produce and earn money for his owner. This pattern of exploitation would continue until the mid-nineteenth century when the Industrial Revolution made the slave an antiquated means of production. New farming methods would also add to slavery's obsolescence. This evolution would have taken place without the arrival of the refugees, but they accelerated the process by at least thirty years.

This restructuring of work on the coffee plantations came to pose in other guises the general problems of manual labor.

The Treaty of Vienna had abolished the sale of slaves. This interdiction in principal inhibited the recruiting of agricultural slaves.[241] The slave trade did not disappear overnight, so to speak, but slave-traders were only able to raise the "strength of the plantations" with great difficulty; prices sky-rocketed.

The scarcity of slaves forced the colonists to turn to free men [of color] to supply manual labor. The French, much more than the Creoles, with the possible exception of the *vegueros* growing tobacco in the West, juxtaposed paid labor with slave labor. On many plantations, free men of color and free blacks, whites also, a world of true farm workers sweated side by side with the slaves. It would be curious to study this overlapping in Cuba of the two modes of labor by comparing the two rates of production.[242] A rapid observation concludes that, on the one hand, this juxtaposition was executed to the detriment of the black slave, and on the other, it converted many minds to the idea of the abolition of slavery. The high yields of the refugees' plantations was assuredly obtained through a better agricultural technology, but also by a more rational use of manual labor. Because of the distribution of tasks among both slave and salaried workers, [planters were able to make direct], daily comparisons of their results determined that the profitability of servile workers was inferior to that of paid employees. The black slave appeared to be an expensive anachronism that was

[241] E. Williams, "The Negro Slave Trade in Anglo-Spanish Relations," *Caribbean Historical Review*, I (December, 1950).

[242] This study was sketched out by H. S. Aimes, "The Transition from Slave to Free Labor in Cuba," *Yale Review*, XV (1906), 68-84. See also by the same author, "*Coratación*, A Spanish Institution for the Advancement of Slaves into Freemen," *Yale Review*, XVII (1909), 412-431.

only justifiable for reasons of social status. The *hacendados* were also convinced to consider the possibility of a tropical economy without slaves, and at the same time as the coming revolution, we see the first war for independence beginning in 1868 with the abolition of slavery. Obviously, here, as elsewhere, the situation was complex, but it is possible to trace back here the confluence of a double French current:

1. The social and economic changes suggested by the results of the large coffee plantations demonstrated the inability of slave labor to compete with paid labor. On the whole, the Creole *hacendados,* who were generally more aware of the output of the French plantations, became abolitionists, whereas the Spanish planters remained unabashed supporters of slavery.

2. The general influence of the ideas of 1789, and especially those of 1848, was superimposed upon this new economic arrangement, excercising its control upon the youth of Cuba through the books they received in school from France by way of Baltimore and New Orleans. Here, the influence of the French planters does not appear to be direct and their exact role in spreading these ideas has not been established. They paved the way, though, in perpetuating the use of French, by certain imitative habits, by certain fashion trends, and by establishing and maintaining links with France.

The local population soon unable to provide sufficient free manual labor. They were obligated to encourage immigration. The *Consulado*, the economic society of Havana recommended it. A royal decree of October 21, 1817, had already encouraged European immigrants, Spaniards preferably, to settle in Cuba. Tax exemptions, land in the eastern provinces, and a reduction in rent for fifteen years were offered to them.[243] The newcomers were drawn to the East because that was where the largest estates of the colored population were, in the provinces closest to Haiti. This infusion of new blood into this part of Cuba reduced the numerical importance of the French refugees and their

[243]"Memoir (translated from Spanish) presented to the Queen of Spain by Don Domingo de Goicouria on the effects of increasing the white population on the island of Cuba," *Revue Coloniale*, II, (1849), series 2, 1-14.

descendants. Thus, the coffee-based economy which had been the direct consequence of French immigration became in its own right the source of an influx necessary for its upkeep and development. The sugarcane plantation had a return then of seven percent on the average, the same as before 1800. On the coffee farms, yield was at thirty percent, but these results were obtained at the detriment of the workers.

Opulence without its problems is unimaginable. Nowhere were slaves the passive instruments of colonial wealth, and there was probably a connection between this high productivity rate and the uprisings which broke out in 1825, 1830, 1831, and 1835.[244]

Next came the fall of the Cuban coffee production before the competition from Brazilian coffee, then the rise of King Sugar. Another balance of power, another world was coming into being, one in which the refugees were less involved because they lacked funding. The detachment of old ties to form new ones, operating slowly over time, caused the amalgamation of the French community into the island's Cuban population, forming a Franco-Cuban blend. Prosperity from sugar brought to Cuba new foreigners and other human unrest. The story of the refugees and their actions as French colonists comes to an end around 1850.

We have only examined their history, only interpreted its meaning and scope by summarizing what Mr. Pérez de la Riva's book has taught us. It is now a matter of clarifying and deepening it by recounting the story of a few Creole families from Saint-Domingue who settled on Cuban soil. It is a matter of following their misfortune and their efforts to rebuild their lives and their fortune. Nothing could teach us more things concerning their installations and the vicissitudes of luck than a few well conducted and detailed mongraphs on the plantations. Yet this work is not accessible to us in France.[245] The papers and souvenirs of this past are kept in Cuba, around Santiago or in the Havana region. One cannot make them come more alive,

[244]This conclusion is closely inspired by observations summarized in several letters by Mr. Pérez de la Riva.

[245]Where, nonetheless, the papers of the Gleize de Maisoncelle family are kept in Notre Dame du Fort, near Nantes.

one cannot better assure their future than by using them for historical purposes and publishing them.

A nineteenth-century engraving of the ruins of a Saint-Domingue plantation.

The Saint-Domingue Refugees in Louisiana, 1792-1804

by Gabriel Debien and René Le Gardeur†

translated by David Cheramie

This essay is the end result of extensive research conducted in collaboration with a colleague who eventually became my friend.

Even before 1955 Mr. [René] LeGardeur* was silently collecting New Orleans books and information about the colonists who came to Louisiana from Saint-Domingue [present-day Haiti] during the French Revolution. Meanwhile in France, I was researching the history of the colonists who fled to Cuba in still greater numbers. Our intertwining inquiries were brought into contact with one-another by Mr. [Sidney Louis] Villeré[1] of the Athénée Club,[2] and they turned out to be complementary. There was work enough for two. There is enough left for many more.

---

* René J. LeGardeur (1893-1973), a descendant of Saint-Domingue refugees, was an authority on early Louisiana history. He authored many articles, the most noted of which is "Les Premières Années du Théâtre à la Nouvelle-Orléans," *Compte-rendu de l'Athénée Louisianais* (1954), 33-64. For a brief biographical sketch of Mr. Legardeur, see Alice D. Forsyth, "René Joseph LeGardeur," in Glenn R. Conrad, ed., *A Dictionary of Louisiana Biography*, 2 vols. (New Orleans, 1988), I, 499-500.

[1]Annotator's note: Sidney Louis Villeré is the author of two works on Louisiana history: *The Canary Islands Migration to Louisiana, 1778-1783: The History and Passenger Lists of the Isleños Volunteer Recruits and Their Families* (New Orleans, 1971); and *Jacques Philippe Villeré, First Native-Born Governor of Louisiana, 1816-1820* (New Orleans, 1981).

[2]Annotator's note: The Athenée Louisianais, a Creole cultural and literary society, was founded at New Orleans on January 12, 1876, by twelve Louisiana Francophones, led by Dr. Alfred Mercier. Mercier's brother Armand served as the organization's first president. The organization's journal, *Comptes Rendus de l'Athénée Louisianais*, functioned as the main literary outlet for French Louisiana writers during the late nineteenth and early twentieth centuries. For additional information, see Reginald Ford Trotter, Jr., "An Index of the *Comptes Rendus* of *l'Athénée Louisianais* and a General History of the Organization, 1876-1951" (M.A. thesis, Tulane University, 1952).

After seventeen years of exchanging information, one ends up with a rough first draft of the history of these refugees, one which is very incomplete though, for, in order to produce a detailed account, a complex network of parochial records—not only from New Orleans, but also from Santiago de Cuba, Baracoa, and Havana; administrative correspondence; notarial minutes; and genealogies would have had to be examined. But enough is enough.

At first, mostly isolated cases were recorded, but, upon further investigation, these isolated cases appear to have been part of larger waves [of immigration]. They thus debarked by groups—colonists, women and children, people of color—both free and enslaved, [and] slaves, first in 1798, after the English evacuation of Saint-Domingue, then in 1803, when the remnants of Leclerc's[3] army left the colony, and finally from May to September 1809, when [Saint-Domingue] refugees were chased from Cuba by the Spanish War.

This influx of French-speaking colonists doubled the number of French-speakers in New Orleans, an important demographic factor. It [the influx] accented its [New Orleans'] Creole character[4] and cast the problem of education in a different perspective. In addition, even if these refugees did not introduce sugarcane farming into South Louisiana, these men from Saint-Domingue established New Orleans' first newspapers. One may characterize them as important reinforcements during the War of 1812. United by their Creole language and culture and by their common misfortune, these newcomers from the islands permitted New Orleans to preserve for a few more years its colonial character, its exotic charm, and

[3]Annotator's note: Charles Victor Emmanuel Leclerc, (1772-1802), Napoleon's brother-in-law and commander of the French army sent in 1801 to subjugate Saint-Domingue's rebellious black population.

[4]Annotator's note: For more information regarding the demographic, economic, and cultural impacts of the Saint-Domingue influx, see Paul Lachance, "The 1809 Immigration of Saint-Domingue Refugees to New Orleans: Reception, Integration and Impact," XXIX (1988), 109-141; and John A. Heitmann, "Revolutions and Beginnings: The Dual Revolution and the Origins of the Louisiana Sugar Industry." (Paper read before the World Plantation Conference, University of Southwestern Louisiana, Lafayette, October 1989).

a life-style similar to that of an island just offshore from the continent, even as thousands of Americans were arriving from the eastern seabord states.

The first planters who left the colony headed east to Santo Domingo, the Spanish part of the island; others went to Cuba, Jamaica, or Puerto Rico; still others travelled to the Dutch island of Saint Thomas or to Danish Saint Eustache. Revolutionaries from Martinique disembarked from the *Trinité*. In 1793 and 1794, civil commissioners Sonthonax[5] and Polverel[6] deported to the continent a number of counter-revolutionaries, partisans of the white supremacy movement. Many refugees, instead of returning to France, went to the United States in the hope of soon being able to return to their plantations or businesses. The fire in Cap-Français (present-day Cap-Haïtien) in late June 1793 increased departures tenfold.

The truth is that all of these departures were not flights to safety. Some colonists left Saint-Domingue more or less at their own leisure, guided by their business relations, by relatives who preceded them, or by a preoccupation with finding a climate

[5]Annotator's note: Léger-Félicité Sonthonax, a "revolutionary agent," was born March 17, 1763, at Oyonnax (Bugey), France. He earned his livelihood as an attorney at the beginning of the French Revolution. During the Revolution, Sonthonax was active in the Parisian revolutionary movement. Joined with Condorcet and Brissot to secure a writ extending civil rights to persons of color in the Antilles. On June 3, 1792, with Polverel and Ailhaud, he was named royal commissioner with extraordinary powers to restore order in Saint-Domingue. He arrived at Cap Français, September 19, 1792. Because of opposition from General Galbaud, Sonthonax and his fellow commissioners were forced to arm Negroes in an effort to restore order to the colony and to prevent an English invasion. Shortly after arming the blacks, Sonthonax and his fellow commissioners promulgated, on August 29, 1793, the order of emancipation for all Negroes in the colony, thereby precipitating a full-scale civil war in the colony, for the whites and free blacks responded by inviting the British to take possession of Saint-Domingue. Subsequently returned to France to face charges of malfeasance. Upon returning to Saint-Domingue in 1797, Sonthonax named Toussaint Louverture to command the forces defending the colony. Returned to France in May 1799. Again charged with malfeasance, he was arrested and exiled to the Department of Charente-Maritime. After being permitted to relocate to Orleans, France, he was permitted to return to his hometown of Oyonnax, where he died on July 28, 1813.

[6]Annotator's note: On June 3, 1792, with Sonthonax and Ailhaud, he was named royal commissioner with extraordinary powers to restore order in Saint-Domingue.

most similar to the one they abandoned for the purpose of establishing new plantations with their remaining slaves.

The evacuation of this society, which went into exile in order to survive and to preserve its cultural identity, was not a phenomena unique to Louisiana. It is a chapter in a much larger movement, but nowhere else did it so significantly affect the history of a country.

We have noticed that these departures conveniently occurred in several phases.

1) From 1791 to 1803 there was a series of independent departures by individuals and families. Their arrival would not have provoked so much discussion if these refugees had not been accompanied by slaves. Coming from a country torn by insurrection, these slaves raised fears of an uprising plotted by "Jacobins" and free men of color. These colonists would later play important roles in the foundation of New Orleans' first theater and in the establishment of Louisiana's first sugar mills.[7]

2) Toward the end of 1803 and again in 1804, the remaining soldiers in Leclerc's army evacuated Saint-Domingue.[8] They are preceded, accompanied, or followed by the last remaining colonists and merchants who clung to this now independent scorched land. They came from the North, the West, and the South. They did not choose their place of refuge but went wherever their ship took them. It is a story of the final scramble for survival which often ended in Louisiana.

3) In 1809 occurred the greatest movement of refugees. At the beginning of the Spanish War, authorities in Cuba and Puerto Rico chased from these islands all French men who had not married Spanish women or had not taken Spanish citizenship. Many individuals booked passage aboard small open boats; but

---

[7]Annotator's note: See the following works by René J. LeGardeur, Jr., *The First New Orleans Theatre, 1792-1803* (New Orleans, 1963); and "The Origins of the Sugar Industry in Louisiana," in *Green Fields: Two Hundred Years of Louisiana Sugar* (Lafayette, La., 1980), pp. 1-28.

[8]Annotator's note: For information regarding the fate of some of these soldiers, see the following works by Simone Rivière de la Souchère de Léry: *A la Poursuite des Aigles* (Paris, 1950); and *Napoleon's Soldiers in America* (Gretna, La., 1972).

other crossings were organized by Louisiana's American government, which made these refugees debark at New Orleans. This wave [of immigration] was dense but of a short duration (October and December 1809).

4) With the end of maritime hostilities in 1815, some Creole families who had gone to France and were still unadapted to life and the winters there, found in Louisiana an atmosphere analogous to the one they knew in happier times. There they hoped to observe the events they awaited in Saint-Domingue where the slaves maintained very tenuous control. The whites fully expected to reconquer the island, or at least to negotiate a more favorable peace. Mothers who had prudently sent their children to France called them back to their fathers' side. Families were reunited. This tendency is only of secondary importance, but one we must mention.

The very last colonists to disembark in New Orleans came from Jamaica between 1835 and 1840 in the days following the abolition of slavery in the British colonies. They were able to rebuild a large domestic staff and the life-style facilitated by it.

We had developed the major themes of this history, assembled the names of many colonists and many families who arrived before 1804, when the unexpected demise of Mr. LeGardeur shattered our project. I abandoned the enterprise.

In 1978 Paul Lachance, professor at the University of Ottawa, made his presence known. He was interested in and aware of the large number of colonists from Saint-Domingue who went to Louisiana. He too had examined parochial records at Saint Louis Cathedral in New Orleans.[9] He came to see the notes and copies of documents that I had gathered and to read Mr. LeGardeur's letters. Our decision was to take up research again, but, alas, without Mr. LeGardeur's note cards. We agreed to share the work which remained to be done. By associating the names that I had with those which my friend had

---

[9]Annotator's note: Abstracts of these records are currently being published by the Archdiocese of New Orleans. See Earl C. Woods and Charles E. Nolan, comps., *Sacramental Records of the Roman Catholic Church of the Archdiocese of New Orleans,* 7 vols. (New Orleans, 1987-1992).

gathered before 1962, I agreed to write the history of the refugees prior to 1804. Mr. Lachance would write about the refugees who went to Cuba and who were expelled from there in 1809.[10]

I

From one colony to the other before the Revolution.
Commerce and passages. Refuge and aid.

Whether French or Spanish, Louisiana sustained a flow of people and business from Saint-Domingue throughout the eighteenth century, not of great importance, but continuous and direct.

Indeed, the development of Louisiana never had the feverish impetus like that of the biggest island in the French Antilles. It ranked in last place among the plantation colonies before the Seven Years' War. It was not of great interest to French commerce because it had neither sugar nor coffee and because all of its other products were found in much greater quantity in the other colonies.[11] Its immense and unfamiliar territory did not offer much of a future to young people concerned with making a fortune.

Louisiana was, nevertheless, of vital interest to Saint-Domingue. It furnished excellent wood to the growing needs of the island's developing cities and burgeoning plantations. The main link between the two colonies throughout the eighteenth century thus was the lumber trade.[12] Comestibles lagged far behind; New Orleans merchants went to Cap-Français to buy sugar, syrup, and European merchandise only after the Spaniards took possession of Louisiana.

Saint-Domingue, with its plains and low hills quickly deforested, lacked the boards and beams necessary for

---

[10]Annotator's note: See above note 4.

[11]Annotator's note: For additional information regarding colonial Louisiana's economic development, see John G. Clark, *New Orleans, 1718-1812: An Economic History* (Baton Rouge, 1970).

[12]Annotator's note: On the development of Louisiana's export lumber trade, see John Hebron Moore, "The Cypress Lumber Industry of the Lower Mississippi Valley During the Colonial Period," *Louisiana History*, XXIV (1983), 25-47.

construction, the stave-wood and hoop-wood for its casks, [and] the fire-wood for its sugar mills' furnaces. One could solve the heating problem by utilizing bagasse.[13] But the carpenters who built the sugar-mills, the boats, and the slave quarters often lacked workable wood. The forests of the Mississippi satisfied Saint-Domingue's needs.

> From Louisiana, they took to the islands squared cypress beams suitable for building. Houses, completely marked and cut, ready to assemble upon arrival at their destination, were often transported; bricks; *essentes*[14] used to cover homes and barns. . . . Transporting the foregoing materials to the islands was quite profitable; profits were ordinarily one hundred percent. Ships from the colony[15] brought back sugar, coffee, and *guildive,* a brandy made from sugarcane which the Negroes liked to drink. They shipped back still other merchandise for use in that country.[16]

The conditions which Le Page du Pratz[17] summarizes here existed as far back as the time of his sojourn in Louisiana (1718 to 1734), and the coffee of which he speaks came from Martinique rather than Saint-Domingue, where its cultivation was only beginning.

---

[13]Dry straw produced as a residue of milled sugarcane.

[14]Flat wooden shingles used to cover houses.

[15]Louisiana.

[16](Antoine-Simon) Le Page du Pratz, *History of Louisiana*, 3 vols. (Paris, 1758), III, 326.

[17]Annotator's note: (Antoine-Simon?) Le Page du Pratz was a Louisiana colonist and historian. Born ca. 1689, he served in the French army during the German campaign of the War of the Spanish Succession. He sailed for Louisiana in 1718 and established himself first along Bayou St. John, near New Orleans, and later at Natchez. In 1728 he became director of the Company of the Indies' plantation near New Orleans. He departed Louisiana for France in 1734. In 1758, Le Page du Pratz published a three-volume work entitled *Histoire de la Louisiane*. He died in 1775. Conrad, ed., *Dictionary of Louisiana Biography*, I, 504.

In the first days of the Seven Years' War, the Chevalier de Pradel[18] announced in a letter to his brother:

> *May 21, 1751.*—We now have in our port more vessels than there were before, and I would gladly use all of those returning directly to France, for many go to Saint-Domingue, carrying lumber and taking on stones as freight [meaning ballast].

> *and April 29, 1753.*—We have a number of boats engaged in the coasting trade with the islands of Saint-Domingue, Martinique, etc. . . . They bring us their surplus goods from France: Negroes,[19] sugar, and sugarcane brandy called *tafia* or *guildive*. It is a bad, stinking drug, but since it inebriates and is cheaper than French brandy, surprisingly large quantities of it are consumed both by the Indians and by the Negroes and [by settlers] in the outposts as well; and in New Orleans, the regimental adjutant there leases the right to distribute the drink for 4,000 *livres*.[20]

The Saint-Domingue sugarmills' accounts provide evidence of the importation of lumber from the Mississippi *via* New

---

[18]Annotator's note: Jean de Pradel, a French soldier and planter, was born at Uzerche, France, on April 12, 1692. He served in the Louisiana garrison from 1714 to the mid-1730s, eventually attaining the rank of captain. He subsequently retired to his plantation, Monplaisir, located across the Mississippi River from New Orleans. He died at Monplaisir on May 28, 1764. Pradel's correspondence with his relatives in France has been compiled and published by A. Baillardel and A. Prioult, eds., *Le Chevalier de Pradel: Vie d'un colon en Louisiane au XVIIIe siècle* (Paris, 1928).

[19]Annotator's note: This slave trade would be officially terminated in 1765.

[20]Martial de Pradel de Lamaze, "A Colonial Officer in Louisiana, the Knight of Pradel," *Revue d'Histoire des Colonies Française*, (1920), 128.

Later Dubroca insists upon the importance of the income derived from this commerce: "The vessels also loaded lumber there which they transported to Saint-Domingue and a shipment of 8,000 pounds had a return, ordinarily, of 35 to 40,000 francs with which they bought sugar in Saint-Domingue. Quadrupling their investment upon return to France, this commerce gave to the colony an annual income of 250,000 pounds." *L'itinéraire des Français dans la Louisiane* (Paris, Year 10 [1802]), p. 86.

Orleans, but very rarely do they specify the type [of wood]. In addition to this lumber, Saint-Domingue imported dried provisions: corn, rice, peas, and beans.

When surveillance of foreign commerce was most stringent, before the Franco-Spanish agreement, La Frénière,[21] a Louisiana colonist, described on April 6, 1775, how this commerce was conducted.

> Never has the settler had so much income. Nothing remains, not even supplies. The many vessels in the river buy up everything. When we arrived, we composed a flotilla of seven boats.... We openly engaged in smuggling with the farmsteads. They come aboard in pirogues to get whatever they need. The settlers upstream, forewarned of the vessels' passage, congregate near Mr. de Livaudais' settlement. This area is called Little Manchac.[22]

From Saint-Domingue's viewpoint, smuggling's main advantage was that Louisiana colonists paid mostly in cash, with those precious "*piastres* which they procured for themselves through their commerce with Florida and New Spain."

At the same time, a small number of men circulated—hurrying to and fro would be an exaggeration—for one travelled more often from Louisiana to Saint-Domingue than in the opposite direction. Individuals and some groups participated in this movement.

Amongst the individual departures, that of one L'Isle, second lieutenant of the Louisiana troops who appears in Saint-

---

[21]Annotator's note: The identity of this individual is uncertain. Nicolas Chauvin de Lafrénière, *père*, died in 1749. His son, Nicolas Chauvin de Lafrénière, *fils*, was killed by firing squad on October 25, 1769. Biographical sketches, family histories, and church records all record the birth of one Lafrénière child, a daughter. Conrad, ed., *Dictionary of Louisiana Biography*, I, 172; Stanley Clisby Arthur and George Campbell Huchet de Kernion, *Old Families of Louisiana* (1931; reprint ed., Baton Rouge, 1971), pp. 241-243; Woods and Nolan, eds., *Sacramental Records*, II, 53.

[22]Marc de Villiers du Terrage, *Les dernières années de la Louisiane française* (Paris, 1903), p. 354.

Domingue as early as 1718, was among the earliest.[23] Following
the Company of the Indies's[24] failure to populate Louisiana,[25]
there must have been a backlash that brought to Saint-Domingue
a certain number of individuals who had not succeeded on
the banks of the Mississippi. But at the same time, Clairin-
Deslauriers, surgeon-major in the Saint-Domingue garrison
went to Louisiana in 1723.[26]   Shortly after 1725, a certain
Durand, formerly a warehouse manager for the Company of
the Indies accused of embezzlement in Louisiana, took refuge
in Saint-Domingue where he issued protestations of innocence.
He was but one piece of human wreckage, probably not unlike
many others.[27]   In 1742, Castelconnel,[28] former ensign in the
Louisiana garrison, requested a position as half-pay ensign in
Saint-Domingue.

Another Louisiana warehouse manager, Duparquier,
established himself in Saint-Domingue in 1754.[29]   He
ultimately supervised the recruiting office in Cap-Français.
His son served there as artillery lieutenant. Joseph Gamon[t]
de La Rochette,[30] an army captain in Louisiana, had himself

[23]National Archives, Paris, France. Colonial Archives, Series E (Individual personnel), carton 287, l'Isle dossier; hereafter cited as AC, E, with the numbers of the carton and the names of the dossiers.

[24]Annotator's note: The Company of the West, and its corporate successor, the Company of the Indies, operated Louisiana as a proprietary colony from 1717 to 1731. For additional information regarding this phase of Louisiana's development, see Pierre Heinrich, *La Louisiane sous la Compagnie des Indes* (Paris, 1908).

[25]Annotator's note: On this subject, consult Marcel Giraud, *Histoire de la Louisiane,* 4 vols. (Paris, 1953-1974), vols. II-IV.

[26]AC, E 82, Clairin-Deslauriers dossier.

[27]AC, E 164, Durand dossier.

[28]AC, E 65, Castelconnel dossier.

[29]AC, E 158, Duparquier dossier.

[30]Annotator's note: Louisiana military records indicated that Gamont de La Rochette had received a commission as captain in the Dauphiné militia on September 1, 1747. He was appointed captain in Louisiana on October 1, 1750. While in Louisiana, he served as commandant of the Arkansas post from 1757 to 1763, when he returned to France.

transferred to Saint-Domingue in 1757. Twenty years later, he held the rank of major at Port-de-Paix.[31] Antoine Bruslé, councilman in the New Orleans Superior Council, was the father of a militia commander stationed in Grande-Rivière du Nord. Retiring to Saint-Domingue to be near his son, he became an important coffee planter.[32] Jean-Maurice Collet, after some years as a surgeon in New Orleans, found it more advantageous—he made a fortune—exercising his talents in and around Cap-Français from 1770 to 1785 where he requested and received an appointment as the chief royal surgeon.[33] At the age of twenty, Modeste Barbier, a "native of Louisiana," was married at Cap-Français to Jean-Joseph Barême. She sought refuge in Nantes at the time of the slave uprising of 1791.[34] In almost all of these cases, it was not a question of officers or civil servants being transferred from one colonial post to another, but of voluntary displacements and individual requests. Some Louisiana families settled in the principal French colony in the hope of sharing in the apparent wealth of the island.

The cession of Louisiana to Spain by the Treaty of Fontainebleau (November 3, 1762) marked the beginning of major changes in the dealings between the two colonies. The merchants from New Orleans, Cap-Français, and Port-au-Prince feared suppression of the unrestricted commerce in lumber, sugar, and supplies.[35] They anticipated an interdiction against smuggling and speculation in *piastres*, which had proved mutually profitable. In 1764, the opening of Môle-Saint-Nicolas, Saint-Domingue, located at the far end of the northern

---

[31]AC, E 197, Gamon de La Rochette.

[32]AC, E 55, Bruslé dossier.

[33]AC, E 87, J-M. Collet.

[34]Archives of the Loire-Atlantique, Nantes, France. Series P, assisted colonists dossier.

[35]The accord allowed French merchants the freedom of commerce with Louisiana in order to be able to collect their active debts up until 1772.

peninsula, as a free port soon came to accommodate many business interests, and the Superior Councils of Cap-Français and Port-au-Prince never lost sight of that fact.[36]

This did not initially alter the status quo, however. When Ulloa,[37] the first Spanish governor, arrived in 1766, he had [Charles Philippe] Aubry,[38] the last French representative, promulgate a temporizing order. With the objective of favoring Louisianians, this order dated September 6 and 7, 1766, allowed "the settlers of the French colonies of Saint-Domingue and Martinique who will bring here wine, flour, and other goods and who, in exchange, will take aboard as cargo lumber and specific commodities until such time as commerce with Spain is established." Prices were controlled by the Spanish authorities. This restriction elicited an immediate protest [from members of the New Orleans mercantile community], who sought

[36]The dean of the Port-au-Prince council to the council of New Orleans, February 9, 1769. National Archives, Paris, France. Colonial estates, Series C 13a (Louisiana: general correspondence), volume 49, folio 208; hereafter cited as AC, C 13a, with the volume and folio numbers.

[37]Annotator's note: Antonio de Ulloa (1716-1795) was perhaps the most outstanding Spanish scientist of the eighteenth-century. As a young man, he participated in a French scientific expedition to South America. He subsequently produced, with Jorge Juan, a report on conditions in Peru. He served as governor of Louisiana from March 1766 to October 1768, when he was forcibly expelled from New Orleans by a colonial insurrection. Ulloa subsequently served without distinction in the Spanish navy.

[38]Annotator's note: Charles-Philippe Aubry was appointed second lieutenant in the Lyonnais Infantry Regiment on November 6, 1742. On April 1, 1743, he was commissioned second lieutenant in the French regular army. Aubry served with distinction in the War of the Austrian Succession. He was assigned to Louisiana with the rank of captain in the colonial troops, 1750. Aubry led a party of French raiders against an English position along the Tennessee River in 1757 and, the following year, commanded a French detachment that successfully defended Fort Duquesne against English and Indian invaders. He was captured while leading an expedition to lift the siege of Fort Niagara, in 1759. Aubry returned to France after being detained in New York for two years as a prisoner of war. While in France, he was awarded the Cross of St. Louis for meritorious conduct. In 1763, Aubry was placed in command of Louisiana's small caretaker garrison. In February 1765, he succeeded Jean-Jacques-Blaise d'Abbadie as acting governor of Louisiana. He governed Louisiana jointly with Antonio de Ulloa, Louisiana's first Spanish governor, from 1766 through 1768. In 1769, he assisted Alejandro O'Reilly in prosecuting French colonists allegedly responsible for Ulloa's expulsion in October 1768. Aubry died in the wreck of the *Père de Famille* while returning to France, February 17, 1770.

unrestricted commerce.[39] Moreover, Spain seemed to extend trading privileges only to the islands' established merchants. In the absence of a formal trade agreement with Louisiana, the French government authorized Saint-Domingue and Martinique merchants to transport sugar and other commodities to New Orleans, from which they were to return with *piastres.* [Louisiana] lumber products [also] continued to reach Cap-Français and Port-au-Prince.[40]

During the early [transitional] years (1763-1768), [many] soldiers and civil servants who were forced to leave the colony by the change in sovereignty later served in Saint-Domingue. However, not all of the officers and clerks left right after the colony's cession to Spain. They had interests to protect and debts to collect or to pay off. Their departures are staggered until 1773.

Among the first to leave were Douin de La Motte, promoted to the rank of captain in the Saint-Domingue army;[41]   De Fontad, captain in the Angoumois Regiment;[42] Louis-Augustin Montault de Montbéraud,[43] whose family had been in Louisiana since 1739;[44] Balthazar Fabre de Mazan[45] who became the royal

---

[39]Order of the king of Spain, September 6, 1766. AC C 13a, 46:89; and Villiers du Terrage, *Les dernières années*, p. 352.

[40]Villiers du Terrage, *Les dernières années*, p . 237.

[41]AC, E 137.

[42]Annotator's note: The Angoumois Regiment was stationed briefly in Louisiana during the early 1760s. See Carl A. Brasseaux, trans. and ed., *A Comparative View of French Louisiana, 1699 and 1762: The Journals of Pierre Le Moyne d'Iberville and Jean-Jacques-Blaise d'Abbadie* (Lafayette, La., 1979), pp. 86, 91, 92, 95, 102.

[43]Annotator's note: Montault de Monbérault was commissioned captain in Louisiana on October 1, 1752. In 1755, he served as commandant of Fort Toulouse. He was characterized by Louisiana Governor Louis Billouart de Kerlérec in 1758 as "severe, muddle-headed, and dangerous." On January 8, 1765, he was appointed British "deputy superintendent of Indian Affairs of West Florida." Montault de Monbéraut was subsequently dismissed from office by British Governor George Johnstone.

[44]AC, E 195.

[45]Annotator's note: In late October 1768, Mazan, the alleged "treasurer of the rebels," was named acting councillor for a special session of the Louisiana Superior Council convoked to consider the expulsion of Spanish Governor Antonio de Ulloa. The following summer, Mazan and Noyan-Bienville represented the revolutionaries before Montfort

lieutenant and commander of Cap-Français.[46] The garrison soldiers who were threatened with service in Saint-Domingue if they refused to serve under Spain were finally repatriated. Only one entered the Legion of Saint-Domingue.[47]

At the same time, approximately half of the Acadians exiled to New England who, after the Treaty of 1763, sought refuge at Saint-Domingue,[48] came to Louisiana in 1765.[49] They disembarked in a state of complete destitution, sharing among themselves only 47,000 *livres* in Canadian card-money which naturally nobody wanted. The Louisiana soil would miraculously stabilize this uprooted, disoriented, unfortunate people.

Alongside the Acadians appeared some young people that the Seven Years War had brought first to Saint-Domingue and later to Louisiana. Driven by an inquisitive and adventurous spirit, Julien Poydras[50] of Nantes, an English prisoner of war

Browne, lieutenant governor of British West Florida, to gauge the British reaction to the uprising. In August 1769, Mazan was arrested by Spanish authorities and charged with sedition. He was subsequently tried, convicted, and sentenced to imprisonment in Morro Castle. He was released in 1770.

[46]AC, E 149.

[47]Report of the king on the troops in Louisiana, April 28, 1766. AC, C 13a, 46:78. Aubry to Bongars, July 15, [1767]. AC, C 13a, 47:13; Aubry to Praslin, October 1769. AC, C 13a, 49:106.

[48]Gabriel Debien, "Les Acadiens à Saint-Domingue," in Glenn Conrad, ed., *The Cajuns: Essays on Their History and Culture* (Lafayette, La., 1978), pp. 255-432.

[49]Annotator's note: Although hundreds of Acadians did actually resettle in Saint-Domingue, the exiles referred to here were from Halifax, Nova Scotia. They had simply changed ships at Saint-Domingue while en route to Louisiana. For more information on these Acadian exiles, see Carl A. Brasseaux, *The Founding of New Acadia: Beginnings of Acadian Life in Louisiana, 1765-1803* (Baton Rouge, 1987).

[50]Annotator's note: Julien de La Lande Poydras was born at Rezé, France, on April 3, 1746. Poydras became a British prisoner-of-war while serving in the French navy during the Seven Years' War, but he subsequently escaped and made his way to Saint-Domingue, where he remained until around 1768, when he migrated to New Orleans. Poydras subsequently established a trading post along False River, in the Pointe Coupée District, later diversifying his business interests by operating a general store, a cotton gin, and a plantation. In 1779, he wrote *La Prise du Morne du Baton Rouge* to commemorate the Spanish capture of British Baton Rouge. He served as civil commandant of the Pointe Coupée District in 1804 and later served as the president of the Louisiana legislative council. Poydras presided over the Louisiana constitutional convention of 1812. He served as president of the state senate in 1812-1813 and again in 1820-1821. He died at New Roads, La., on June 23, 1824. Conrad, ed., *Dictionary*

from 1760 to 1763 and later a soldier of fortune at Cap-Français, left Saint-Domingue around 1768. He remained a year at New Orleans and later established himself in Pointe Coupée, where he became one of the richest planters of the colony.[51]

On the other hand, for many years, importation of slaves from Saint-Domingue was banned. A decree of the New Orleans Superior Council explains the prohibition: "gunfire being incapable to stopping the corruption of Negroes, the masters are forced to burn the guilty parties. Evil is so pervasive that the prisons are always full and the councils have been obliged to tolerate executions at the farmsteads."[52]

These developments were followed in 1768 by the official Spanish act of possession for Louisiana and by the decree of March 23 which imposed Spanish mercantilism, authorizing direct commerce with only nine "accredited" ports on the [Spanish] peninsula.[53] Minds were already closed in New Orleans. One may be assured that this order precipitated the rebellion of 1768. "The widespread hatred for Mr. Ulloa and promulgation of His Catholic Majesty's decree depriving this colony of its commerce with the French colonies were the primary causes of the revolt."[54]

---

of Louisiana Biography, II, 660-661.

[51]Alcée Fortier, *A History of Louisiana,* 4 vols., (New York, 1904), II, 66.

[52]Villiers du Terrage, *Les dernières années,* pp. 161, 222.

[53]"Royal Decree Providing the Rules and Conditions under which Commerce May Be Carried on Between Spain and the Province of Louisiana," March 23, 1768, in Lawrence Kinnaird, ed., *Spain in the Mississippi Valley, 1765-1794,* Annual Report to the American Historical Society for the Year 1945, 3 parts (Washington, D.C., 1949), Part 1, 45-51.

[54]Note from Aubry to O'Reilly, August 20, 1769. AC, C 13a, 49:31. Also see James E. Winston, "The Causes and the Results of the Revolution of 1768 in Louisiana," *Louisiana Historical Quarterly,* XV (1932), 181-213. Annotator's note: See also, John Preston Moore, *Revolt in Louisiana: The Spanish Occupation, 1766-1770* (Baton Rouge, La., 1976); and Carl A. Brasseaux, *Denis-Nicolas Foucault and the New Orleans Rebellion of 1768* (Ruston, La., 1987).

It was fundamentally a struggle between the merchants of New Orleans and the new Spanish authorities who intended to scrutinize foreign trade and to prohibit contraband. Ulloa was expelled by the malcontents who supported the Superior Colonial Council. In truth, it would have taken a lot more for all of the French colonists to be united against Ulloa, as suggested by the Count of Montault. On October 31, 1768, he wrote to his brother, who had already arrived in Saint-Domingue:

> At the very moment that I am writing to you, my dear brother, the entire colony has taken up arms. The settlers have revolted against the Spanish, and the governor has been forced to leave. I dare not give you any details of this unprecedented act. It has profoundly shaken me. That is all I can tell you. You well know that I hold my honor much too dearly to have participated in, much less approved of, an uprising of this sort.[55]

In the end, the *coup d'état* failed. [Alejandro] O'Reilly[56] was sent to reestablish the royal authority. As soon as he arrived in New Orleans, he reimposed the [commercial] restrictions and tried the movement's leaders.

The sentence of October 24, 1769, condemned to death six of the

---

[55]Villiers du Terrage, *Les dernières années,* p. 261. About the Montaults, see National Archives, Series T 1725, carton 4, dossier 4; hereafter cited as AN, T 1725. Annotator's note: For a brief account of the family, see Fontaine Martin, *A History of the Bouligny Family and Allied Families* (Lafayette, La., 1990), pp. 280-283ff.

[56]Annotator's note: O'Reilly was born in 1725 at Dublin, Ireland. He was educated at Spain's Colegio de las Escuelas Pias de Zaragoza and subsequently enrolled in the Regimiento de Hibernia. O'Reilly commanded the Spanish army during the invasion of Portugal and served as inspector-general at Cuba and Puerto Rico, 1764-1765. He led an army of over 2,000 men to Louisiana in 1769. Charles III bestowed the title of conde de O'Reilly upon him on July 19, 1769. In 1775, O'Reilly organized and led the unsuccessful Spanish invasion of Algiers. He served as governor of Cadiz from 1780 until his retirement in 1789. He died on March 23, 1794. Conrad, ed., *Dictionary of Louisiana Biography,* II, 620.

leaders, including Jean-Baptiste Payen de Noyan,[57] brother of a Saint-Domingue colonist, and Joseph Milhet.[58] Six others were imprisoned, including Joseph Petit, life imprisonment; Jean Milhet, Hardi de Boisblanc,[59] Julien-Jérôme Doucet[60] and Poupet,[61] ten years. All of their possessions were confiscated.[62]

[57]Annotator's note: Payen de Noyan was born in Louisiana around 1745. He was the son-in-law of Nicolas Chauvin de La Frénière, Louisiana's attorney general and the leader of 1768 New Orleans rebellion. Payen de Noyan participated in a meeting, held at New Orleans around January 1, 1765, in response to Louisiana's cession to Spain. *Ibid.*, p. 234; Conrad, ed., *Dictionary of Louisiana Biography*, II, 610.

[58]Annotator's note: Joseph Milhet was a prominent New Orleans merchant. In 1763, he signed a public declaration of support for Governor Kerlérec. The following year, he joined with several other New Orleans merchants to protest the issuance of a trade monopoly with the Indian tribes of Upper Louisiana. In 1765, he was reportedly an organizer of a meeting called in response to Louisiana's cession to Spain. Marc de Villiers du Terrage, *The Last Years of French Louisiana*, trans. by Hosea Phillips, ed. by Carl A. Brasseaux and Glenn R. Conrad (Lafayette, La., 1982), pp. 150, 216, 234, 289, 290, 296, 350, 354, 388.

[59]Annotator's note: Pierre Hardi de Boisblanc was a native of La Rochelle, France. During the early 1760s, he served as an attorney for vacant estates in the Louisiana Superior Council. He was selected by *Commissaire-ordonnateur* Denis-Nicolas Foucault to serve in the Superior Council hearing on the petition to expel Antonio de Ulloa. Following his arrest by Spanish authorities on August 19, 1769, he was tried and sentenced to six years in Morro Castle. He was released in December 1770 through the influence of his brother, an influential French Recollet. Conrad, ed., *Dictionary of Louisiana Biography*, I, 378.

[60]Annotator's note: Julien Jérôme Doucet was a native of Switzerland. During the late 1760s, he was an attorney in New Orleans. Doucet was arrested by Spanish authorities on August 19, 1769, and charged with sedition stemming from his support of the 1768 New Orleans Rebellion. He was sentenced to ten years' imprisonment. Conrad, ed., *Dictionary of Louisiana Biography*, I, 253.

[61]Annotator's note: Pierre Cyprien Poupet, a native of La Rochelle, France, went to New Orleans in 1763 as the representative of a La Rochelle mercantile house. Poupet allegedly served as treasurer for the insurgents who expelled Ulloa from Louisiana in October 1768. Poupet was arrested by Spanish authorities in 1769 and charged with sedition. He was subsequently tried, convicted, and sentenced to six years in Morro Castle. Conrad, ed., *Dictionary of Louisiana Biography*, II, 660.

[62]O'Reilly to Arriaga, October 28, 1769. Seville, Spain. General Archives of the West Indies, Saint-Domingue Hearings, ledger 80-1-7; hereafter cited as AGI, SD. O'Reilly to the Marquis of Grimaldi, October 27, 1769. AGI, SD, 80-1-7, Buccareli to Arriaga, December 12, 1770 AGI, SD, 80-1-9. O'Reilly to Grimaldi, October 17-27, 1769. AC, C 13a, 49:121. Annotator's note: For an account of the trial of these individuals, see David Ker Texada, *Alejandro O'Reilly and the New Orleans Rebels*, U.S.L. History Series No. 2 (Lafayette, La., 1970).

The prisoners were incarcerated at Morro Castle in Havana, but shortly thereafter, the Spanish king pardoned them. Yet he did not allow them to return to Louisiana. In December 1770, they were transported to Puerto Rico. From there, they went to Cap-Français, where nearly all of them settled and where their families joined them. Jean Milhet's[63] daughters thus married Moreau de Saint-Méry[64] and Baudry des Lozières,[65] who would later go to Louisiana.[66]

Captain-general O'Reilly also deported others during the trial: the Durand brothers,[67] the Boudet brothers, the Duralde brothers from Geneva, all merchants; Jean Sauvestre, Elias Hugues Paprion, Doraison, Fornie, Jean Brunet, Blache,[68] Jean

---

[63]Annotator's note: Jean Milhet was reputedly one of the wealthiest men in Louisiana. In 1764, he carried to France a petition from New Orleans merchants protesting Louisiana's cession to Spain. Failing to secure the nulification of the cession, he returned to Louisiana in 1767. Milhet was arrested on August 19, 1769, and charged with participation in the New Orleans Rebellion of 1768. He was tried and sentenced to six years' imprisonment. Milhet was released in December 1770 and subsequently returned to his native France. He died around 1780. Conrad, ed., *Dictionary of Louisiana Biography*, I, 568.

[64]Annotator's note: Médéric Louis Elie Moreau de Saint-Méry was born at Fort Royal, Martinique, in 1750. As a young man, he practiced law in Saint-Domingue and published in Paris a six-volume legal reference work entitled *Loix et constitutions des colonies françaises de l'Amérique sous le vent* (1784-1790). Moreau de Saint-Méry was a founder and president of the Museum of Paris. He was active in the revolutionary movement in Paris in 1789. He fled to the United States because of political persecution in 1794 and subsequently opened a Philadelphia publishing house and bookstore. He returned to Paris in 1798 and served as an administrator in Parma, Piacensza, and Guastalla between 1802 and 1806. He was recalled to France by Napoleon in 1806. Moreau de Saint-Méry died in 1819. *Webster's Biographical Dictionary* (Springfield, Mass., 1963), p. 1052.

[65]Annotator's note: Louis Narcisse Baudry des Lozières (1761-1841) wrote *Voyage à la Louisiane, et sur le continent de l'Amérique septentrionale, fait dans les années 1794 à 1798, contenant un tableau historique de la Louisiane* (Paris, 1802); and *Second Voyage à la Louisiane, faisant suite au premier de l'auteur de 1794-1798. Contenant la vie militaire du Général Grondel, qui commanda long-temps à la Louisiane* (Paris, 1803).

[66]A-L. Elicona, *Un colonial sous la Révolution: Moreau de Saint-Méry* (Paris, 1934), p. 12.

[67]Concerning the Durand brothers' affair, see AN, T 1725, Dossier 2.

[68]"A malcontent, a nuisance harmful to public safety," writes O'Reilly to Praslin, October 27, 1769. AGI, SD, 80-1-7.

Vincent,[69] almost all merchants also; Poquet, clerk in the New Orleans treasury; Maison, chief process-server of the Superior Council; Reignier, chief surgeon at the hospital;[70] and three "undesirable" Jews:[71] Brito, Meto, and Monsanto, asked to leave [Louisiana] for having engaged in smuggling.[72] The total includes twenty-one persons. Twelve were obliged to leave Louisiana after the trial. They did not all take refuge in Saint-Domingue, but it seems that many did.

A small migration to Saint-Domingue accompanied or followed these expulsions.[73] It continued for three or four years, encouraged probably by the attitude of Port-au-Prince's Superior Council at the time of the insurrection. Many Saint-Domingue colonists shared the Louisianians' resentment regarding Ulloa in the wake of his blunders, and the [Saint-Domingue] superior councils, mouthpieces for colonial public opinion, openly exhibited their sympathy for the Louisiana Creoles. The senior member of the Port-au-Prince Superior Council had warmly congratulated the New Orleans council upon its energetic intervention in Ulloa's expulsion.[74]

Martin[75] assures us that during the summer of 1770,

[69]Merchant and clock-maker, who may have married Jeanne Godard. O'Reilly to Praslin, October 3, 1769. AC, C 13a, 49:150.

[70]Bobé to Praslin, October 3, 1769. AC, C 13a, 49:150.

[71]Annotator's note: For the best available history of New Orleans's early Jewish community, see Bertram Wallace Korn, *The Early Jews in New Orleans* (Waltham, Mass., 1969).

[72]O'Reilly to Arriaga, October 17, 1769. AGI, SD, 80-1-7. There were some Monsantos in Cap-Haitien.

[73]Winston, "The Cause and Results of the Revolution of 1768," 181-213.

[74]The senior member of Port-au-Prince to the High Council of New Orleans, February 9, 1769. AC, C 13a, 49:208. Aubry to the minister, May 23, 1769. AC, C 13a, 49:20.

[75]Annotator's note: François-Xavier Martin, a pioneer Louisiana historian, was born at Marseilles, France, on March 17, 1762. He joined his uncle at Martinique around 1782 and, after the failure of his uncle's business, moved to Newbern, North Carolina, where he studied law. Martin was appointed Superior Court judge of the Mississippi Territory in 1809 and, the following year, he was named Superior Court judge for the Territory of Orleans. He served as Louisiana's first attorney general and as a member of the state supreme court from 1815-1846. He died at New Orleans on December 10, 1846. Conrad, ed., *Dictionary of Louisiana Biography*, I, 511.

after O'Reilly's departure,[76] "most" New Orleans merchants and artisans withdrew to Cap-Français and that many colonists followed them there. These departures were supposedly so numerous that O'Reilly tried to block them by refusing to issue passports. Martin must be alluding to the merchants expelled in August and October of 1769 and he assuredly exaggerates when he speaks of "many colonists." Besides, undertaking the voyage was not an easy venture. [Governmental] authorization was required, and these departures were more like escapes. However, in 1773, Colonel Israël Putnam[77] notes in his *Journal of an Expedition to the Natchez*[78] that he met a schooner at the mouth of the Mississippi aboard which were about forty French passengers "who, tired of the Spanish government, were going to Cap-Français." His testimony is verified by some correspondence of September and October 1772 which signal other departures.[79]

But several officers, armed with all necessary authorization, were able to leave in 1773 or before: administrative officials like Bobé-Desclozeaux, *commissaire ordonnateur*;[80] militia officers

---

[76]Fortier, *A History of Louisiana*, II, 22. O'Reilly was governor from August 18, 1769, up to December 1 of the same year, but continued his functions as captain-general until his departure in March 1770.

[77]Annotator's note: Israel Putnam was born at Danvers, Mass., around 1739. He was a soldier in the French and Indian War and served during Pontiac's Uprising. In 1775, he was appointed major general in the Continental Army. He was incapacitated by a stroke in 1779 and died in 1790. *Webster's Biographical Dictionary*, p. 1223.

[78]John W. Caughey, *Bernardo de Galvez in Louisiana, 1776-1783* (Berkeley, Cal., 1934), p. 51. A copy of this diary is available at the Library of Congress.

[79]These letters are deposited in the Archives of the Ministry of Foreign Affairs, Political correspondence, Spain, volume 567, folios 56, 281, 296, 394; hereafter cited as Foreign Affairs. One knew that in Cap-Haitien and Port-au-Prince that rich families from New Orleans planned to leave Louisiana for Saint-Domingue and that they were expected. But they changed their minds or rather the refusal to issue a passport must have forced a change in plans. Foucault to Praslin, November 22, 1768. AC, C 13a, 48:78.

[80]Villiers du Terrage, *Les dernières années*, p. 363. Annotator's note: The *commissaire-ordonnateur* functioned as the administrative chief in Louisiana's bi-polar government. See Brasseaux, *Denis-Nicolas Foucault*.

like Nicolas Champfort de Longueval,[81] army officers like Garderet, infantry officers or army engineers like Hippolyte Amelot, fortification engineer. Amelot was not in Louisiana for a very long time, but he had married a Creole there, Félicité Dubreuil, who bore him two daughters.[82] During the insurrection, he remained faithful to the Spanish authorities[83] and was named ordinary *alcalde* of the *cabildo*.[84] They would all perish at sea while en route to Cap-Français[85] at the end of 1773. The widow and daughter of Alexis-Joseph Carlier, former naval scribe and comptroller at New Orleans, perished with them.[86]

Though stern, O'Reilly was also clever. He recognized the importance of Louisiana's lumber trade with Saint-Domingue

[81]AC, E 290 (1777-1780).

[82]Félicité, who died in New Orleans in 1829, at the age of 66, widow of Jean Canon, and probably Adélaïde, wife of François Dutillet.

[83]Ulloa to Grimaldi, October 26, 1768, in Kinnaird, ed., *Spain in the Mississippi Valley*, Part 1, 77.

[84]The *cabildo* was a sort of high council, but invested with quite special powers according to the Spanish laws, but, at the same time, with those of city council and chamber of commerce. It had been established November 25, 1769, by O'Reilly to replace the French Superior Council. At first, it was composed of eleven members: 6 *regidores perpetuales*, buying their charge, two ordinary *alcaldes*, one attorney general, one tax collector and one registrar.

[85]François X. Martin, *The History of Louisiana from the Earliest Period*, 2 vols. (New Orleans, 1827-1829), II, 30-31.

[86]Carlier had left the colony in 1769 to go to Saint-Domingue to join his son Alexis-Joseph, he too an officer in the Navy's administration fulfilling the function of commissioner of War and Classes in Port-au-Prince. He had gone by way of France; from Paris, in January of 1770, he had written to Choiseul that the French were groaning in Louisiana under Spanish domination and implored that the Spanish government be begged to take under its special protection his wife, his two daughters, and all his possessions that he had left in Louisiana which they had been charged to liquidate. Upon arrival in Port-au-Prince, he had serious confrontations with Rochemore, General Commissioner of the Navy, former head of payroll in Louisiana. When he died in 1773, nothing had been settled yet. AC, E 63 (1770-1773).

The son married in Port-au-Prince on November 28, 1792, Jeanne-Catherine Eugénie Peneault, Creole from Port-au-Prince, who, widowed on July 16, 1794, remarried in the town of Jérémie on November 10, 1798, to Louis-Joseph-Simon Le Gardeur de Tilly.

and, while awaiting orders from the royal court, he took it upon himself to authorize its exportation. He knew that it was an important exchange. He restricted it only by limiting it to Louisiana's ships.[87]

His successor, Luis de Unzaga[88] (December 1, 1769-January 1, 1777), was tolerant and through his policy of reconciliation most Louisiana Creoles adjusted well to the new administration. Smuggling found an existence parallel to that of the customs agencies. This very fact is what forced France and Spain to sign, on July 8, 1776, a commercial convention to avoid a worsening of the situation. Thereafter, one could transport Louisiana wood, grains, tobacco, "and other fruits" for the subsistence of the French colonies. The French ships would be admitted provided that they were carrying a passport signed by two French commissioners residing in New Orleans who would buy the lumber and everything to be exported to the island. These ships would come to New Orleans in ballast and would only pay for their cargoes in cash or in valid letters of exchange. However, the commissioners were chosen not by the minister but by the general administrators of Saint-Domingue. They were Claude-Joseph Villars Dubreuil[89] and Guy-Charles Fabre-Daunois,[90] both Louisianians. Dubreuil had served in Saint-Domingue as captain then as infantry major from 1770 to 1774.[91] In

[87]O'Reilly to Arriaga, October 27, 1769, in Kinniard, ed., *Spain in the Mississippi Valley*, Part 1, 103-105.

[88]Annotator's note: Luís de Unzaga y Amezaga was born at Málaga, Spain, in 1721. He served in the Regiment of Havana from 1740 to 1772, rising from the rank of captain to brigadier-general. Unzaga accompanied Alejandro O'Reilly to Louisiana in 1769 and succeeded O'Reilly as governor of the colony on December 1, 1769, serving in that capacity until January 1, 1777. He held the post of governor-general of present-day Venezuela from June 17, 1777, to December 10, 1782. Unzaga died in Spain on July 21, 1793. Conrad, ed., *Dictionary of Louisiana Biography*, II, 804-805.

[89]Born in New Orleans in 1744, he had wed on May 25, 1779, in New Orleans Marie-Eulalie Livaudais, widow of Pierre de Saint-Pé. Archives of St. Louis Cathedral.

[90]Annotator's note: Charles-Philippe Favre Daunoy received a salary of 4,000 *livres* per year. He died at New Orleans in October 1780. Villiers du Terrage, *Last Years*, p. 411.

[91]Since he was in 1774 one of the representatives of the Louisiana refugees established in the Cayemites.

a way, they held the office of consuls for Saint-Domingue in New Orleans: Daunois until his death in 1780, Villars Dubreuil until 1784. These functionaries were not there to encourage bashfulness on the part of the Saint-Domingue colonists, nor to suppress their spirit of independence.[92]

However, French Creoles could not go to France without the Spanish king's permission. Denis Braud, one of the *cabildo's regidores*, was dismissed from office at the end of 1773. His office was auctioned off and his belongings confiscated for having undertaken one such voyage without permission.[93]

[Bernardo de] Gálvez who succeeded Ungaza (January 1, 1777-January 2, 1785) followed a more liberal political policy. Making Louisiana a buffer between the English colonies and New Spain was his first priority. This required a large population base and almost complete freedom of trade.

His proclamation of November 21, 1777, announced that, to encourage agriculture, the king had permitted, since the preceding March 10, the importation of slaves from the French islands. Mulatto slaves, however, were banned. Slaves could be used as payment for the wood exported to the Antilles.[94] Ships no longer had to come into the port of New Orleans laden only with ballast; French wines, fabrics, merchandise were acquired at Cap-Français and imported to Louisiana. Bordeaux wine merchants even found a way to ship merchandise [to Louisiana] directly from France. Their ships called at Cap-Français, thus pretending that the trip began in Saint-Domingue. These vessels then sailed to New Orleans and from there returned directly to France.[95]

[92]This convention ceased to be applied in 1785—at least in principle. Tallyrand to the Directory, Germinal 20, year IX (April 2, 1798). Archives of Foreign Affaires, Political Correspondence, Spain, volume 651.

[93]Caughey, *Bernardo de Galvez*, pp. 45-49.

[94]Proclamation Concerning Louisiana's Commerce, November 21, 1777, in Kinnaird, ed., *Spain in the Mississippi Valley*, Part 1, 242-243.

[95]Note from Las Horas, Spanish council in Bordeaux, addressed to the Count of Floridablanca, January 9, 1778, in Whitaker, *Documents Relating to the Commercial Policy of Spain in the Floridas, with Incidental Reference to Louisiana* (DeLand, Fla., 1931), p. 4.

We know what was done in Cap-Français to welcome the refugees who were not all well-to-do merchants. In fact, "most of these immigrants [were] people who brought nothing or almost nothing with them."[96] Rations were distributed among them, to permit them to continue their voyage. They were then allocated a portion of the enfranchisement tax receipts, when the *ordonnateurs* were authorized to do so by the governor and the intendant, who had earlier designated Jérémie's southern dependency as the prospective settlement for immigrants wishing to establish plantations.[97] In order to distribute plots of land that would be close to each other, numerous undeveloped concessions were returned to the royal domain and then conceded to the newcomers. This measure had caused quite an uproar.

In that vast canton called the Désert, between the Corail and Baradères[98] rivers, a few refugees planted coffee. Some friends initiated a subscription to aid them. Shares of this "patriotic association" were sold for 500 *livres* in money, commodities, or cattle," to be able to buy tools . . . and Negroes."[99] A circular from the administrators promoted the subscription.[100] These new colonists had two representatives named by the governor: in 1773, Villars Dubreuil, who would be tapped in 1777 as royal commissioner at New Orleans, and Payen de Noyan, ship's ensign, residing in the Grand-Anse district, of which Jérémie, the Cayemites, and the Désert were a part. This Payen was a close relative of the Payen who was executed by firing squad at

[96]The administrators of Saint-Domingue to the minister, October 14, 1775. National Archives, Paris, France. Funds of the Colonies, Series F 3 (Moreau de Saint-Méry Collection), volume 25, folio 33; hereafter cited as AC, F 3, with the numbers of the volumes and folios.

[97]P. A. Cabon, *Histoire d'Haiti*, 4 vols. (Port-au-Prince, 1930-39), volume II.

[98]This name indicated the fertility of the land offered.

[99]Announcement of a patriotic association for the settlers of Louisiana who withdrew to Saint-Domingue, December 1773. AC, F 3, 25:350.

[100]Circular of the administrators, December 28, 1773. AC, F 3, 25:332.

New Orleans in 1769, and Villars Dubreuil's mother was a Payen de Noyan.[101]   Moreau de Saint-Méry, who had just married Louise-Catherine Milhet and who had done so much to preserve the memory of Saint-Domingue's generous colonist, was on the association's board of directors.

This effort to create a settlement in this new district did not endure. The concessionaires abandoned the district preferring military or judicial positions. Such was the case of Jérôme Gauvain who had himself appointed port captain in Cayes-Saint-Louis.[102] The example of the Chevalier François Fabre de Mazan is typical. A bodyguard in Noailles' company since 1731, he had succeeded in 1735 in becoming second ensign in the Louisiana troops. After serving twenty-three years, during the course of which he had been wounded in the arm and appointed a knight of [the Order of] Saint Louis, he retired in September of 1754. He settled in Louisiana where he had a plantation and diverse properties that his son would later appraise, generously, at 800,000 *livres*. He was implicated in the disturbances of 1768. He was arrested and condemned to life imprisonment. His belongings were confiscated.[103]   He was heavily in debt, but by admitting this he was able to pay off the debts from the proceeds of the sale of his property. Through the French king's intercession, he was pardoned, and 100,000 *livres* were restored to him—the remaining proceeds from [the sale of] his confiscated property, which had been placed in the safe custody of the Spanish government to safeguard the interest of his creditors. The recovery of his wife's property was worth twenty-five slaves to him. He left for Jérémie with them where he had been accorded a concession of 400 *carreaux* (over 450 hectares). But there was no longer any available land. The surveyors had mislaid their surveys or had taken bribes from the negligent former concessionaires who had been evicted by the order returning the land to the royal domain. His concession was

---

[101]According to Arthur and Huchet de Kernion eds., *Old Families of Louisiana*, pp. 105-111.

[102]AC, E 200, J. Gauvain (1782-1791).

[103]Villiers du Terrage, *Les dernières années*, p. 310.

never "situated," as was the case with many surrounding ones. Also in April 1773, although he had retired from service fifteen years before, he was named regimental adjutant at Fort-Dauphin in the North, where he died January 21, 1775.[104]

Many other "former settlers" of Louisiana, assembled for a short time in the solitude of the South, returned to the cities and asked for another form of aid. After 1775, there must not have remained many Louisianians around Jérémie nor even in the South in general: Jean-Baptiste Gautherot-Dutheil and his sons Honoré and Claude, obtained positions, one in the offices of the Navy,[105] the other in the constabulary;[106] Jacques Bertrand, from La Rochelle, and Gabrielle Gabion, his wife, did not relish the colonial life in Saint-Domingue any more than they had the one in Louisiana.[107]

Among those who toiled feverishly to build a plantation or to stay in the South, three names survive: Jean-Jacques, Michel Verret,[108] and Barthélémy Charbonnet, who moved to Jérémie. He came from Natchitoches, where he had married in March of 1768 Nathalie Pain, a Louisiana Creole. They went to Saint-Domingue around 1772. They probably died in Jérémie where one of their children was born.

During the last years of the century, just before the Revolution, the direction of the migration shifted, now usually moving from Saint-Domingue to Louisiana. The growing difficulty in amassing a quick fortune turned the more ambitious toward

---

[104]AC, E 308. There is another Mazan dossier in E 149.

[105]AC, E 200, Gautherot-Dutheil (1775-1792).

[106]AC, E 379, Tizonneau (1774-1778).

[107]AC, E 28, Bertrand dossier. Request for aid in 1775.

[108]Jean-Jacques Verret, born in Cannes-Brûlées, near New Orleans, on June 17, 1745, went to Saint-Domingue in 1772. He set himself up as a windmill builder for the sugar mills in Saint Louis du Sud, in association with Michel his brother, then together as entrepreneurs of bridges and hydraulic works. Michel died at the age of fifty in Jérémie May 30, 1790. AC, E 385, Verret dossier; and Médéric Louis Elie Moreau de Saint-Méry, *Description topographique, physique, civile, politique, et historique de la partie française de l'isle Saint-Domingue . . .* , 3 vols. (1796; reprint, Paris, 1958). See the index under Verret.

other horizons. This movement is parallel to the one that, in France, caused more and more young people to emigrate to the islands of the Indian Ocean.

After the end of the American Revolution, when Spain had been France's ally, the English and American threat had spawned a policy of reinforcing Louisiana. The discussions regarding unrestricted commerce and immigration at New Orleans led to the royal *cedula* of January 22, 1782.[109] For a period of ten years beginning with the promulgation of peace,[110] Spanish and Louisiana ships were authorized to go to New Orleans or Pensacola directly from French ports having a Spanish consulate and then to return to France with Louisiana goods, payment in specie remaining strictly forbidden. The importation of slaves was now duty free.

Saint-Domingue immigrants followed in its wake. Just to illustrate this point, here are a few examples, almost all having left from Cap-Français:

In early adulthood, Symphorien Gaillavet, from Bordeaux, son of a member of *parlement* and of Marie Tuart, went to Saint-Domingue where he became a militia officer in Cap-Français, married on June 1, 1785, in New Orleans Marie-Rose Carrière, a Creole. On January 24, 1806, he died in New Orleans at the age of fifty-four, having lived in Louisiana since his marriage.[111]

On February 15, 1785, Antoine Terrasson, a native of Cap-Français, requested permission to settle at New Orleans. Witnesses declared that he had brought all of his belongings to Louisiana and that he apparently intended to take up permanent residence there.[112]

Jean-Baptiste Olivier, born at Cap-Français around 1762, son of Joseph, from Marseilles, and Marguerite Martin, from

[109]"Real Cedula Concdiendo Nuevas Gracias para Fomento del Comercio de la Luisiana," in Whitaker, ed., *Documents*, pp. 30-39.

[110]It was promulgated in Louisiana in early 1784.

[111]Marital and Burial records of Saint Louis Cathedral, New Orleans.

[112]Laura L. Porteous, trans., "Index to the Spanish Judicial Records of Louisiana," *Louisiana Historical Quarterly*, XXVI (1943), 1188.

Canada, went to New Orleans and married there Madeline-Adélaïde Mioton, a Creole, on June 9, 1785.[113]

An entire family, François Féraud, Rose Bernard, his wife, and their daughter Françoise, arrived in New Orleans around 1785. The daughter, born at Cap-Français, is said to have been "reared from early childhood in New Orleans," and because she married Pierre Lavigne, a Louisiana Creole, on May 6, 1803, one may conclude that she was born around 1783-1785.[114]

Louis Cornu de Livornière, son of Louis-Michel, captain of the Cap-Français militia, and Anne-Madeleine Faucher, owners of two houses in Cap-Français, married in New Orleans on November 26, 1770, Thérèse-Viviane B(r)unet, a Louisiana Creole.[115]

A certain Guérin, disappointed by his brief stay in Saint-Domingue, traveled to Louisiana in 1786, where he hoped to find a better fate.[116]

Jean Langouran was a native of Bordeaux. For several years he engaged in trade with Saint-Domingue, where he married Marie Fortier[117] and acquired a plantation employing about forty slaves. But, cursed by bad luck, or so he believed, the slaves died one after another, perhaps from poisoning. Around 1785, he sought better fortune in New Orleans with his wife where they found family members and their daughter Adélaïde. His hopes faded quickly, however, for in 1788, he left for Honduras to engage in commerce. His unfettered eloquence and his Voltairian views attracted notice and resulted in his being turned over to the tribunal of the Inquisition in 1792.[118]

[113]Marriage records, Saint Louis Cathedral.

[114]*Ibid.*

[115]*Ibid.*; *Etat d'indemnité . . .* (Paris, 1832), p. 98.

[116]AC, E 214, Guérin dossier (1786).

[117]Related to the Fortiers of New Orleans.

[118]Houdaille, "Les Français et les Afrançados," 313-314. His remaining daughter in New Orleans served as godmother on September 30, 1800. She married William G. Garland from Virginia on March 19, 1801. Their daughter, Virginia, born in New Orleans on February 7, 1804, was baptized on February 7, 1805. Baptismal and marital records, Saint Louis Cathedral.

One must not include among these refugees Father François Colomban, a Capuchin who had been apostolic prefect in Saint-Domingue and who arrived in Louisiana in 1790 to regain his health. He died in New Orleans on February 14, 1791.[119] Nor was Jean-Baptiste-Frédéric Colson, son of Pierre and of Marie Dubourg, born at Port-au-Prince on September 25, 1788, and baptized in New Orleans on October 1, 1790, a part of this group. He was not able to come with his parents before early 1790.[120]

The great fire of March 1788 that ravaged New Orleans revitalized both the generosity of the Saint-Domingue colonists and the generally healthy relations between the Creoles of the two colonies. From Cap-Français came assistance in the form of 29,407 *gourdes*[121] for the most destitute victims.[122]

Until the onset of the French Revolution, Saint-Domingue and Louisiana were bound together by ongoing, mutually profitable commercial relations, and by the innumerable reciprocal exchanges of congeniality. It is thus hardly surprising that, among the first colonists who abandoned their plantations in northern Saint-Domingue at the beginning of the French Revolution, many thought of migrating to New Orleans.

II
First Refugees (1792-1798)

We can identify fewer than 100 refugees who disembarked at Louisiana between 1792 and 1798. Instead of colonists, many [of

---

[119]Burial records, Saint Louis Cathedral.

[120]Baptismal records, Saint Louis Cathedral. He died a bachelor on April 11, 1835. Burial records, Saint Louis Cathedral.

[121]*Piastres* or dollars. Miró to the Captain-General, September 1788. Pontalba papers, conserved with Baron Alfred de Pontalba at the castle of Mont-l'Evêque near Senlis, France.

[122]François Barbé-Marbois, *Histoire de la Louisiane et de la cession de cette colonie aux Etats-Unis* (Paris, 1829), p. 161.

these refugees] appear to have been whites of modest social standing who had not yet set down roots in Saint-Domingue. Yet by their side, one finds well established [colonists] with familial ties to Louisiana.

First, there was the Count of Montault, officer in the Mississippi country who had taken up his duties in Saint-Domingue after the New Orleans insurrection. He was in the South where he had been named royal regimental adjutant at Cap-Tiburon in the Grand-Anse sector.[123] With other colonists from the South, who, like him were probably implicated in the political agitations at the start of the Revolution, he left Saint-Domingue for Jamaica in late 1791 or early 1792. From Kingston on March 2, 1792, he writes to his friend Livaudais, already established in New Orleans, the following letter which is probably our oldest account of the colonial immigration from Saint-Domingue to Louisiana:

> To my friends and compatriots in Louisiana,
>
> My unlimited attachment for my country, for my best friends, and my former comrades is known to them and to everyone. Fleuriau, Reggio, Saint-Cyr, Marigny, Macarty, Foucher, Trudeau, Le Blanc, Robert, and you, my dear Livaudais, have seen more closely than the others the extreme regret which I manifested the first time I left Louisiana with the intention of returning there to die after having reunited my friends and a large family which I cite lastly, certain I am that they know the place they hold in my heart. My brother never had any other way of thinking, [or] plans other than mine. He and I would have preferred remaining and working in Louisiana to continuing our service in France, thereby avoiding the catastrophe that we foresaw for our compatriots.[124] An enlightened father, whose loss is etched at this very moment upon my mind by fresh pangs

[123]AC, E 315 and T 1725, 4.

[124]The failure of the Rebellion of New Orleans in 1768.

of grief, preserved us from the mistake which claimed many as victims. We awaited receipt of our retirement pensions in order to ask for the permission that we should surely have obtained to enjoy it amongst our relatives and friends. We fortunately escaped a revolution that we always abhorred and that we now justifiably disdain because of the rabble's blind ingratitude and injustice. We are now back among you, my dear friends and compatriots, a little sooner than we had planned. Such, as you will see for yourselves, are our intentions, which are as ardent and pure as our very souls. We do not doubt that you will do for us what we would do for you if our situations were reversed. I find myself with my wife six months pregnant, feeding a son not yet eight months old; my brother is more unfortunate than I, for he is without his wife and his child who were compelled by poor health to remain temporarily at Saint-Domingue. We were constrained to abandon our possessions and our Negroes, who have shown us fidelity and attachment, which did not permit us at the last minute to hide from them our route and our plans. 'What is going to become of us,' these poor unfortunates said to us, 'if you abandon us in this lost and ruined country? Take us with you, any place you want to go; we will follow you anywhere. As long as we die with you, we will be happy.' Moved by this speech that each of them expressed in his own way, and all in a manner that appeared natural to us, how could have we conceal from them the uncertainty clouding the attempt which we, acting out of gratitude, must make to bring them to Louisiana. We could only promise to request permission.

My dear friends, we confidently anticipate that, motivated by your friendship, your zeal, and your humanity, you will solicit support for our cause in your dealings with, and petitions to, Louisiana's governor.

In receiving the passports we dare hope that the governor would well accord us, for us and for the

families who are allied to us and who have the greatest
desire to withdraw with us to Louisiana, the ships
travelling between the Leeward and Windward islands
and New Orleans being for the most part too small to
contain us all together, we ask you, my dear friends,
to try and obtain for us two separate passports, one
for Madame de Montault, my sister-in-law,[125] M. and
Mme. de Bruhier, Monsieur and Madame Pradines,
his brothers and sisters, brothers-in-law and sisters-
in-law and their children, *nègres bossales*,[126] related
subjects and their belongings in Saint-Domingue; and
another passport permission for my brother-in-law, my
wife, and myself. Address the first of these passports to
Madame de Montault in Aux Cayes;[127] send the other
to me here in care of M. MacLean, a businessman.
Our gratitude will be equal to the very sincere and
inviolable attachment to you that my brother shares.
We ask you, dear friends and dear compatriots, to
extend our reassurances to all those who are still
fortunately interested in our country. No one will be
able to disapprove the fact that, I addressed my letter
to you because of your proximity to the city[128] and asked
you, my dear friend, to communicate it to all the others,
whether or not they are named in this letter, so that you
may all act, as I am sure you will, in such a manner as

[125]Mme de Montault de Saint-Civier. Chevalier Montault de Civier married on Saint-
Domingue Geniviève-Renée Bruhier de Varvilliers, daughter of a coffee planter from Torbeck in the South who had presided in 1790 over the Provincial Assembly of the South.
The sister of Mme Montault de Civier, Madeleine-Thérèse, had wed Louis-Auguste Colla
de Pradines-Vauroux, from a family from the Cayes. A Mme. de Pradines was a refugee
in Marseille in 1802, but we could be dealing with the widow of the former president of
the Provincial Assembly of the South, *née* Madeleine-Gabrielle Madec du Pouldu or with
Marguerite-Rose Boyer de la Gautraie, married to another Colla de Pradines-Vauroux.

[126]That is to say, Negroes born in Africa, thus [considered] more reliable. A certain
choice was thus made.

[127]Where numerous colonists retreated from neighboring sectors.

[128]New Orleans.

to rejoin friends who were unable to control the circumstances that drove them away [from Louisiana]. . . .

In addition, kindly extend our respectful regards to your ladies and to assure them of the earnest desire ours have to make their acquaintance and to deserve from them [the Livaudais women] the same friendship for them [the Montault women] that they [the Livaudais women] now feel from the bottom of their hearts.

I reiterate to you with pleasure, my dear Livaudais, assurances of my faithful attachment.

Montault, Chevalier de Saint-Louis, retired infantry lieutenant

P.S. The exportation of cash from Saint-Domingue being forbidden, we will be obligated to take whatever one will be willing to offer us in exchange for our belongings. Consequently, do us the pleasure of letting us know the colonial commodities and the merchandise[129] . . . [available in] Louisiana.[130]

This migration was essentially a retreat. One prudently "withdrew" to Louisiana, a familiar country. This group of families was leaving a troubled land, seeking to find a life analogous to the one in Saint-Domingue. Departure was planned to proceed in stages, the men first in order to prepare the general moving. But there was the question of the slaves.

Montault wanted to take his slaves with him to Louisiana. This obstacle was almost insurmountable. He probably knew through his friends' unsuccessful attempts to do the same thing. Issued at Madrid in May 1790, orders, secret ones at that, banning the importation into Louisiana of all blacks from the

---

[129]Several illegible words here.

[130]Favrot Papers, volume III, folios 139-141; hereafter cited with only volume and folio numbers. This collection is conserved at Tulane University. Annotator's note: This collection has recently been published.

French and English Antilles. And one also knew what to expect from Louisiana's slaveowners because they feared a domestic uprising like that of Saint-Domingue.

The first document concerning the departures for Louisiana thus relates the difficulty of importing potentially dangerous slaves from Saint-Domingue. This prohibition which would become more and more restrictive invariably influenced the movement of refugees.

One does not know the kind of reception Montault's request received. He gave assurances that the slaves he wanted to import were faithful slaves. It appears probable that it met with refusal for if the chevalier was in New Orleans before the month of May 1793, the count, his brother, remained in Jamaica, where as a refugee and former soldier, he joined the British army which occupied Saint-Domingue from 1793 to 1798. In 1795,[131] he was second colonel in the constabulary regiment of scouts, one of the Saint-Domingue regiments created by the English.[132] The chevalier's wife died in Cap-Français of a putrid fever in early 1793. Perhaps she was preparing to leave for New Orleans.[133] Montault de Saint-Cirié then married Marie-Anne Claudine Planchard, New Orleans Creole.[134] They had two children.[135] On November 1, 1799, he died in New Orleans at the age of "45 to 50 years old."[136] There is no trace in Louisiana of the Count

[131]David P. Geggus, "The British Occupation of San Domingo (1793-1798)," (Ph. D. dissertation, University of York, 1978).

[132]*Précis des Annales historiques de Saint-Domingue*, 1st. Vol. It is very likely that one is speaking of the Chevalier Montault de Saint-Civier in the brochure *Les Volontaires du Petit-Goave à MM. les officiers du régiment du Port-au-Prince, sous les auspices de M. de Montault, leur major, sont venus les soustraire à l'oppression le 29 décembre 1790* (Port-au-Prince, 1791).

[133]Letters of Montault de Monbérault, from Kingston, to his brother in New Orleans, May 8 and August 10, 1793, accompanying an act from the notary public Esteban de Quinones from New Orleans, February 1794.

[134]Parochial records, Saint Louis Cathedral, February 26, 1794.

[135]Louis-Joseph, born May 31, 1795. Baptismal records of Saint Louis Cathedral, September 7, 1795, and another child born August 14, 1797, baptized January 15, 1798.

[136]Burial records of Saint Louis. His widow remarried on January 20, 1805, François-Joseph.

Montault de Monbérault nor his family.

In 1792, one finds at New Orleans André Bouquet, a former soldier in the Bourbon regiment who had been living in Saint-Domingue since 1788. Remaining a bachelor, he had practiced the trades of ironsmith and gunsmith. He would not establish permanent residency in Louisiana. In 1804, he was in Veracruz, Mexico.

Denis-Gaston *dit* Saint-Léonard, from Saint-Léonard in Limousin,[137] established in Saint-Domingue since 1780, left for Louisiana in 1793 with his mistress, a woman of color. He did not stay long, for he was in Cuba in 1803.[138]

In late 1792 or early 1793, Mme de Gripière departed for New Orleans with her child and her mother, Mme d'Anglade. This departure was more like a chartered cruise than a hurried escape, but it took considerable wrangling to persuade the captain of the coastal schooner, who was planning to sail along the southern coast, near Cavaillon, to embark the five or six slaves who wanted to accompany Mme de Gripière. Their baggage included several barrels of coffee.[139]

Louis Duclot escaped "during the slave uprising," probably after the fire in Cap-Français on June 21, 1793. A printer and engraver, he moved to New Orleans, where, with the governor's permission, he published the *Moniteur de la Louisiane,* whose first edition is dated March 3, 1794. It was Louisiana's first newspaper. He was associated in 1796 with J.-B. Lesueur-Fontaine whom he had first known in Cap-Français and who had first been a refugee in New York.[140]

[137]Workers and colonists from Saint Léonard were numerous in Saint-Domingue.

[138]Gabriel Debien, "*Les Colons de Saint-Domingue, réfugiés à Cuba (1793-1815),*" *Revista de Indias,* XII (1954), 573.

[139]"*Vie de Madame de Payrac,*" p. 9. Manuscript communicated by the General d'Aboville, 1935.

[140]Edward Larocque Tinker, *Les Ecrits de langue française en Louisiane au XIXe siécle* (Paris, 1932), p. 202. Lesueur-Fontaine was to die in New Orleans on July 4, 1814.

The three Dusseau de Lacroix brothers had some rather complicated ties with Saint-Domingue and with Louisiana. They were from Dauphiné, more exactly from Gap. Two carried the name Joseph.

Joseph, the elder it seems, born around 1732,[141] served in the artillery. He married in New Orleans a Creole, Marie-Thérèse Ofrère (or Aufrère) by whom he had two children, François-Emmanuel[142] and Balthazard[143] who do not seem to have left Louisiana.

The other Joseph was a lieutenant in the regiment at Cap-Français and married in the colony a Creole, Charlotte Defau, by whom he had two children: François[144] and Françoise.[145] A letter from Carondelet[146] to Luis de Las Casas, captain-general in Havana, dated March 28, 1794, indicates that Dusseau was then in New Orleans with the Chevalier de Montault.[147] He took

[141]Deceased in New Orleans on October 22, 1804, parochial records, Saint Louis Cathedral.

[142]Who married on October 29, 1793, in New Orleans Marie-Françoise-Geniviève Zoé Le Breton d'Orgenois, Creole. He died on October 7, 1803. Two daughters were born from this marriage: Marie-Rose-Zoé and Marie-Rose born on January 3, 1802, baptized the following February 4. The *Moniteur de la Louisiane* of March 8, 1806, announces the sale of François-Emmanuel Dusseau de La Croix's plantation.

[143]Born in St. Charles Parish, he wed Marie-Françoise de Priacourt, from New Orleans, who died at the age of twenty-one on August 19, 1794.

[144]Who would marry in New Orleans Anne-Marie Cavelier, Louisiana Creole, on February 2, 1800. Parochial records, Saint Louis Cathedral. They had a son François-Emmanuel-Frédéric, born January 1, 1801, baptized the following May. *Ibid.*

[145]Who probably wed in Saint-Domingue Marie-Etienne, knight of Fléchier, former captain in the regiment in Cap-Français who died on April 19, 1817. Burial records, Saint Louis Cathedral. Their son, Eugène was born in Saint-Domingue around 1792. He died in New Orleans. *Ibid.*, December 27, 1831.

[146]Annotator's note: Luis Francisco Hector de Carondelet (1747-[1807]) entered the Spanish military service in 1762. After serving the Spanish monarch in the Caribbean area, Carondelet participated in the 1781 siege of Pensacola. He was appointed governor of San Salvador in March 1789 and, on March 13, 1791, assumed the duties of governor of Louisiana. Carondelet left New Orleans, in 1797.

[147]Luis Hector, baron of Carondelet, to Luis de Las Casas, March 28, 1794. Archivo General de Indias, Seville, Spain. Papeles Procedentes de Cuba, legajo 152-2.

refuge there with his wife and children before the remnants of his regiment were sent back to France. It is known that he died before February 2, 1800, but his burial certificate cannot be found in New Orleans.

The third Dusseau de LaCroix was a colonist and property owner at Cap-Français. He had married a cousin, a Miss Lagarde, niece of a Dusseau de LaCroix from Saint Charles Parish, Louisiana. With his family, "victims of the Revolution," Dusseau first took refuge at Philadelphia, probably sailing aboard the convoy that left Cap-Français in the days following the fire of July 22 and 23, 1793. He died there [Philadelphia]. There, his widow, through gratitude she says, married a musician, also a refugee, by the name of Chevalier. She made the trip to New Orleans to secure her inheritance from Mr. Desmalters, an uncle who had lived in Louisiana.[148]

In most cases, one can well distinguish the relationships with kinsmen, neighbors, or regimental comrades-in-arms which explain these departures for Louisiana.

Alexandre Baudin arrived at New Orleans, probably in early 1793, with his wife, Julie Michon, and their daughter, Marguérite-Joséphine. He shows up without having any ties whatsoever to Louisiana. He was from Ile de Ré[149] and his wife from Ancenis. On May 27, 1793, a second daughter was born, Louise-Pauline, who on November 5, 1814, married Henri-Nicolas Poulet.[150] One of the witnesses was Jean-François Baudin, her uncle; he, too, had probably come from Saint-Domingue.

Ursin Durel was one of the six Frenchmen identified by Carondelet[151] to the Duke of Alendia, a [Spanish] minister, on

---

[148]Pontalba to his wife, April 20, 1796. Pontalba letters.

[149]He was the son of François Baudin and Suzanne Guillaube.

[150]Marriage records, Saint Louis Cathedral. A third child, Samuel-Alexandre was born March 24, 1799.

[151]"Carondelet to the Duke of Alcudia, [1793]," in *Annual Report of the American Historical Association for the Year 1896*, 2 vols. (Washington, D.C., 1897), II, 974-977. The names of these Frenchmen were: Pierre Sauvé, Jean Lanolier, Ursin Durel, Jean Mercier, Etienne Baruel, and J.-B. Molleret.

April 23, 1793, as fanatical partisans of the [French] Republic and recently established Louisiana merchants. The Durels, however, had been in New Orleans for a long time. Ursin may have been a refugee, but one who owned no property whatsoever in Saint-Domingue in 1791. Françoise Dejean, his wife, was a New Orleans Creole. François Durel, perhaps Ursin's brother, had married Marie Dejean, probably Françoise Durel's sister. The fact that Jean-Ursin, son of Ursin and Françoise Dejean, would marry a Môle Saint-Nicolas Creole, Marie-Polymnie Rochefort, on November 16, 1816,[152] at New Orleans, and that Jean-Baptiste Neuville-Durel, son of François, would marry on January 21, 1821, Louise-Eugénie Dupuy, another Creole from Môle, leads one to believe that the Durels came from Saint-Domingue.

Charles Longro, Saint-Domingue Creole, was captain in the dragoon militia and married to Louise Lachapelle, born at New Orleans. He was the son of François Longro, from Lille, and Marie Ducavinet, a Creole from Saint-Domingue. Their daughter, Euphrasie, born March 17, 1793, perhaps in Saint-Domingue, was baptized March 8, 1794, in New Orleans, giving rise to speculation that her parents had arrived in Louisiana in 1793 or in early 1794. The godmother was Françoise Longro, maybe an aunt to the child, she too a refugee.[153]

Between 1794 and 1796, the Saint-Domingue refugees came in greater numbers, this time by groups. First, there were those who came from the South, the sectors around Aux Cayes, Sale-Trou, and Jacmel. They had escaped the massacres committed by the mulatto Faubert. They were joined by political deportees from these same sectors, by some Saint-Domingue actors, and, in 1796, by colonists returning to France *via* Bordeaux. At the same time, a number of colonists who had orginally sought refuge in the Eastern Seaboard ports began to congregate in Louisiana.

Mme. Henriette Perroneau, *née* Druilhet, came from Baynet and Jacmel. The widows Mmes. Marie and Madeleine Mac

---

[152]Marriage records, Saint Louis Cathedral.

[153]Baptismal records, Saint Louis Cathedral.

Gill Mestayet as well as Jean Marsenat had all lived on Bernard Bret's plantation in Aux Cayes but had been deported from Jacmel in 1794. Marie-Madeleine Castaignet, born at Aux Cayes, the spouse and most likely the widow of Alexis Lesmartes, had two of her children baptized in New Orleans: Hyacinthe-Germain, born on July 24, 1787, and Marie-Delphine, born on February 4, 1790, "baptized privately—perhaps in Saint-Domingue by a Castillian Capuchin whose name is unknown." [Such an entry] suggests a hasty flight from the colony, the father's probable massacre, and an emergency baptism. She was forced to take refuge in Louisiana between February 4, 1790, and April 30, 1794.

Baudry des Lozières had married in Cap-Français a daughter of Jean Milhet, a Louisianian shot by firing squad in 1769. He is not what is normally considered a refugee from the sedition against Ulloa.[154] He had been in New Orleans only a short time, but undoubtedly only because of his wife's origins there. In late 1792, he returned from Saint-Domingue to France and on November 9, 1793, he arrived in the United States. He was in Norfolk on February 26, 1794, and in Philadelphia on Pluviôse 3, year III (January 2, 1795) whence he did not seem to move afterward. He could have reached New Orleans only sometime between March of 1794 and January of 1795 since he wrote a travel account which appears to be based on a little more than hearsay. He was back in France in 1798. In 1802 when Louisiana was a popular subject of conversation, he hurried to write *Voyage à la Louisiane et sur le Continent de l'Amérique septentrionale fait dans les années 1794-1798*[155] and the following year *Second voyage à la Louisiane faisant suite au premier de l'auteur de 1794 à 1798.*[156] The very abundant papers left by this long-winded defender of the colonial situation prior to 1789 give us absolutely no account of his stay in Louisiana.[157]

---

[154]A. Drépréaux, "Le Commandment des Lozières et la phalange de Crête-Dragons," *Revue d'Histoire des Colonies Françaises*, (1924), 1-41.

[155]Published in Paris, 1802.

[156]Published in Paris, year XI (1803), in two volumes.

[157]They are in the National Library, Paris.

Jean-Louis Isnard, born at Grasse, in Provence, on January 10, 1764, the son of Jean-Barthélémy and Marie-Jeanne Thémèse, had married in Port-au-Prince Marie-Euphrosine Marchand, Creole daughter of Pierre and Anne Chevalier. They were owners of mercantile houses in Port-au-Prince.[158] They disembarked in New Orleans in 1796 for their son Auguste-Louis, born May 9, 1796—in an unknown place—was baptized in Saint-Louis on August 2, 1796. The godparents were Auguste de Bréars and Eulalie Gardet from Saint-Domingue. They were later to have two other children in New Orleans: Jean-Baptiste and Jean-Louis. Isnard died on November 14, 1815[159] and his wife [sic] married a man named Planché, apparently also from Saint-Domingue.

Nicolas Laissard-Marafet was born at New Orleans to Etienne-Gabriel and Hélène Fazende. His mother was related to a Fazende who went to Saint-Domingue with his family shortly after 1770. Nicolas had gone to Cap-Français under undetermined circumstances and had married there Marie-Jeanne Desmortiers, a Creole from the Plaisance sector where her parents, René and Marie-Thérèse Leclerc, were colonists. The household had first taken refuge at New York, and then had gone to New Orleans, apparently at the very end of 1794. Indeed, their son Louis-Etienne, born at New York on October 1, 1794, was baptized in New Orleans on June 25, 1795.[160] The father died at the age of forty in New Orleans on January 1, 1795, probably shortly after his arrival there.[161] In 1824 Nicolas Desmortiers was running a store in New Orleans.[162]

Not directly from Saint-Domingue, but from Philadelphia, Jacques-François Pitot disembarked in New Orleans probably

---

[158]*Etat détaillé des liquidations opérées à l'époque du 1 janvier 1832 par la commission chargé [sic] de répartir l'indemnité* . . . (Paris, 1832), p. 316.

[159]Burial records, Saint Louis Cathedral.

[160]Baptismal records, Saint Louis Cathedral.

[161]Burial records, Saint Louis Cathedral.

[162]*Michel's New Orleans and Commercial Register . . . for 1834* (New Orleans, 1833).

in 1796. He first appears in Louisiana on June 21 of that year. At that time, he was married to Marie-Jeanne Marty, a native of Saint-Marc,[163] whom he must have married during his six-year stay in Saint-Domingue, where he learned the science of sugar refining. He was born at Villedieu in Normandy in 1761. In 1796, he had already become an American citizen. From August 1798 to May 1799, he undertook an overland trip in the United States from which he would gather information used to write his *Observations* that Henry C. Pitot, his descendant, has published.[164] Claiborne later named him to the New Orleans city council in March of 1804 and two months later, mayor.

François Luscy arrived in 1796. He was originally from Marseilles, the son of Antoine and Marie Flandin, and had probably married at Cap-Français Marie-Louise-Catherine Chédôme, the Creole daughter of Vincent and Rosalie Boutin who owned a bakery in Limonade, near Cap-Français.[165]

André-Daniel Chastant, born at Cap-Français, the son of Jacques and Thérèse Gaze, married on January 30, 1795, in New Orleans Madeleine-Clothilde Soubie, from that [Louisiana] city. They had two children. He was appointed militia lieutenant in 1806,[166] and was identified as a goldsmith in 1822. He died at the age of sixty-two, on November 21, 1828.[167]

Joseph-Honoré Martelly, from Marseilles, had wed Marie-Louise-Victoire Chancerel, from a well-known Cap-Français family. In 1798 and 1800, two children were born to them in New Orleans. At the baptism of the eldest, Marie-Louise-Victoire, on April 22, 1800, a refugee, Marie-Celeste Carrère, was the godmother.[168]

---

[163] Daughter of Jean-Nicolas and Marie Lemonnier. Deceased in New Orleans on November 30, 1815. Burial records, Saint Louis Cathedral.

[164] James Pitot, *Observations on the Colony of Louisiana, from 1796 to 1802*, trans. by Henry C. Pitot, ed. by Robert D. Bush (Baton Rouge, 1979).

[165] *Etats des liquidations*, 1830, p. 50.

[166] Clarence Edwin Carter, comp. and ed., *The Territorial Papers of the United States*, 28 vols. (Washington, D. C., 1934-1975), IX, 629.

[167] Burial records, Saint Louis Cathedral.

[168] Baptismal records, Saint Louis Cathedral.

Jacques-Marie Lavit, a Creole from Fort-Dauphin, widow of a road-surveyor massacred on June 22, 1793, arrived at New Orleans in 1797 with her two children, at least such might be deduced from the chronology of the rather vague memoirs left by one of her daughters.[169] She left behind her only a house in Cap-Français, estimated at 10,600 *francs,* and a small coffee plantation at Grande-Rivière de Jérémie.[170] This land bought for speculation, and the Indemnity Commission estimated it at only 16,800 *francs.*[171]

The journalist, Mrs. Frank Leslie (1836-1914),[172] originally from New Orleans, was the granddaughter of Firmin-Auguste Follin who married in New Orleans in 1798 and whose father, Jean-August, was in Cap-Français, and whose mother, Marie-Joseph Hébert, was an Acadian.[173]

Marie-Adélaïde de Charlieu, from Nippe in the South, had married the Count Tringant de Beaumont, naval officer, at Port-au-Prince a bit before 1784.[174] In 1795, she took refuge in New Orleans with her four children. Her husband, then serving in France, failed to send her news of his whereabouts. He later emigrated [from France], but returned there soon thereafter. Taking advantage of new laws in effect, he divorced, then remarried. With her two children, she eventually settled at Natchez, remaining there until 1856. Her son Louis died at New

---

[169]Cited by J.-P. Allaux, *Ulysse aux Antilles* (Paris, 1935), pp. 170, 180, 210, 235.

[170]*Ibid.*

[171]*Etats des liquidations, 1829 and 1832.*

[172]Annotator's note: Her husband, Frank Leslie (1821-1880), was born Henry Carter. His name was legally changed to Frank Leslie in 1857. He founded *Frank Leslie's Ladies' Gazette of Paris, London, and New York Fashions* in 1854, and, the following year, established *Frank Leslie's Illustrated Newspaper,* one of the most widely read American newspapers of the 1850s and 1860s. *Websters Biographical Dictionary* (Springfield, Mass., 1963), p. 890. For a biographical sketch of Mrs. Frank Leslie, see Conrad, ed., *Dictionary of Louisiana Biography,* I, 506.

[173]Bégouin-Desmeaux, *Mémorial d'une famille havraise,* 5 vols. (Paris, 1948-1967), II, 253.

[174]AC, E 73.

Orleans on February 20, 1880, apparently without children.[175]

What of Egron? If he did not go to Louisiana as a refugee, he went as an agitator of refugees, or at least as an information-gathering agent, in early 1796. This former Saint-Domingue jurist held a position at the French legation in Philadelphia, where he edited the *Niveau de l'Europe et de l'Amérique*, a newspaper published by Tanguy Boissière, another Saint-Domingue refugee living in the United States. Adet, a French minister presumably acting upon the Convention's instructions, had sent Egron to Louisiana on a special mission, where he was quickly recognized as a spy. It was exactly at the same time he was in Louisiana that there were rumours about the slave uprising in Pointe Coupée.[176]

On February 25, 1796, Pontalba describes his expulsion:

> In town this morning, we had invested the house of Madame Latil in order to arrest one Egron who was taken aboard a dinghy and brought to Plaquemines whence he will depart with the first ship leaving for his homeland. Since this man had engratiated himself with me, I was asked four hours after his departure to render my opinion of him: In a word, I did not believe him to be dangerous, and he gives every indication of being simply a very inconsequential man. It appears, however, by all that the auditor had communicated to me, that this man was suspicious. According to several people, he said that within three months the colony would be under French rule and that he would govern as the French representative. He has been accused of having attested to the trustworthiness and fidelity of his domestic when it had been demonstrated that this Negro had incited several slaves to kill whites in Saint-Domingue as a means of securing their freedom. Others

[175]Maxime Trigant de Beaumont, *Les Tringant, souvenirs de famille* (Bergerac, 1895), p. 72.

[176]Adet to Latombe: order to pay $500 to Egron for his special mission to Louisiana. Egron's receipt, Brumaire 19, year IV (November 10, 1795). Foreign Affairs, Political correspondence, United States, supplement 191-328.

have assured me that Egron was largely responsible for the disasters of the Convention and that consequently he was wanted by the Convention. In the final analysis, we are rid of him, and I think that this is good.

Michel de Coigné, [former] royal lieutenant at Saint-Marc, had come to Saint-Domingue with other Canadian officers in the days following the fall of Quebec. He had two sons, officers like himself, the elder serving as captain in the Foix Regiment, the younger as lieutenant in the Flanders Regiment. Through their mother, they were the nephews of Loppinot, an Acadian who represented briefly the Princes in the Antilles. They were also nephews of J.-B. Coigné, naval scribe at Saint-Marc, a royalist who, it was said, had organized a servile insurrection in the surrounding hills and who had been assassinated there in March 1793. Upon his uncle's recommendation to Pontalba, the younger Coigné arrived in the Illinois territory in late 1795, and reached New Orleans around March 25, 1796, in sorrowful shape—"naked, after a two-year long journey, during which time he had always lacked the barest of necessities." Pontalba put him up in his home and got him back on his feet. He almost restored his fortune by having him marry a rich heiress. A yellow fever epidemic which ravaged the city carried Coigné away on October 29, 1796. As indicated in his act of burial dated the following day, he was thirty-five, single, a native of Canada whose parents were unknown.[177]

We will quote here Pontalba's letter of May 3, 1796, about Dr. Robert Dow, a Scot and one of the best-known physicians in Louisiana. Had he settled in Saint-Domingue, or had he taken a trip there?

Mr. Dow's son has just arrived from Saint-Domingue. He had left only two weeks ago. He claims that over there, the Negroes are the absolute masters, that the principle positions are filled by them, and that there were

---

[177]Burial records, Saint Louis Cathedral; and Charles de Bonnault, "Les Canadiens en France et aux colonies après la cession, 1760-1815," *Revue d'Histoire des Colonies Françaises* (1924), 425-600.

no more than thirty or forty whites in Cap-Français, more mistreated by the Negroes than if they [the whites] were slaves.

It seems that they want to be free of all whites, even from the French Republic. A Spanish frigate which entered the Port of Cap-Français was forced to leave. The Negroes did not want to grant it permission to enter and even threatened to sink it. It was forced to withdraw.

That same day, Pontalba announced that Pierre Basty, "a dangerous man linked to the revolutionaries of Saint-Domingue" has been in New Orleans since the previous day.

Pierre Darrigarde, originally from Ascan, near Saint-Jean de Luz, left Saint-Domingue around 1797 to go to New Orleans. His parents' names are unknown. He was supposedly a bachelor and a naval carpenter. He died on October 12, 1802, at the age of approximately forty.[178]

The wife of General Ferrand, from La Chapelle, who, from 1803 to 1808, commanded the Spanish part of Saint-Domingue, which had been ceded to France in 1795 by the Treaty of Basel, was a native of Louisiana. As a refugee in the United States, she made a living by private tutoring. After returning to New Orleans, she died there in 1800.[179]

From research on the origins of theater in New Orleans,[180] many of the names of the actors in the [city's] first [theatrical] presentations are known. Several were from Saint-Domingue and arrived in 1795. Not all of them, however, went there directly.

The first to be cited is Denis-Richard Dechanet-Desassarts. Although he was the son of an actor from the Comédie Française and one day walked the boards in New Orleans, it is really not appropriate to group him with the other actors. But we are oversimplifying.

[178]Saint Louis Cathedral records.

[179]Trigant, *Les Tringant*, p. 118.

[180]LeGardeur, "Les Premières Années du Théâtre à la Nouvelle-Orléans," 33-64.

He was born at Langres to Denis Dechanet *dit* Desessarts and Marguerite-Louise Massin. His father, a former public prosecutor, had tried his hand at acting in the provincial theaters, having played the role of Lisimon in *Les Glorieux* by Destouches in October 1778, then that of Lucas in *Le Tuteur.* On April 1, 1773, he succeeded Bonneval, the famous actor at the Comédie Française, in the lead role of *Les Financiers.* His obesity lent itself to the part. In October 1793, he died at the age of fifty-five in Barèges.[181] The *Affiches Américaines*, then the only newspaper in Saint-Domingue, on October 5, 1785, advised the public that a man named Desessarts, working with the show in Cap-Français, was going to perform. The October 26, 1791, edition of the *Journal des Débats de l'Assemblé Coloniale* announced the departure of a Déchanet Desessarts for the continent. One can easily put these two bits of information together.

He appeared in New Orleans on January 15, 1794, as godfather to Denis-Richard Henry, born the preceding November 4, son of Jean-Marie Henry, builder of that city's first theater. With Henry, he witnessed free mulatto Rosalie Villeré's will, and on July 19, 1801, he became godfather to a young Prévost.[182] In November of 1802, an accident almost claimed an eye. He barely escaped with his life.[183]

Over the last five years, he made a living as a tutor, particularly for the Destréhan children. In early 1803, he announced his intention to leave for France, but did he make the trip?[184] On December 25, 1805, he attended the wedding of Christophe-Joseph Le Prévost,[185] and in the *Moniteur* of August 13, 1806, started a subscription to build a schoolhouse on the

---

[181]J.-B. Colson, *Répertoire du théâtre français ou trois cent soixante tragédies et comédies*, 2 vols. (Bordeaux, [vers 1819]), II, 7, 113 notes. A Colson, maybe a relative, was director of a theater in New Orleans in 1820. J. Fouchard, *Artistes et reepertoires des scènes de Saint-Domingue* (Port-au-Prince, 1955).

[182]Baptismal records, Saint Louis Cathedral.

[183]*Moniteur de la Louisiane*, November 13, 1802.

[184]*Ibid.*, March 12, 1803.

[185]Marital records, Saint Louis Cathedral.

Second German Coast.[186] This project, already submitted to the Spanish authorities in September of 1801 had been set aside by Governor Salcedo. Desessarts had acquired a plantation in this sector precisely where the Destréhans were colonists. On December 6, 1806, he would be named clerk of court in this sector.

He would not remain in that position long, for soon the newspapers announced that the Deserter ballet, great pantomine-ballet in three acts, would be performed in the St. Phillip Theater, and among the actors—moreover almost all of whom are from Saint-Domingue—one was the name Desessarts. In April of 1808, he announced to the public that he, Master of Arts, had closed his school on the German Coast and that henceforth he would teach in town.

Shortly before 1806, he married Marie-Geneviève Trouard, whose parents had been coffee planters in southern Saint-Domingue.[187]   His first child died May 1, 1809. Governor Claiborne of Louisiana appointed Desessarts principal assessor of the third district.[188] In reality, he was French, but his long residency in the country and the dignity of his life earned him this function. He did not die in New Orleans.

Actor Joseph Destinval went from France to Port-au-Prince in 1785, and remained active in theater until 1791. He was in Philadelphia in 1794 and in 1797 he joined the New Orleans theater, but as an amateur.

Jeanne-Marie Chapiseau, born at Faubourg Saint-Germain of Paris in 1746, was the daughter of Louis Chapiseau and Aimée Droit. At the age of eighteen, she married Pierre Legendre from Marsan. In 1775, she went to Martinique to act in the Saint-Pierre Theater where she distinguished herself. Around 1780, she went to Cap-Français, where she continued to enjoy success until 1790. Her husband died in 1787. She made appearances in the New Orleans theater in 1795, 1796, and 1797. In March 1803,

---

[186]Annotator's note: St. John the Baptist Parish, Louisiana.

[187]*Etat détaillé de l'indemnié*, 1834, pp. 612, 628, 630.

[188]Dunbar Rowland, ed., *Official Letter Books of W. C. C. Claiborne, 1801-1816*, 6 vols. (Jackson, Miss., 1917), VI, 358.

she acquired a home in New Orleans. She died on February 25, 1807.[189]

Jean-Baptiste Lesueur-Fontaine, born at Paris around 1744, was in Cap-Français as theatrical director in 1775, but he seems to have previously been engaged in other activities in that sector before becoming a thespian. He owned in Limonade a distillery appraised at 96,754 *francs* in 1834.[190] He went to Saint-Domingue with Marianne Leprévost whom he had married in Paris.[191] They took refuge in New York in 1793 presumably aboard the convoy that departed Cap-Français after June 21 or 22. He went to New Orleans—probably in 1795—where he appeared many times on stage while, at the same time, running the first newspaper in Louisiana, the *Moniteur*.[192] He died at the age of seventy around July 5, 1814.

Louis-François Clairville, born at Paris, was a musician and actor at Cap-Français where he had married Scholastique Labbé on January 28, 1785. She, too, was an actress. He signed the Lafon contract on May 4, 1797, and appeared in the New Orleans theater in 1806 and 1808.[193]

By the same contract, Mme. Delaure, an actress from Cap-Français, bound herself to perform [at New Orleans].

These former Saint-Domingue colonists, who had almost all gone to France in 1793, requested passports in 1796 for travel to Louisiana by way of Bordeaux. Were they able to reach New Orleans?

Take the case of Marie-Elisabeth Hernaudin, wife of Bernard Castaing. She and her husband operated a farm near Port-au-Prince, but she was forced to go to France with her daughter Aménaïde, fifteen years old, after having sold the movables she salvaged from the November 1791 Port-au-Prince fire. She

---

[189]Moreau de St-Méry, *Description générale*, II, 361; Fouchard, *Artistes et répertoires*, pp. 50-60; burial records, Saint Louis Cathedral.

[190]*Etat détaillé de l'indemnité*, p. 60; 1834, p. 28.

[191]Burial records, July 5, 1814, Saint Louis Cathedral.

[192]*Moniteur de la Louisiane*, November 10, 1797.

[193]Moreau de Saint-Méry, *Description générale*, II, 34.

wished to rejoin her friends in Louisiana.[194]

Antoine and Ferdinand Chabert, sons of Antoine Chabert, militia captain in the Port-Margot sector and a settler in Jacquezy (1783-1791)[195] had campaigned in favor of Saint-Domingue's representation to the States General. They had returned in 1791. They sought to rejoin their mother in New Orleans.

Pierre Chatard *fils* and Jean and Frédéric Raverzie, his children who were Saint-Domingue landowners, wanted to go to New Orleans to obtain funds from Saint-Domingue that had been sent to them there [New Orleans].[196]

Citizen Saint-Martin, a Creole, offered no reason whatsoever for obtaining a passport, as did Pierre Pascal, a fifteen-year-old Creole from Cap-Français, and Didier Bérard; whereas Henri-Joseph Bourdié (the elder) and J.-B. Bourdié, both from Cap-Français, went there on business.[197] The occupation of Martinique by the English troops who maintained slavery there reduced to a trickle the movement of these colonists toward Louisiana. In the years 1793-1795 there were only a small number of refugees from that island.

Pierre Humbert, son of Pierre and _____ (his mother's name is unknown), arrived unmarried at New Orleans on August 21, 1793.[198]

Emmanuel-Marius Pons Bringier, the son of Pierre and Agnès Arnoul, was a native of Aubagne, near Marseilles. With his wife Marie-Françoise Durand who was also from Marseilles, he had left France for Martinique in 1780.[199] They went to Louisiana around the beginning of the Revolution and settled there. Two of their children: François, born March 9, 1786, and Fanny—probably Elisabeth—born April 24, 1788, were

[194]Archives de la Gironde, Bordeaux, France. Collection 3 L 181; hereafter cited as ALG, with the serial number.

[195]ALG, 3 L 178.

[196]ALG, 3 L 181.

[197]Burial records, Saint Louis Cathedral.

[198]Grace King, *Creole Families of New Orleans* (New York, 1921), pp. 413-414.

[199]Baptismal records, Saint Louis Cathedral.

baptized together in New Orleans on November 22, 1795, most likely in the days following their arrival in Louisiana. In 1803, Elisabeth wed Augustin-Dominique Tureaud, and another daughter married Christophe Colomb, a Saint-Domingue refugee. Widower Emmanuel-Marius-Pons Bringier, took as his second wife Marie-Anna Roudanez, a refugee, the daughter of the late Pierre Roudanez of Angoulême and Anne-Elisabeth Henry. They were coffee planters from Dondon.[200] He had gone into partnership with Tureaud and, in 1805, had served as adjutant of militia.

Father Flavian, from Besançon, left France in 1790, and went first to Guadeloupe, then to Saint-Domingue, Martinique, and finally took refuge at Philadelphia in 1794. He then went to Saint Charles on the German Coast and then to New Orleans where, at Saint Louis Cathedral, he signed his first act on February 5, 1798. He died at the age of approximately sixty.[201]

Rose Taton, born at Fort-Royal, Martinique, wife of Pierre Hardi de Boisblanc from Saint-Jean d'Angély, was the grandmother of a Hardi child baptized in New Orleans on April 19, 1795, and of a Mérieult child baptized on March 30, 1799.[202]

Because names mentioned in the baptismal, marriage, and burial registers are the only evidence we have for most of these refugees (bachelors appear only in burial registers), it is difficult to pinpoint their arrival at New Orleans. The scattered names in this fragmentary information are not classified in strictly chronological order. Any other order would have been artificial. We have preferred to provide [the reader with] a simple enumeration, however arbitrary that may be. We hope the reader will excuse us. This list constitutes merely a very tentative enumeration, for we know that many refugees would not have escaped our attention had we examined the graveyard inscriptions and the parochial records in and around New Orleans after 1835, the ending date of our research.

---

[200]In Mare-à-Laroche, *Etat détaillé . . .*, 1830.

[201]Burial records, February 9, 1802, Saint Louis Cathedral.

[202]*Ibid.*

III
1798-1803

When British troops evacuated Saint-Domingue during the summer of 1798, many colonists seized the opportunity to leave [the colony]. Some had served, more or less voluntarily, in the colonial corps recruited by the English. Others maintained their administrative or judicial positions during the occupation, or had accepted newly created posts.

The agreement negotiated by General Thomas Maitland, commander of the occupational forces, and General Toussaint L'Ouverture, governor of Saint-Domingue, permitted the colonists to either remain on the island or accompany the English. Slaves, with few exceptions, were not allowed to depart, a proscription applying also to the men of color recruited locally for the corps. There were insufficient means of transportation, and, besides, such a migration would have created problems for Jamaica.

General Hédouville, special agent for the Directory who had been banned from participating in the negotiations between Maitland and Toussaint L'Ouverture, restricted the colonists' freedom to remain in the colony. With the exception of militiamen entering the service before arrival of the English, he classified soldiers who had served them [the English] and all civil servants remaining under their [English] authority as immigrants.

Departing with these soldiers and civil servants were those colonists who feared that, under the Toussaint L'Ouverture regime, their most robust slaves would be claimed by military levees, that their crops would be seized, and that they would be vulnerable to massacres. Very few of them tried to return to France, for direct communications [with that country] were practically nonexistent. They went to Jamaica, Louisiana, or Cuba.

In Jamaica, they significantly increased the number of refugees who had arrived since 1792. Most of them lacked both a marketable skill and slaves to establish a small plantation.

The local population did not look upon them favorably, for they feared anything coming from Saint-Domingue. They thought that, among these newcomers, there must certainly have been some French republicans, who were then equated with revolutionaries. They [Jamaicans] were afraid that they might organize some sort of slave uprising. Many of them [refugees] were forced to leave for Cuba or Louisiana.

We shall identify only a few of those departing refugees because only rarely can we distinguish those who came from Saint-Domingue in 1798 from the earlier immigrants.

Many of those who abandoned Saint-Domingue upon the English withdrawal were from the South. Among them were Simon Dupin, Julien-Bernard Journu; Peyrol and Dupoix,[203] two Béarnais; all of them were from Aux Cayes. Peyrol was the authorized agent for Hebellynk, a merchant [with offices in] Paris and Dunkirk. He decided to leave in early 1799.[204] Jean-Baptiste Gérard, who had been a representative from the South in the Constituent Assembly, must have encountered Peyrol and Dupoix at New Orleans in 1804. Peyrol would not stay long in Louisiana. He would be in Paris as early as 1806.[205] From Jérémie, in the South, we find Louis-Roland Charbonnet, who would marry Marie-Mélanie Fleuriau at New Orleans on April 29, 1799.[206] But Marie-Désirée Michel, born at Cap-Français in 1792, would be baptized at New Orleans on December 26, 1799.[207] The parents, Jean-André, born at Arles, and Anne-Henriette Bouet, from Marseilles, arrived with her. She would marry, on October 1, 1807, Pierre-Marie-Thérèse Godefroy, from Cap-Français.[208]

Philippe de La Marnière, royal naval lieutenant at Port-

[203]Perhaps a difformation of Dupoey.

[204]Blanche Maurel, *Le Vent du large; ou le destin tourmenté de Jean-Baptiste Gérard, colon de Saint-Domingue* (Paris, 1952), p. 328.

[205]*Ibid.* p. 451.

[206]Marriage records, Saint Louis Cathedral.

[207]Baptismal records, Saint Louis Cathedral.

[208]Marriage records, Saint Louis Cathedral.

au-Prince, a rank he maintained under the English,[209] is another example of these emigrants. Familial oral tradition vividly describes the circumstances of their [the emigrants'] departure. They supposedly left at the very last minute, with only the clothes on their backs. Protected by a few faithful slaves, they embarked aboard an English ship.[210]

The fate of Louis-Joseph-Simon Le Gardeur, a British army officer, can be easily distinguished from those of his companions. He was born at 1769, most likely in Petit-Trou de Nippe, in the South, son of Etienne-Simon Le Gardeur de Tilly and of Marie-Rose Loménie de Marmé, who had had six children.

On September 1, 1794, he was commissioned as cornet in the white Regiment of the British Hussars. But at the time of the evacuation, he did not leave with the English regiments, for on November 10, 1798, he wed at Jérémie Jeanne-Catherine Pénault,[211] widow of Alexis-Joseph Carlier, who had been a naval administrative officer. Louis-Joseph Le Gardeur arrived at Louisiana with his wife a few months later. His eldest brother, Nicolas-Charles-Etienne, naval ensign, was with his three daughters, "on the American continent," on November 9, 1798. Their parents, having stayed behind, left Saint-Domingue for Cuba only in 1803. [From Cuba,] they would go to New Orleans in 1809.

Another officer, Joseph Villars-Dubreuil, was born at Louisiana in 1744. At a young age, he travelled to France, where he embarked upon a military career, becoming lieutenant-colonel in 1790. The date of his arrival at Saint-Domingue is not known, but he and his family lived at Léogane. In 1793, leaving two of his children with their mother, he boarded an American ship for Philadelphia. He was accompanied by two of his other

[209]Historical overview in the *Annales de la Révolution,* anonymus manuscript, volume II, folio 137.

[210]G. de Chateaubriant, *Les Réfugiés de Saint-Domingue. Quelques notes et documents* (Angers, 1942), p. 80.

[211]Contract received on Brumaire 19 Year VII (November 9, 1798) by Alafargue, notary in Jérémie.

children. An English corsair intercepted the ship captured its French passengers, and transported them to Kingston, Jamaica.

They returned to the colony in 1794 with the troops of occupation. The commander-in-chief named Villars-Dubreuil to his private council. In 1798, when the British forces withdrew, he chose to go to Louisiana where his mother—a Livaudais—and his cousins Fleuriau, Dugué, and Marignac were living.[212] We do not know if his wife and children were able to join him.

Madame de La Biche, whom J.-B. Gérard also encountered at New Orleans, had arrived there [New Orleans] in 1799. She was the widow of a [former] councilman in the Cap-Français Superior Council. He had owned a sugar mill estimated at nearly one million *livres* and cotton fields in Baynet in the South, in Cavaillon, near Aux Cayes. If the sugarmill had been pillaged and burned in 1793, the cotton fields were still intact when the English landed at Grande Anse in September 1793. Her husband used his personal connections in the [Superior] Council's private sessions, convoked by the local commanders-in-chief, through which he acquired several prime plantations owned by absentee landlords.[213] He had remained in the colony after the English had departed, but he was massacred. His wife did not linger in Saint-Domingue.[214]

The Charest de Lauzon family had taken the longest route to go to Louisiana. In the days following the Treaty of Paris in 1763, they had left Canada for Saint-Domingue. Ethem Charest had been the last lord of the Lauzon estate near Québec. His son François, a colonist at Limonade, near Cap-Français, had become a militia officer of this sector.[215] We later encounter him in Louisiana as a member of a large group of refugees.[216] In

---

[212]Arthur and Huchet de Kernion, eds., *Old Families of Louisiana,* pp. 105-111.

[213]AC, E 236, Le Gardeur dossier.

[214]Maurel, *Le vent du large,* p. 343.

[215]P. Wright and G. Debien, "Les colons de Saint-Domingue passés à la Jamaïque, 1792-1835," *Bulletin de la Société historique de la Guadeloupe,* XXV (1975), 52, 77, 105, 135, 173.

[216]AC, E 72, Dossier Charest de Lauzon.

Saint-Domingue, he had married Perrine-Thérèse de Gournay, great-great aunt of Louis Malabre, historian of the French refugees in Jamaica.[217]

[Pierre-Louis?] Berquin-Duvallon was not a Creole, but was a native of Bordeaux, where he was born at 1747.[218] His family owned plantations in southern Saint-Domingue. He came to claim his property and had himself named royal prosecutor for the seneschal's court in Cap-Français area. He was in that city in June 1793, at the time of the struggle between the Civil Commissioner Sonthonax and Governor Galbaud du Fort. He was able to go aboard one of the ships anchored in the harbor which, in June, brought to the continent several thousand whites and slaves. He disembarked at Baltimore. He was accompanied by several domestics and a few other slaves, which permitted him to live until 1800. Hoping, along with many other refugees, to find a better situation in the Spanish colony, he subsequently arrived in Louisiana with his slaves. He encountered great difficulties because of them: his slaves had no sooner set foot on the Mississippi levee[219] than they were jailed,[220] and it was only with much trouble that he was able to secure their release, one by one, by bribing Judge Vidal, an old, corrupt Spaniard. Berquin claims to have been unaware of the ban upon the introduction of slaves from Saint-Domingue, which seems a bit curious to us.

In the face of this rather unfriendly welcome, it is not surprising that he chose to leave New Orleans. He travelled extensively throughout the colony, and took notes on all he heard and saw. He settled on the Chapitoulas coast and wrote the book that was to be published in Paris the following year. Naturally,

---

[217]"Biographie et généologie des familles françaises de la Jamaïque par C.L. Malabre," 3 vols., manuscript in the Library of the Jamaican Institute in Kingston.

[218]Gragnon-Lacoste, "Lieu de naissance de Berquin," *Recueil des actes de l'Académie de Bardeaux* (1863), 111.

[219]This must have been in Plaquemines.

[220]Pierre-Clément de Laussat, *Mémoires sur ma vie, à mon fils* . . . (Pau, 1831), p. 161, notes that it was a matter of some "very bad subjects" that the governor and the auditor (Vidal) rendered with little trouble.

his description of Louisiana is not very flattering.[221]

> There is not a single petty scoundrel, born in this
> wilderness colony and reared exclusively along the
> Mississippi's banks, never having tasted any water but
> that of this river, who does not believe himself justified
> by the examples of their leading citizens as well as the
> jackass in the fable to insult an unfortunate stranger. I
> refer even to Frenchmen, colonists like themselves, who,
> having been spared the upheavals and massacres of Saint-
> Domingue and having sought refuge in this country with
> the meagre remains of their fortunes—all because the
> scoundrel is in his homeland and the foreigner is not, and
> because the former senses the support of friends, while
> the latter is isolated. . . .

The welcome reserved for the Louisiana refugees by Saint-
Domingue in 1768 had been quite different. They were greeted
with open arms. Several had "even occupied honorable and
lucrative positions." Just as touching must have been the noble
and generous conduct of several American states, especially
Maryland, toward the Saint-Domingue colonists fleeing *en masse*
to this country. In Baltimore, they had been treated, lodged,
clothed, fed, and assured of monetary aid over a period of six
months.

Which brings us to a touchy subject:

> They did not stop with these early demonstrations of
> generosity. There exists, in these States, a fundamental
> law which formally forbids the introduction, across
> their boundaries, of blacks and foreign slaves . . .
> Disregarding this fundamental law, or, better said, with

---

[221]Berquin-Duvallon, *Vue de la colonie espagnole du Mississippi ou des provinces de Louisiane et Floride occidentale, en l'année 1802, par un observateur résidant sur les lieux*
(Paris, 1803), where he insisted upon the opposition of the Yankees and the Creoles
regarding the refugees from Saint-Domingue.

respect to the sacredness of a law sovereign over all other laws, which must bow down before it . . . and which the ancient Romans designated under the beautiful name of *Caritas humani generis (Love of the Human Kind)*, the government of Maryland, seated in Annapolis . . . unanimously decreed that the slaves . . . who had followed their masters to this land, would be admitted there, like them, with the help accorded in proportion to their situation, and would continue to serve them as usual, with the sole obligation, on the part of the masters, to declare this fact to the municipal offices of the areas where they went. And yet, the Saint-Domingue colonists were foreigners . . . as well by their government as by their language and customs . . . finally, this Province being populated by slaves, they could have pretended . . . that the introduction of blacks coming from St.-Domingue and who had followed their masters, could have produced an occasion for the fermentation of trouble amongst those in the State, by way of their reciprocal communication, and from there, they may have been able to conclude that this prohibitive law was, for their sake, more strongly desirable than ever . . .

This spirit of hardship and inhospitality in this country is such that an individual, who showed some interest in the lot of a woman from Saint-Domingue taking refuge here with her children, and whose three female Negro servants were being held, for over a year, in the city's prisons, daring to say, in the presence of some Louisiana gossipers, that this lady, burdened with children, far from home, and having few means, was very unfortunate not to have at least one of her three servants to prepare the meals and to wash her family's clothes and to be forced to take from her paltry savings enough to pay for a cook and a washmaid. 'Ah!,' then said, with a languishing voice full of bitterness and irony, one of these charitable gossipers, 'She is well to be pitied, this beautiful lady from Cap-Français! If she doesn't have enough to pay for a cook and a washmaid,

let cook her own meals and wash her own clothes': and all
the others were quick to applaud unanimously through
bursts of vulgar laughter and snickering. In the end,
however, and despite the good will in her behalf on the
part of the people of her sex, she got her three servants
after fifteen months of apprehension and having paid out
three hundred *piastres* in expenditures and costs on this
subject.

In a word, in this indigenous conduct of the
Louisianians toward their unfortunate compatriots and
their former benefactors, all that was missing to crown
this work was to demand the payment of a fine of 400
piastres per Negro admitted, to benefit their country, in
accordance with a Law promulgated here and nowhere
else; and that is assuredly what would have come to
pass if the Government had not stepped in . . .

And let it not be said that there was an imminent
danger in permitting the entry of these families
from Saint-Domingue with their domestics, whereas
according to the facts, it was sufficiently demonstrated
that this danger had never been real nor imaginary in
the American States where over six hundred slaves are
to be counted . . . After all, what was to be feared from
such a negligible number of domestics, who had time
and time again proven their fidelity and attachment to
their masters, by leaving St.-Domingue, their native
soil or their adopted nation, where all engaged them
to remain . . . and especially, when these masters
gave their word to answer personally for the conduct
of their domestics? One well feels that there was not,
in these prohibitive measures, any direct view toward
the public's best interest, any fear well founded fear..
but rather a frame of mind . . . a vile yearning which
seemed to become indignant before the past prosperity
of these Colonists from St. Domingue, cheering on their
present misery. . . . Behold what were and what are the
sentiments of the Louisianians towards their former
compatriots from St.-Domingue. . . . Also, very few of

the latter went to seek refuge in this inhospitable wilderness, and the small number of those whose unfortunate destiny forced them to go there had ... every reason to repent, with the exception of a few refiners and workers, who were needed to establish the sugarmills, and who were well received, in proportion to how useful they could be to this end. Almost all the colonists from this ill-fated island, wandering far from home, far from their estates, but well informed of the trials and tribulations they could expect here, preferred lugging about their life and sorrow amongst the Americans, the Danes, the Dutch, the Spanish, even the English, at war with their homeland ... to going to this formerly French colony, and which still is by the origins of most of the Colonists, by its external customs, and by the language, but not at all by its character. ...

One might imagine, moreover, after what has just been reported, that these same Colonists from St.-Domingue, whose right, in this area, even to breathe air and to live here peaceably with their humble resources has been disputed, must not have received the slightest aid from the government nor, even less so, from individuals. That's the way it is. Upset about everything, far from being protected, insulted instead of pitied, abandoned by all, and entirely isolated in this country which was, itself, at the time of its establishment, a haven from exile, which it still could be in many ways, these unfortunate ones, small in number luckily, and that a local woman, speaking of them and joking about their plight, ironically called, *The Saint-Domingue Escapees,* did not waste time in shaking the dust from their feet and fled this savage land, as soon as circumstances permitted; and a few of them were in such a hurry to leave that they did so before the cessation of hostilities, at the risk of being taken by enemy corsairs, who, more humane than the Louisianians, did not always plunder an unfortunate person and, on the contrary, sometimes helped him out.

The same bad impression has been given to us by Paul Alliot,[222] a doctor who arrived from Saint-Domingue in December 1802, with his wife and children. He soon began practicing his profession. He operated, in his own words, marvellous healings in the case of deafness, colics, snake bites, smallpox, and yellow fever. He administered his treatments without the proper authorizations. Did he incur the jealousy of others? We do not know. It is probable that he dabbled in politics. He was accused of inciting slaves to revolt. On March 18, 1803, he was arrested, deported to France, and imprisoned upon his arrival at Lorient. He must have been exonerated or else he defended himself well for he soon obtained the permission to return to America. He was in New York on April 6, 1804, where he addressed a curious note to President Jefferson concerning his misfortune.[223]

It is quite true that almost all [Louisianians] did not look favorably upon the arrival of Frenchmen amongst them and considered their conduct at Saint-Domingue as the ruination of their homeland. They would have preferred to be governed by the Americans. . . . The small Negro insurrections have left them [the Spanish government] aghast and they [Spaniards] have forbidden the introduction [of Negroes], which has done much harm to all the farmers. It is very true that if these unfortunate people were better fed, clothed, and well treated in their servitude, they would have for their masters the regards and the respect, the gratefulness and the attachment that these men have in general for their

---

[222]Annotator's note: Paul Alliot was arrested at New Orleans on March 18, 1803, and accused of practicing medicine without a license. Alliot pleaded ignorance of the local licensing requirment. He was later accused of attempting to incite a servile insurrection at New Orleans. Alliot was consequently deported to France following a short jail sentence at the Crescent City. Following his arrival at Lorient, France, in July 1803, he penned *Historical and Political Reflections on Louisiana,* a scathing indictment of the Spanish administration of Louisiana. Conrad, ed., *Dictionary of Louisiana Biography,* I, 11.

[223]Paul Alliot, "Réflexions historiques et politiques sur la Louisiane," in James A. Robertson, *Louisiana Under the Rule of Spain, France, and the United States, 1785-1807 . . . ,* 2 vols. (Cleveland, 1911), I, 29.

benefactors and never would they think of an insurrection.[224]

The testimonies of malcontents Berquin-Duvallon and Alliot must be tempered by the more friendly and indulgent one offered by Perrin du Lac, another refugee. But to be honest, Perrin also repeats words of defiance and hostility.[225]

An accurate reflection of reality must be rendered. Amongst the refugees there certainly existed a high proportion of poor souls who arrived possessing nothing but who were determined to survive. They [persons who arrived with nothing] were not those one talked about, the ones who inspired antipathy, but rather those who, having saved a few resources, were able to establish some sort of commerce or a plantation. We must remember the reputation the colonists from Saint-Domingue had before the French Revolution, sojourning in Paris and leaving in the hotels a strong reputation of pretentious arrogance. There must have been something of this attitude and this reaction in New Orleans. Saint-Domingue was also known in Louisiana as a land of audacious wealth and grandiose plantations. Many refugees took some pride in this and kept a certain way of holding their heads and modulating their voice. This attitude was not conducive to inspiring sympathy and a friendly welcome.

No doubt also, the Louisianians did not look favorably upon these colonists who were able to have a few slaves enter the country and to be able to rent them out in town in order to make a quick profit from them as domestics, as cooks, wig makers, or coachmen. With the assurance that these slaves were in their personal service, the authorities looked the other way. However, they were often leased out according to the custom used in Saint-Domingue where, in the city, the master allowed their slaves to be free to seek work at their convenience in exchange for a flat

[224]*Ibid.*, I, 66-68. One finds Alliot in New Orleans in 1807 where he published in the *Moniteur de la Louisiane* on September 16 a generous tableau of his miraculous cures of cases of putride fever.

[225]François-Marie Perrin du Lac, *Voyages dans les deux Louisianes . . . en 1801, 1802, and 1803* (Lyon, 1805).

weekly or monthly rate. This practice was in opposition to certain local habits.

Moreover, these refugees, both blacks and whites, remained concentrated in the city, only scattering themselves out very slowly into "the parishes," thus increasing a floating population of which one was instinctively wary. Manual labor for agriculture was in greatest demand. For these final years of the eighteenth century, we were able to assemble only a few of the names of the new arrivals, as follows:

Charles Savary, a man of color who was allegedly the brother of Vincent Ogé, and who had been one of the signatories of the Concordat of the West with the free men of color. As mayor of Saint-Marc, he favored seeking assistance from the Spanish, but not the English.[226] Under their [English] occupation, he commanded the colonial infantry corps, called the Prince de Galles [Regiment]. He left Saint-Domingue for Jamaica with the British troops, then went to New Orleans. In 1814-1815, he distinguished himself in the campaign against the English and again in Texas where he participated in the revolutionary struggle against the Spanish.

René Théart, architect, had come to Saint-Domingue at the time of the Revolution, but without our knowing the exact date nor under what circumstances. He married at New York Marie-Rose Robert, a Creole from Cap-Français whose father, Joseph-Modeste, spouse of Marie-Jeanne Mary, was a planter in Petite-Anse.[227] In New York, they had a first child, René-Nicolas, then in New Orleans, Marie-Constance, born March 2, 1798,[228] and who married on December 15, 1816,[229] Antoine Deyrem, probably a refugee. The parents settled in Assumption Parish, where they most probably passed away.

François-Auguste-Amant Hulin, son of François and Marie-

---

[226]Jean-Philippe Garran de Coulon, *Rapport sur les troubles de Saint-Domingue*, 4 vols. (Paris, year V- year VII [1797-1799]), III, 59, 60, 157, 250.

[227]*Etat détaillé de l'indemnité*, 1831, p. 14.

[228]Baptismal records, April 14, 1799, Saint Louis Cathedral.

[229]Edward Laroque Tinker, *Bibliography of the French Newspapers and Periodicals of Louisiana* (Worchester, Mass., 1933), p. 465.

Madeleine Duchêne, born at Rouen, a refugee(?), married, on May 3, 1800,[230] Mélanie Vitaud, a native of Cap-Français. He died on August 27, 1828.[231] He had arrived at Louisiana shortly before 1800.

Marie-Célestine Carrère was godmother to Marie-Louise-Victoire Martely, probably born at New Orleans March 2, 1798, baptized the following July 14. This child was the daughter of Joseph-Honoré Martely, born at Marseilles and of Marie-Louise-Victoire Chancerel.

Dom Nicolas Dollet, a Benedictine, was buried in the Saint Louis parish cemetery on August 6, 1799. He was born at Béthincourt (Pas-de-Calais), son of Louis and Augustine Béguin. He had immigrated to the United States "at the most ardent period of the French Revolution," residing there six or seven years and having been named curé before his death.

IV
The Entry of Slaves Controversy

If we assemble so few names of refugees before the Great Wave of 1803 and if amongst them we find so few rich colonists, it is not only because freight is quite scarce,[232] it is also because one knew in Saint-Domingue that a person with slaves would not be well received. The Count of Montault's letter, dated March 3, 1792, had already echoed Louisianians' fears.

For several years, slaves from the French Antilles had been looked upon with suspicion. In his *Bando de Buen Gobierno* of 1786, Don Esteban Miró, governor of Louisiana, noticed that "experience has showed that the admission of blacks born at the English or French Antilles is harmful to this province. It is

---

[230]Marriage records, Saint Louis Cathedral.

[231]Burial records, Saint Louis Cathedral.

[232]As it is shown in the portrait of the entries to the port of New Orleans drawn by Juan de Castanedo, member of the *cabildo* and city treasurer in his report dated December 31, 1796 (City Hall Archives): Ships coming from the Spanish colonies, 47; from the United States, 33; from Jamaica, 3; from Saint-Domingue, 1.

necessary to erect a major barricade, and I order the merchants to cease introducing them."[233] The events of 1789 in France and the first signs of trouble in Martinique and Saint-Domingue gave a clear indication of what kind of trouble the admission of island blacks could produce in New Orleans. Spain feared the spread of revolutionary ideas, knowing Louisiana to be very vulnerable. Thus, as early as May 11, 1790, a secret royal order forbade the entry blacks who fled the French colonies or who were bought there.[234] And a few days later other orders further decreed that those who had already crossed the Louisiana's border were to be deported.[235]

A quickly suppressed[236] slave revolt in Pointe Coupée in July 1791,[237] had supposedly unmasked free mulattoes from Saint-Domingue as instigators. During the trial of the free black suspects, Pierre Bahy, a free mulatto, had testified that, with his companions, he was awaiting orders from Cap-Français to start a coup that would have resembled the one in Cap-Français.[238]

A month before leaving his command, Miró renewed his decrees and reminded the minister of all the measures he had taken to prevent the entry of all persons coming from France of the French Antilles.[239]

Nevertheless, the first deliberation at the Cabildo where it was question of the French slaves was not before February 10, 1792. It was an allusion to the harm they would do in the area. We do not have an indication of the strong fears that would follow. The promulgation of a new ordinance was not demanded, but rather

[233]Minutes of June 2, 1786, Cabildo Archives, volume III, page 111.

[234]Indias las Reales Ordenes, May 11, 1790. Pontalba Papers. Transcripts of the Louisiana Historical Society Library, New Orleans.

[235]*Ibid.*, May 17-20, August 23, September 26 1790.

[236]*Ibid.*, August 28 and October 4, 1791.

[237]*Ibid.*, Miro to the Minister, no. 205, July 15, 1791.

[238]Cabildo Museum Collection, Judicial Records, 1782-1800, Docket 2855, file 1488, October 7, 1791.

[239]Indias las Reales Ordenes, no. 318, November 28, 1791.

the rigorous application of the laws already in existence; the governor controlled the entry of all ships. Before sailing up to New Orleans, they had to undergo an inspection by the Fort Plaquemines commandant; the powers of the Spanish governors allowed the prevention of the disembarkation of all suspicious persons without the Cabildo's having to make a request.

Carondelet, the new governor, had not yet taken any special measures, and a few slaves did enter. That day, the attorney-general informed the Cabildo that Negroes from Cap-Français had just arrived in Louisiana. He recommended petitioning the governor to ban the importation of slaves not only from Cap-Français, but also from any colony that had endured an insurrection under penalty of severe fines and other penalties. Thus, fear was growing. Still, very few slaves must have entered [Louisiana] from Saint-Domingue, most probably trustworthy domestics.

Carondelet had attended that meeting. Under pressure from the Cabildo, he prohibited, on July 23, the debarkation of all slaves from the French and English Antilles under penalty of a 400-*piastre* fine per slave seized. No exceptions appear to have been allowed.[240]

This measure was actually directed against only Saint-Domingue and Martinique slaves who were arriving either directly from, or by way of, Jamaica. The king at first approved the measure, then revoked it by an edict of January 24, 1793.[241] Yet, Carondelet could ignore it,[242] because when he received it, Spain was at war with France. The ordinance of July 23, 1792, was not, in all probability, immediately executed and when it was, not with much enthusiasm, but it most likely did stop many a colonist who would have been able to leave Saint-Domingue with his best slaves.

On February 1, 1793, when the Convention declared war on Spain, New Orleanians again grew apprehensive, and this time

---

[240]Frederick Jackson Turner, "Carondelet on the Defense of Louisiana, 1794," *American Historical Review*, II (1896-1897), 474-505.

[241]Carter, ed., *Territorial Papers*, IX, 172.

[242]Annotator's note: the royal edict of January 24, 1793.

their fears were justified. Indeed, plots against Louisiana were devised by Citizen Genêt,[243] French minister to the United States,[244] and by his lieutenants Mangourit, consul at Charleston, and Auguste [de] La Chaise. They had some allies in the New Orleans population, though not very many, but they knew how to exploit a few malcontents from Saint-Domingue. The danger was not imaginary but it was blown out of proportion. Furthermore, Carondelet remained vigilant, and Genêt committed so many blunders that Washington demanded his recall. Nevertheless, they continued their skulduggery.[245]

Genêt's master plan was to intercept the convoys leaving Quebec, Havana, and New Orleans and then to strike Louisiana and the Floridas with a force of adventurers and refugees from Saint-Domingue.[246] Although the matter was discussed throughout the continent, only a small number of former colonists in the United States joined his cause, even fewer among those [refugees] in Louisiana. They realized that this land-and-sea offensive would sever relations between Saint-Domingue and the continent. All they saw in this scheme was

[243]Annotator's note: Edmond-C. Genêt (1765-1834) was appointed *chargé d'affaires* to Russia on October 13, 1789. He was banished from the Russian court by Empress Catherine II in 1791. Genêt nevertheless remained at Saint-Petersburg until July 19, 1792. On November 14, 1792, he was appointed French ambassador to The Netherlands, a post he held for only one month. In December, he was reassigned to the United States with the rank of ambassador. Genêt's political intrigues resulted in his removal from office. The former ambassador, however, remained in the United States, became a naturalized citizen, and married a prominent American woman.

[244]Frederick J. Turner, "The Origins of Genêt's Projected Attack on Louisiana and the Floridas, " *American Historical Review*, III (1897-1898), 650-671; Louise Phelps Kellog, ed., "Letters of Thomas Paine, 1793," *American Historical Review*, XXIX (1923-1924), 501-505; "George Rogers Clark to Genêt, 1794," *American Historical Review*, XVIII (1912-1913), 780-783.

[245]"General Collot's Reconnoitering Trip down the Mississippi and his Attack on Louisiana in 1796, by Order of the Baron de Carondelet, Governor of Louisiana," *Louisiana Historical Quarterly*, I (1918), 303-326.

[246]Meade Minnigerode, *Jefferson, Friend of France, 1793; the Career of Edmond Charles Genêt, Minister Plenipotentiary from the French Republic to the United States . . .* (New York, 1928); and "The Mangourit Correspondence in Respect to Genêt's Projected Attack upon the Floridas, 1793-1794," *Annual Report of the American Historical Association for the Year 1897* (Washington, D.C., 1898), pp. 569-577.

Jacobin madness inspired by Genêt, "Brissot's man, friend to the blacks," and by Sonthonax, one of Saint-Domingue's civil commissioners, "the colonists' enemy."[247] They presented this project as a social adventure which would disturb the internal peace of the United States and which would lead them into war with England.

As early as April 23, 1793, in a letter to the minister the Duke of Alcadia, Carondelet remarked that a few New Orleans Frenchmen were secretly plotting something. He gave the names of those he thought to be the leaders, none of whom appear to have been from Saint-Domingue.[248] He adds:

> among the fanatical partisans of the new republic . . . I am sure that no Creole landowner is to be found. . . . The conspirators are all merchants, some of which have only recently been established in the colony.[249]

Some unrest was feared amongst the slaves and, in fact, on August 1, 1793, Mangourit submitted a plan to Citizen Pelletier of New Orleans "for starting a revolution in Louisiana"[250] and on October 29, 1793 a refugee wrote from Charleston to Larchevêque-Thibaud, then in France:

> Already in Virginia a horrible machination has been discovered and an important person is suspected to be its chief, and seeing that Genêt and the consuls are partisans of Brissot, suspicion will soon fall on them also. In this state a few discoveries have been made and we are on our guard. It seems that even an ordinance by the governor forbids the entry of mulattoes and free Negroes.[251]

---

[247]Ernest R. Liljegren's study, "Jacobinism in Spanish Louisiana, 1792-1797," *Louisiana Historical Quarterly*, XXII (1939), 47-97, is of no help here.

[248]We may have some doubt about Sauve and Mercier.

[249]*Annual Report of the American Historical Association for the Year 1896, 2* vols. (Washington, D.C., 1897), I, 174.

[250]Library of Reims. Tarbé collection, manuscript 59.

[251]Jean Delaire to Larchevêque-Thibaud, cited by Garren de Coulon in his *Rapport sur*

In the December 9, 1793 edition of his *Journal des révolutions de la partie française de Saint-Domingue*, which he published in Philadelphia, the refugee Tanguy Boisière specified:

> A Frenchmen has just received some letters from Charleston. They announced a plan which had been formulated to promote the system of freedom for Negroes in the Southern American states, to arm them and to give them as leaders free Saint-Domingue mulattoes, and to have them march against Louisiana and the other Spanish possessions. One of the commissioners[252] was identified as the secret agent of this project. Only time will inform us of the accuracy of this news. Governor Moultrie of South Carolina issued a proclamation, dated October 5, which ordered all free Negroes and other men of color coming from Saint-Domingue to leave the said State within ten days' time upon the notice that he received that there were amongst them suspicious men who planned to incite an insurrection by the Negroes of this state.

According to the *Le Courrier de la France et de ses Colonies,* edited at Philadelphia by Gatereau, another Saint-Domingue refugee, the man behind the uprising was not a man of color but a white who had only recently arrived in the United States from Saint-Domingue: Auguste de la Chaise, a person well known by the refugees and no less familiar in his native Louisiana. He was the grandson of one of the commissioners sent [to Louisiana] in 1722 by the Company of the Indies and the youngest son of Jacques de la Chaise, one of the alcades at the Cabildo in 1770, and Marguerite d'Arensbourg.[253] His parents

---

les troubles de Saint-Domingue, IV, 418.

[252]One of the civil commissioners sent to Saint-Domingue. He is probably speaking of Commissioner Sonthonax.

[253]Charles E. Gayarré, *History of Louisiana,* 4 vols., 4th ed. (1903, reprint edition; New Orleans, 1965), III, 31.

had remained under [Louisiana's] Spanish regime, but he went to serve in France. His enemies in Saint-Domingue added "that he had been one of the body guards found on the civil list, and . . . one of the agents of Monsieur [the king's brother]."[254] This situation was most likely due to the realities of war. We do not know under what circumstances he arrived in Saint-Domingue, nor when he left. We find him on July 30, 1790, as one of the governor's commissioners for the Port-au-Prince volunteer corps.[255] He was one of the co-founders of the Society of the Friends of the Revolution in Cap-Républicain[256] where he supposedly established, in October 1792, a "black-list" of 143 people. He had demanded the immediate departure of all those who filled or had filled public posts. In this manner, he had pressured Governor d'Esparbès and Colonels Cambefort, commander of the Cap-Républicain regiment, and Touzard to leave. He "had fought with distinction against the insurgent Negroes and during all the agitation he had demonstrated that he was one of the most ardent revolutionaries as long as it was only a matter of combatting the landed aristocracy and the government's party."[257] He did not join "the independents' party." As Garran de Coulon put it "he conserved for France the tender attachment that this interesting colony [Louisiana] always showed him." Cambefort, with whom he was to come face to face in the United States, accuses him in the *Précis de [sa] justification* . . . (January 26, 1793)[258] of having been sent on February 8, 1792, by the municipality of Jérémie to exculpate himself before the Colonial Assembly, but of having instead "provoked a new land distribution and [having] appeared before

---

[254]Garran de Coulon, *Rapport sur les troubles*, IV, 42.

[255]La Rochelle Chamber of Commerce Archives, carton XV.

[256]Pierre-François Page, *Discours historique sur les effets que la Révolution a produits à Saint-Domingue* (Cap-Républican, 1792), p. 40.

[257]Garran de Coulon, *Rapport sur les troubles*, IV, 419.

[258]Joseph-Paul-Augustin de Cambefort, *Précis de la justification de Joseph-Paul-Augustin, colonel du régiment du Cap* . . . (Paris, 1921), p. 165.

the municipality armed and accompanied by a crowd of men he had whipped up in order to strengthen his cause."

We suppose that he had been a member of parliament on the continent.

In Philadelphia, he was a member of the Jacobin Society.[259] It seems almost certain that with George Rogers Clark he was supposed to command the expedition being prepared against Louisiana. Genêt had sent him to Kentucky in order to recruit men for the operation.[260]

On February 12, 1794, Carondelet addressed a proclamation in French to Louisiana's inhabitants:

> Avoid the devastation with which you are being threatened by these scoundrels, those who expelled from Saint-Domingue, but not before assuring its destruction. They have been sent to the Ohio region by Genêt, the so-called minister from the Convention. . . . Their adherents are very few and they are poorly armed. . . . If you join us, I promise you that these enemies will not get beyond Nogales.[261]

When in April 1795 the slaves on the Poydras plantation began to revolt in Pointe Coupée, forty leagues upstream from New Orleans, Carondelet and all the colonists believed that they had been incited by agents of the French government. They were persuaded that La Chaise was still lurking behind the scenes with a few henchmen from Saint-Domingue who had entered the country through the northern ports.[262] Pontalba wrote to his wife on September 13, 1796:

[259]King, *Creole Families*, p. 165.

[260]Gayarré, *History of Louisiana*, III, 340-342.

[261]"Circular addressed by the Government to all the inhabitants of Louisiana," February 12, 1794, in Kinnaird, ed., *Spain in the Mississippi Valley*, Part III, IV, 255-257.

[262]Minutes from the Cabildo's records, May 2, 1795.

Mme. Marré of Charleston[263] declared that La Chaise had told her that he was the instigator of the troubles in Pointe Coupée; that he had missed his chance this time, but that he would try again to do better the next time.

A refugee, Dr. Paul Alliot, echoes this statement in his "*Réflexions historiques et politiques sur la Louysiane*," addressing to President Jefferson the rumors of the day:[264]

An inhabitant of New Orleans well known in Jérémie, Island of St. Domingue, because of his murders, thefts, [and] devastations, has gone to the United States, to the Ohio River, and [*via*] the Mississippi to Pointe Coupée, an area more heavily populated in slaves than anywhere else. Hoping to disrupt everything to profit from the colonists' misery, he made the acquaintance of several black men and convinced them to revolt by showing them how happy those [blacks] in St.-Domingue were. If the Spanish government, which had been warned of these stormy developments in time [to take action], had not reestablished order by dispatching troops and by having about sixty of the renegades hanged, the colonists would have found themselves without means of support. Seeing his attempt fail, the head of this insurrection fled to the United States, and the Negroes left behind by this villain returned to their farms. This extreme example completely reestablished the tranquility of this great and rich area.

This movement overexcited the fears of the settlers, and Carondelet published on February 19, 1796, a new proscription on the entry of any slaves whatsoever. Louisianians always believed that the Pointe Coupée insurrection was a direct result of the troubles in Saint-Domingue and their anxiety over this

---

[263] A refugee, Madame Marré d'Azincourt, *née* Cauvin, had owned large sugar-mills in the Archaya sector, estimated at 750,000 *francs*.

[264] Alliot, "Réflexions historiques et politiques," I, 116 and 118.

region [Pointe Coupée] would not abate.

It was at this time that Egron, of whom we have already spoken, was arrested. He was coming from the United States, where he was seen as a political agitator and was consequently sent back on the first ship. Some said that he had incited a handful of slaves to join him in killing all the whites; others said that he had been one of the principal troublemakers.[265]

Then, in March 1795, there was another abortive servile revolt at Pointe Coupée. It was scheduled to start on Easter Sunday. All of the whites from the German Coast to Pointe Coupée were to be taken by surprise. The details of the plot were discovered. Fourteen blacks and mulattoes were arrested and confessions were extracted.[266]

A ship loaded down with slaves came into the mouth of the river. It did not come from Saint-Domingue, but the authorities in Plaquemines [Parish] made some leave the ship and held two blacks and three men of color thought to be from there. One was even wary of the whites from this island. A young lady, Miss de La Garde, who went to New Orleans to settle the estate of her uncle, Dusseau, and who married her cousin, Count de La Croix, in Cap-Français, was considered suspicious.[267] Pierre Bahy, a man of color, who had just disembarked from Saint-Domingue, seems to have been admitted without any difficulty upon his arrival on May 2, 1796. Pontalba admits his stupefaction:

> The baron[268] who has maintained, until now, surveillance of suspicious people, has become lax; he has permitted Pierre Bahy, who arrived again last night, to stay here. He returns well instructed about what is going

---

[265]On August 1, 1796, Carondelet sent the following orders to Favrot who commanded in Plaquemines: "All ships must fly the Spanish pavillion, have a passport signed by the ambassadors, intendants, or consuls of Spain, or else wait in Plaquemines for the decision of the governor . . . Non-Spanish blacks and mulattoes will be detained in Plaquemines awaiting their departure for the United States." Favrot Papers, V, 4.

[266]Pontalba to his wife, March 27, 28, 29, 30, 1796.

[267]*Ibid.*, April 20, 1796.

[268]Baron de Carondelet.

on in Saint-Domingue and assuredly will not miss his chance to indoctrinate his comrades.[269]

Pontalba released him after a short detention period.

From that moment on, he was convinced that Louisiana would return to the French control and that all the slaves would be liberated. The future of their society was at stake—the end of their colonial society. This liberation would be begun by those in Santo Domingo, the Spanish part of Saint-Domingue which had just been ceded to France by the Treaty of Basel (September 1795). The Spanish government will end up following this [Louisiana's] example in all of its colonies.[270]

When a French corsair docked at the port of New Orleans, the crew's tricolor cockade had made an unfortunate impression upon the slaves.[271] Rumors of Louisiana's cession to France persisted: It would be given [to France] in exchange for Santo-Domingo's return to Spain. The slaves acted as if they had already won. The end was near. In October, Carondelet himself no longer doubted that the king would proclaim a general emancipation in three or four months. Pontalba began selling his belongings as well as his land. On October 24, all he had left was an adult and a few children.

Not all of the white population was overwhelmed by the fear of an uprising and many did not believe in a conspiracy.

Robin writes:

> Around 1796, at the time of the upheavals in Saint-Domingue, where the inhabitants of all the colonies were stricken with terror, the Pointe Coupée settlers, more particularly frightened, because they were surrounded by greater danger, discovered the trace of a conspiracy among their Negroes, which may have existed only in their imaginations.

[269]Pontalba to his wife, May 3, 1796.

[270]*Ibid.*, April 30 and July 25, 1796.

[271]*Ibid.*, September 13, 1796.

However, many planters feared a slave revolt. On November 9, 1804, under the American regime, they again expressed their dread to Governor Claiborne: "The news of the revolution of Saint-Domingue and other places has become common among our blacks."

One of the most visible results of the precautions taken by the authorities, permanent vigilance against the introduction of revolutionary ideas, was to alleviate the general mistrust against the Saint-Domingue refugees. They were often believed to be the active agents of Jacobinism, and the Republican spirit. Antipathy grew. This exacerbated the growing antipathy toward the refugees, spawned along the banks of the Mississippi by the increasing birth-rate for native Americans.

Another result of this surveillance and the law forbidding access to slaves detained by Baron Carondelet was to raise "the price of farm Negroes in New Orleans from 1,000 to 1,200 *piastres*." "The price of Negroes in New Orleans was more expensive than it has ever been in any colony; the fear caused by the insurrection in Saint-Domingue had rendered their importation extremely difficult."[272] Naturally, this increase failed to satisfy the Louisiana colonists. They found fault with the bad faith of certain refugees.

The prohibitive measures of 1792 and 1796 had been for a large part inspired by the Cabildo. One may wonder if the fear of an uprising, which was both permanent and significant, was the only motive in this defensive response. In the last decade of the eighteenth century, the Cabildo counted amongst its members a large number of businessmen, many of whom were French Creoles. They practiced *agiotage*, commerce in contraband Negroes, almost always with the tacit permission of the authorities. By forbidding the entry of slaves from Saint-Domingue, in spite of the shortage of manual labor, the businessmen in the Cabildo were most likely hoping to impede the entry of other slaveowning businessmen and to conserve as long as possible their lucrative, illegal trade.

[272]*Ibid.*, II, 122, 126.

At this period, the everyday man in the street, the small merchant, the cooper, the carpenter, the artisan, was gaining esteem for republican sentiments. They had a tendency to look upon the large planters as unpatriotic monarchists. The New Orleans merchants were also, for the most part, royalists, but they took advantage of popular sentiment to protect their commerce.

This hostility has been extensively described by Berquin[273] who had to wait for a more fraternal welcome. Certainly there was a taint of bitterness in his testimony. Laussat recognized that he portrayed the colony "with bilious colors," but that he was not always far from the truth.

According to him, the country is a land of swamps and reptiles, inhabited by pretentious and dishonest people, vain and ignorant women.

The refugees had thought

> rightfully that a small number of slaves who had abandoned everything, even the seductive offer of freedom, to follow and to continue serving their masters, in a foreign country, could not be dangerous, neither by their sentiments, nor by their quantity. The event has justified, in all, their way of thinking in this matter. . . .[274]
>
> In protecting itself with an inhumane law, Louisiana has rendered it impossible to allow the entry of poor blacks faithful to their masters.

The people of New Orleans, by

> means of their Cabildo, . . . have had. . . . this law rigorously enforced, with no consideration whatsoever, nor with any possible exceptions for the French colonists huddled together in North America, (in a country with a different language and climate), and who, in the

---

[273]Berquin-Duvallon, *Vue de la colonie espagnol du Mississippi*, pp. 232-242.

[274]*Ibid.*, p. 233.

absence of this rigorous interdiction, would have come to settle in large numbers here, bringing what was left of their fortunes and talents, if only they could have brought along with them a few faithful domestics who had never abandoned them.

Furthermore, armed with passports delivered by His Catholic Majesty's ambassador to the United States, some of these colonists, having no knowledge of this internal regulation, or else believing that after a few years it had been overturned or was no longer enforced, travelled across North America to this country, intending to settle with their families and servants. Though already tacitly admitted by the Spanish government . . . it was not long before they were denounced, harassesed by the rabble of Louisiana, stripped of their servants (women and children), dragged into prison where these miserable creatures were detained, more often than not at their master's expense, with immediate and repeated levies. This was part of a plan, conceived by heartless and cold-blooded persons, to drive them out of this country. This lasted until the Spanish government, having let the agitation run its course, was able to discretely return them [the imprisoned slaves] to their owners.[275]

V
The Evacuation of Saint-Domingue

In the years around 1803, but especially 1804, we see the refugees disembarking in large numbers, because the ultimate success of the servile insurrection was followed by a general evacuation of the colony. This is particularly true of the remnants of Leclerc's army, but, while the soldiers, the wounded, and as many of the sick as possible [withdrew], the merchants and the colonists also fled the country by the hundreds. Another tragedy, or at least another aspect of the same

---

[275]*Ibid.*, p. 235.

tragedy, occurred in November 1803 when Louisiana was ceded from Spain to France who, shortly thereafter, sold it to the United States. These events coincide and caused much turmoil among the New Orleans Creoles and the refugees. They complicated the arrival of still more refugees.

Rumors of an imminent transfer of Louisiana to France had been circulating since 1796. In 1802, they had become more accurate. Arriving in early 1803 to take possession of the colony Laussat, the colonial prefect, observed: "We had our suspicions that this would happen for the last two years. . . . Last year, our suspicions were confirmed."[276] Refugees were already making plans for Louisiana. It was to become, they hoped, the meeting place for all colonists exiled in the United States, a colony which would replace Saint-Domingue.

Father Louis-Guillaume-Valentin Dubourg, future bishop of New Orleans,[277] was born at Cap-Français on February 13, 1766. He was reared in France and was living there in 1789. He emigrated first to Spain, then to the United States, then to Cuba. When he was in Baltimore, he founded a school—the St. Mary's School—mainly for the children of refugees. As soon as he heard rumors of Louisiana's transfer to France, he decided to transfer his school to New Orleans. The French consul in Baltimore encouraged his project for, he believed, continued development of the school in Maryland, where the refugees, upset and bitter over France, alienated themselves little by little from the mother country, would be plaqued by difficulty. In Louisiana, on the contrary, a French school would counterbalance "the ambition of the Americans [who] would have one believe that all of islands in the Gulf of Mexico belong to them."[278] Father Dubourg came to the United States in 1802.[279]

[276]Laussat, *Mémoires.*

[277]Annotator's note: Dubourg is generally regarded as the second bishop of the Diocese of Louisiana and the Floridas. Technically he was the third prelate of the diocese. Francisco Porro y Reinado was appointed to succeed the first bishop, Peñalver y Cardenas, but Porro y Reinado refused the post.

[278]The French consul in Baltimore to the Minister for Foreign Affaires, 10 Fructidor year X (August 29, 1802), letter published by Mrs. D. M. Quynn, "Dangers of Subversion in American Education: A French View," *Catholic Historical Review*, XXXIX (1953).

[279]Annotator's note: Dubourg was appointed administrator of the Diocese of Louisiana

Louisiana's sale to the United States caused this project to be abandoned, but not before prompting several members of the Dubourg family to establish themselves at New Orleans. First came young Arnould-Louis Du Bourg de la Loubère, born at 1790 in Cap-Républicain, who had at first taken refuge at Jamaica with his mother. He went to New Orleans in 1802. In 1815, he would be named judge of Plaquemines Parish and would die a bachelor in New Orleans on April 29, 1829.[280] Next was Pierre-François Du Bourg de Saint-Colombe. Born at Cap-Français on December 30, 1767, he had arrived in Jamaica in late 1801 or early 1802 with his wife Elisabeth-Etiennette Charest de Lauzon,[281] whom he married in Kingston on February 18, 1797. [Accompanying them were] their little girl Aglaé, his father-in-law François Charest de Lauzon, and his mother-in-law Perrine-Thérèze de Gournay. On February 8, 1803, he received permission from Governor Salcedo to send from Jamaica eight slaves by promising to "use them exclusively to cultivate his lands and not as an object of commerce." Joseph Faurie served as his bondsman. This Du Bourg was the founder of all the American branches of this family.

The intention of establishing a French school in New Orleans belied a desire to preserve Creoles' cultured upbringing and character, the last vestiges of French life in Saint-Domingue.

Even if one knew early on that France was going to retake Louisiana, one did not find out about the sale to the United States—[through the] treaty of April 30, 1803—until June or July.

and the Floridas in 1812. He was consecrated bishop of the diocese on September 24, 1815, during a visit to Rome. He returned to America in 1817, but took up residence in St. Louis, Mo., instead of New Orleans. Dubourg visited the Crescent City for the first time in 1820, but spent only six months there before returning to St. Louis. He left New Orleans for France in 1826. In France, Dubourg served as bishop of Montauban and, later, archbishop of Besançon. He died at Besançon, France, on December 12, 1833. Conrad, ed., *Dictionary of Louisiana Biography*, I, 258.

[280]Burial records, April 30, 1829, Saint Louis Cathedral.

[281]Born in La Marmelade on October 11, 1782, died in New Orleans on May 12, 1811.

Laussat himself would not be informed of the accord between the two countries before June 8. Earlier, he had termed this news as "nonsense." But the *New England Palladium* of Boston made the announcement on June 28, and the *National Intelligencer* of Washington[, D. C.,] confirmed it on July 18.[282]

President Jefferson and the American authorities in general foresaw some very serious difficulties upon taking possession, some emanating from Spain who had not given Louisiana to France only to see it waltz so quickly into the arms of America; others, more serious, would be caused by the opposition of the French Creoles, so shamelessly given away. A policy of bad faith was imputed to Laussat.

On October 31, 1803, Jefferson appointed commissioners to receive Louisiana: General James Wilkinson,[283] commander of the forces assigned to New Orleans, and W. C. C. Claiborne[284] governor of Mississippi for the two previous years. They so feared hostilities by the French population that the commissioners had been given command of troops from neighboring states and territories. On November 17, Daniel Clark,[285] United States consul at New Orleans, wrote to Claiborne that the Spanish governor, the Marquis de Casa-

[282]Carter, ed., *Territorial Papers*, IX, 114.

[283]Annotator's note: Wilkinson, a native of Calvert County, Md., became an officer in the Continental Army in 1775 and served throughout the American Revolution. He was appointed major general in the United States Army in 1792. Wilkinson served as the commandant of Detroit in 1796 and as commander of the Southern military district in 1798. With W. C. C. Claiborne, he received Louisiana from the French representatives. He died in Mexico City, Mexico, December 28, 1825. Conrad, ed., *Dictionary of Louisiana Biography*, II, 846-847.

[284]William Charles Cole Claiborne, born in Virginia in 1775, died in 1817, representative elected to Congress from the State of Tennessee, named by Jefferson governor of the new Mississippi Territory on May 25, 1801, and provisional governor of the Louisiana Territory on October 31, 1803.

[285]Annotator's note: Daniel Clark (the younger) (1766-1813) was a merchant, land speculator, and politician. He arrived at New Orleans in 1786 and subsequently worked as a clerk in his uncle's mercantile firm. Clark served as American counsel in New Orleans from 1801 to 1803. He was elected as the first delegate from the Territory of Orleans to the United States Congress. He retired from political life in 1809 and subsequently devoted himself to business affairs.

Calvo, would not oppose the transfer,[286] but that the measures taken by the French were to be feared.

The American authorities had to confront these complex circumstances when considering the question of new Saint-Domingue refugees, both civilian and military. They would double the number of malcontents.

In October 1803, the frigate *L'Express,* an American ship commanded by a Frenchman, left Môle Saint-Nicolas bound for France with soldiers and some women and children, numbering 450 in all. They stopped at Santiago de Cuba to take on provisions. Then the wind drove them not eastward, but toward Havana, but without allowing them to put ashore. They were forced to return to Santiago. They again departed for Charleston, but winds again prevented them from docking there. They were thus forced to settle for Louisiana, arriving at the mouth of the Mississippi. A large number of passengers, if such a term may be used for such a huddle mass of mankind, perished, probably from yellow fever.[287]

On December 12, 1803, Clark notified two commissioners that, upon arriving at Jamaica, a ship's captain had indicated that 1,200 French troops had been captured by the English around Cap-Républicain about seventeen days earlier. Taken to Kingston, these men were immediately placed aboard three Danish ships bound for the Mississippi.[288] They were forewarned that the soldiers were destitute.

Meanwhile, *L'Express* entered port on January 16. Its supply of provisions was exhausted. It carried sick people, refugees, and the 450 soldiers who were able to enter the vessel, four or five of whom died daily. Only 206 soldiers were left. Contagion was a real threat. The ship's captain requested for immediate permission to go up river to New Orleans.

Claiborne warns him on January 20, 1804:

[286]Carter, ed., *Territorial Papers*, IX, 114.

[287]*Ibid.*, 165, 170; Rowland, ed., *Official Letter Books,* I, 353.

[288]Carter, ed., *Territorial Papers*, IX, 137.

Being informed that your crew and company are infected by a Contagious disease, it becomes necessary to the safety of the good inhabitants of this Province, that you should on the receipt of this order, fall down the River and *come* to below the Post of Plaquemines, without suffering any persons to Land from your Vessel. I lament the necessity of this rigorous treatment, but it is enjoined by the Principles of Self-Preservation and the obligation attached to my particular Station.

The Officer commanding at Plaquemines has orders to do every thing in his power, for your comfort, and that of the unfortunate fugitives who accompany you, and every additional comfort in my power to offer you, will be most cheerfully contributed![289]

Wilkinson and Claiborne asked Laussat to place the soldiers near Plaquemines in barracks identical to those of the American troops. The prefect disliked this solution. He wanted to interpret more broadly the right to asylum. He insisted that all the refugees be able to go to New Orleans and be allowed to remain in the country if they so desired.[290]

However, the American authorities had cause to see things otherwise.

I have myself thought that we were bound to extend to these People, humane and hospitable attentions; but that the means of doing so ought to be left to our own Discretion. I have also thought that the duty of neutrality made it necessary that we should cause them to depart as soon as their situtation will enable them to proceed. . . . Were they admitted to this City, the Soldiers would locate themselves in the Country, and the officers would await opportunities to return to France in some neutral Vessels.[291]

---

[289]Rowland, ed., *Official Letter Books*, I, 343.

[290]Carter, ed., *Territorial Papers*, IX, 177-180.

[291]Rowland, ed., *Official Letter Books*, I, 353.

These were everyday preoccupations.

Indeed, the problem was enormous. Laussat, forewarned by Clark, banned the ships from the river, but authorized shipment of all necessary provisions to them. Clark, unsure of the favorable consequences of these measures, feared massive disorder if the debarkation was stopped.

> Every Hour evinces more & more the necessity of a strong Garrison here . . . our puny force has become a subject of ridicule, and the old women begin to exclaim 'quel triste governement[.]' . . . [Wilkinson feared] that we are exposed to lose much or all, by some sudden explosion of the inflammable spirits, which at once animate & enslave the people of this Country. . . . The Jealousies of the People of Colour & the Whites seem to be increasing, & if I may judge from what I see & hear, the former are most to be relied by us for they have universally mounted the Eagle in their Hats & avow their attachment to the United States—while the latter still demonstrate their love for the Mother Country and do not conceal the fond Hope, that some incident of the depending War, may return them to Her Bosom. . . . It is my Opinion a single envious artful bold incendiary, by rousing their fears & exciting their Hopes, might produce those Horrible Scenes of Bloodshed & rapine, which have been so frequently noticed in St Domingo.[292]

On January 16, 1804, New Orleanians learned that another French shipment was coming directly from Saint-Domingue, with 207 soldiers, refugees, and sick,[293] all without provisions, waiting at the mouth of the river for the authorization to ascend the river to New Orleans.[294]

---

[292]Carter, ed., *Territorial Papers*, IX, 159-160.

[293]Most probably stricken by yellow fever.

[294]*Carter, ed., Territorial Papers*, IX, 165.

I instantly, with the concurrence of Governor Claiborne, dispatched an order to the Officer Commanding at Placquimenes [sic], to forbid this vessels [sic] ascent & also the landing of Her company, but . . . to furnish every comfort & relief to the sufferers in his Power. . . . I stand ready with a handful of men to reinforce Plaquimenes in Person, should it be deemed necessary— The case is painfully embarrassing, but one thing is clear to me—should this Corps be suffered to enter the province, in the present manifest ill temper & disposition of many, a commotion will be the consequence, the end of which cannot be foreseen; I shall therefore oppose their admission, by every means in my Power, on the ground of self preservation.[295]

. . . A more weighty reason, on Our Minds, existed, in the Consequences to be apprehensed, from admitting, such a Number of French Officers, in Addition to those now here, whose Conduct, countenanced as it is, by the Colonial Prefect, is exceedingly hostile to that Spirit & to those feelings, which the Interests of the United States, Require to be cherished; in Short, the State of Things here, at the present Moment, is such, that the Arrival of these French Officers and Troops in the City, would probably have been Immediatey [sic] attended, with, Consequences more or less serious to its tranquility, & more Remotely might have endangered, our Quiet Possession of the Province. . . .[296]

Military officers seem to have been much less numerous than Claiborne and Wilkinson indicate, and they do not remain very long in Louisiana. The one we hear the most about was only passing through himself. Brigadier-general Humbert did not come at the time of the evacuation, but had been sent back to France by General Leclerc for "dirty dealing."[297] He did not go to

[295]*Ibid.*

[296]*Ibid.*, 178.

[297]General Leclerc to the Minister for Foreign Affairs, Cap-Républican, Vendémiaire 15, year XI (October 7, 1802) in Paul Roussier, ed., *Lettres du Général Leclerc, commandant*

New Orleans or else stopped only long enough to get the urge to return there. After his dismissal on 23 Niviose, year XI (January 13, 1803), he would be authorized, on July 9, 1812, to enter in the services of the United States. He would retire at New Orleans where he would die in 1823.

Among those we have been able to identify are: the Chevalier de Touzard, colonel and attaché on General Leclerc's staff, a "counter-revolutionary dangerous yet admired for having lost an arm in the American War;"[298] Louis-Joseph-Paul Garrigues de Flaugéac,[299] an infantry officer; and [Fernand Victor] Pothier, adjunct officer to the corps of engineers arriving in Louisiana in December 1803.[300]

Claiborne, apparently to reassure Madison, indicated to him on January 24, 1804, that there were only eight or ten French officers, "but several of them are seditious and undisciplined."[301]

Unfortunately, they arrived with

> between twenty and thirty young adventurers from Bordeaux and St. Domingo who are troublesome to this Society, they are men of some information, desperate fortunes, and inflated with the Idea of the invincibility of Bonaparte, and the power of the French nation. . . .[302]

en chef de l'armée de Saint-Domingue en 1802 . . . (Paris, 1937), p. 258.

[298]Abridged memoire, belonging to Mr. Clavier in 1960, p. 211. Anne-Louise de Touzard (1749-1817), artillery officer of La Fère, regimental adjudant in the Tours artillery, in America with Lafayette, lieutenant-colonel in the Cap-Républicain regiment, suspended by the convention: returned to service. Vice-consul of France in Louisiana.

[299]Annotator's note: This individual, who later served as a surveyor in southwestern Louisiana, did not use the particle in his signature.

[300]Laussat, *Mémoires*, p. 134. Annotator's note: Pothier also served as a surveyor in southwestern Louisiana.

[301]Rowland, ed., *Official Letter Books*, I, 345.

[302]*Ibid.*

The governor requested incessantly instructions from the president, but all he received were the belated responses of a procrastinating diplomat.[303] In the end, upon Claiborne's insistence, Laussat sent almost all of the soldiers back to France aboard the frigate *Argo,* which may have been the one that took them to New Orleans.[304] One gets the impression that all civilians so desiring were able to stay. The soldiers were mostly Frenchmen from France; the civilians were generally Creoles.

Not all of the soldiers had raised serious social or political fears. They had just escaped from a ravaged country, blockaded by the English navy. Those who had landed at New Orleans before November 1803 and the Great Evacuation had reason to believe that they were on French soil. But after November, this was no longer the case. In November 1803, Americans had taken possession of the land. It was no longer a question for these soldiers to reach safe harbor, but rather to find a way to return home to France.

At the same time as the evacuation of the troops, a large number of civilians, mostly Creoles, disembarked some coming directly from Saint-Domingue, but many others from Jamaica, where they had long taken refuge.

On February 26, 1804, Claiborne wrote:

> The Emigration from the West India Islands to this Province is considerable, there are now on the Mississippi River Several hundred French Emigrants from Jamaica, and two or three other Vessels filled with Passengers are daily expected.[305]

On April 9, 1804, he indicates:

> Enclosed is a Copy of an inflamatory production which was posted up at the Market House in this City in the

---

[303]*Ibid.,* II, 15.

[304]*Ibid.,* I, 387.

[305]*Ibid.,* I, 388.

course of last night. . . . The Author is not known, but the general Suspicion attaches to some of the late Emigrants.[306]

The inflamatory hand Bill . . . has not produced the effect intended, the Mass of the people in Louisiana are well contented with the change of Government and if left to themselves would remain a peaceable amiable people, but the Emigration from France and the West India Islands is considerable, many of the Emigrants are men of desperate characters, and revolutionary dispositions.[307]

On April 13, 1804, he informed his superiors that:

The emigration from the West Indies apparently increases, there is now in the river a Vessel with One Hundred and fifty French passengers from Jamaica, some of these Emigrants are doubtless worthy men but I fear a majority of them will be useless, if not bad Citizens.[308]

Claiborne wrote on May 29, 1804:

. . . many adventurers who are daily coming into the Territory from every quarter, possess revolutionary principles and restless, turbulent dispositions. . . .[309]

The arrival of the five-cannon corsair, *Soeur Chérie*, commanded by the famous Jean Lafitte, generated its share of troubling news from April to August. It had been outfitted at Aux Cayes on October 7, 1803, pursuant to the General Brunet's orders. Upon leaving Saint-Domingue he had a crew of fifty. A storm shook them badly and, before entering the Mississippi, he had lost many of his men, mostly through desertion. At

[306] *Ibid.*, II, 84-85.

[307] *Ibid.*, II, 88.

[308] *Ibid.*, II, 95-96.

[309] *Ibid.*, II, 176.

Plaquemines, he had to talk fast: the ship was armed but was taking on water and was out of provisions. He obtained permission to go up-river to New Orleans for repairs and supplies. The men continued to desert: eighteen or nineteen sailors left, several of whom were Saint-Domingue blacks. Alert! The crew was eventually put back together with the help of the Saint-Domingue refugees newly arrived either directly from the island or from Jamaica.[310] There were that many less to worry about.

In the months which followed, still more refugees arrived. Some were coming from Jamaica, others from Cuba, a few from the Spanish part of Saint-Domingue. This is the second stop in their life as refugees. The luckiest ones were able to save a few slaves, as in the case of the Danish schooner *Nancy*, Captain Belhomme, which came from Kingston with refugees and servants.[311] It was difficult not to accept all these slaves. It was set up to present them to customs at the same time as Africans. Claiborne reassured Madison as much as he could.

In a letter dated July 12, 1804, he imparts:

> Slaves are daily introduced from Africa, many *direct* from *this* unhappy Country and others by way of the west India Islands. All vessels with slaves on bord [sic] are stopped at Plaquemine [sic], and are not permitted to pass without my consent. This is done to prevent the bringing in of Slaves that have been concerned in the insurrections of St. Domingo [sic]. . . .[312]

On October 16, 1804, he writes:

> A few distressed French Families, who were exil'd from Jamaica, and sought an assylum [sic] in Louisiana, were permitted to land their faithful

---

[310]*Ibid.*, II, 100, 276; Carter, ed., *Territorial Papers*, IX, 234.

[311]Rowland, ed., *Official Letter Books*, II, 151.

[312]*Ibid.*, II, 245.

Domestics, upon giving satisfactory proof, that they
had not been concern'd in the Troubles of St. Domingo,
and I have never understood, that this permission,
which Humanity dictated, was disagreeable to the
Louisianians.[313]

Local fear remained intense. The settlers had learned what
John Watkins, future mayor of New Orleans, had reported to
the governor, for whom he was inspecting several parishes.
[Watkins] had pointed out, on February 2, 1804, that a few
weeks before a ship had:

passed up the Fork[314] . . . , a Vessel having on Board
twelve Negroes said to be Brigands from the Island
of St. Domingo. These Negroes in their passage up,
were frequently on shore, and in the French Language
made use of many insulting and menacing expressions
to the inhabitants. Among other things they Spoke of
eating human flesh, and in general, demonstrated great
Savageness of Character, boasting of what they had been
and done in the horrors of St. Domingo.[315]

One easily understands they were driven by rather complex
emotions. Fear was mixed with a certain jealousy, which probably
originated with the refugees' arrival. They wanted slaves but
not those from Saint-Domingue. Yet merchants "criminally
introduced them."[316]
The Alien and Sedition Acts, approved by Congress
shortly after the arrival of large convoys of colonial refugees
had armed the president with discretionary powers for
the surveillance of foreigners. Much of these powers were

[313]*Ibid.*, II, 358.

[314]Annotator's note: Bayou Lafourche.

[315]Rowland, ed., *Official Letter Books*, II, 5.

[316]Laussat, *Mémoires*, p. 31.

transferred to the territorial governors. With regard to white refugees, Claiborne had been generous. Slaves were harder to keep watch over. He focused all of his attention on them.

He was an opponent of slavery, and had come from the Mississippi Territory where, two years earlier, slave sales had been banned by an act of April 7, 1798. His beliefs induced him to follow the same policy in Louisiana, but there were planters who desired as much manual labor as possible, especially the new sugarcane farmers who were growing more numerous by the day. There were also the ship-fitters and merchants who had traditionally found the slave trade to be quite lucrative. The interdiction against the importation of foreign slaves was considered to be a serious blow to Louisiana's interests.[317] It also caused resentment because South Carolina still permitted this commerce. In reality, slaves to be sold were able to enter Louisiana due to its precarious status. The act of October 31, 1803, "to enable the President of the United States to take possession of the territories ceded by France,"[318] was interpreted by Jefferson, who communicated his orders directly to Claiborne, to mean preservation of the status quo. French or Spanish statutes remained in effect for a long time. The governor determined the desirability of granting entry to Negroes from the Antilles.

> As to the particular description of Negroes that shall or shall not be admitted into the Country, Claiborne wrote to Boré, mayor of New Orleans, who requested a blanket rule and criteria for making determinations], and the means of making the discrimination, it is a power devolving particularly upon myself nor can I transfer it to any other body. You may be assured however that such measures shall be taken in that affair as may be best calculated to secure the public good. [319]

[317]Rowland, ed., *Official Letter Books*, II, 25.

[318]Carter, ed., *Territorial Papers*, IX, 89.

[319]Rowland, ed., *Official Letter Books*, II, 51.

At the same time, he sought to convince Louisianians of the treaty's disadvantages by frequently citing the experience of the Saint-Dominguans. "But the opinion of the Inhabitants remains the same," he admitted, "and nothing will satisfy them on this point, but an uninterrupted Trade to Africa, for three or four years."[320]

Claiborne only had to close his eyes for a few short months, because Louisiana's provisional government came to an end on October 1, 1804, when the region was to accede to the level of territory, pursuant to the congressional act of March 26, 1804. The prospect of an inevitable prohibition against importation of all foreign slaves. The prospect of an inevitable prohibition against importation of all foreign slaves brought forth even more determined efforts to introduce slaves.

On May 8, 1804, Claiborne wrote to Madison:

> The emigration from the West Indies to Louisiana continues great; few Vessels arrive from that quarter but are crowded with passengers, and among them many Slaves. I am inclined to think that previous to that 1st of October thousands of African Negroes will be imported into this Province; for the Citizens seem impressed with an opinion, that a great, very great supply of Slaves is essential to the prosperity of Louisiana: Hence Sir you may conclude that the prohibition as to the importation Subsequent to the 1st of October, is a source of some discontent. . . .[321]

Claiborne foresaw that they would seek to smuggle all sorts of blacks without consideration to their origin or past, including the undesirables from the English islands and the "rogues from Saint-Domingue." After October 1, only the worst persons would be able to circumvent [the ban].[322] The governor, while

---

[320]Carter, ed., *Territorial Papers*, IX, 222.

[321]Rowland, ed., *Official Letter Books*, II, 134.

[322]*Ibid.*, II, 245, 254.

increasing surveillance, ultimately disbelieved the supposedly imminent danger of the situation. By reviewing individual cases,[323] Claiborne showed himself to be as humane as possible before October 1, 1804.

Thereafter, the influx of refugees stopped. He would mention slaves from the islands in his correspondence until 1809. They were probably still arriving but in numbers too small to mention.

VI
A Few Names of Refugees from 1803-1804 [324]

In the middle of 1803 and again throughout 1804, hundreds of colonists sailing aboard ships of rather small tonnage arrived in New Orleans. [These immigrants can be divided into a few] fairly broad categories: They were generally merchants and soldiers, [with] few men of color, few women travelling alone or with children, few families. A few colonists brought along some slaves. This at least is what we conclude from the evidence.

We know the names of several hundred of these newly arrived refugees, but they only represent a small fraction [of the total]. Since we do not have immigration registers for the early nineteenth century, we know only their names, not the conditions in which they arrived, nor the circumstances, or the dates of their disembarkation. We are thus forced to assume that their arrival was around the time indicated in parochial records, realizing that several must have arrived a few months before any evidence of their existence was recorded.

Those who left the colony before its massive evacuation were able to go to Louisiana more or less grouped according to neighborhood, for they generally had assembled at a port after having abandoned their beleaguered plantations. The colonists from the North left by Cap-Français, those from Artibonite by

---

[323] *Ibid.*, II, 358.

[324] In certain cases we did not find it necessary to indicate in footnotes the source of information on the baptisms, marriages or burials. It is clearly understood here: St. Louis parish records.

Saint-Marc, those from the West by Port-au-Prince or Léogane, and those from the South by Aux Cayes. Depending upon the circumstances, they boarded ships more or less hastily, fortunate when they were able to take along some clothing, a few quarter-casks of coffee, or a half-dozen servants.

It would be useless to attempt classification of these newly arrived refugees by type of colonist, distinguishing sugarcane from coffee planters, the diverse types of merchants, [or] civil servants; this procedure would be inconclusive. We do not always know the principal activity of these refugees. The safest approach would be to look to their original neighborhood. One day, when we determine the conditions under which the evacuation took place, we will be able to know the date and probably the circumstances surrounding the departure of many of them.

The northern refugees—almost all of whom departed Cap-Français and its immediate surroundings: Petite-Anse, Limbé, Petite and Grande-Rivière du Nord, Plaisance, Port-de-Paix, and Môle Saint-Nicolas—will thus [be the first to] pass in review.

Next came colonists from the West, who were able to leave *via* Port-au-Prince, Saint-Marc, Gonaïves or Léogane; from the South, they left by Aux Cayes, Jérémie, or Jacmel.

This compilation of names does not attempt to avoid monotony, for its style remains consistent. A compilation of vital statistics, it seeks only accuracy.

Almost everyone from Cap-Français left empty-handed. For example, Joseph-Marie Bourguignon undoubtedly returned rather hastily to France with his wife and little girl, for their names are to be found on the list of former colonists aided by the Department of the Bouches-du-Rhône.[325] In addition, Pierre-Auguste-Charles Bourguignon, whose relationship, if any, to the preceding family is unknown, married his second wife, Marie Lartigue, at New Orleans. She died on June 1, 1813.[326]

Louis-Marie-Elisabeth Moreau-Lislet, born in 1767 at Cap-

[325]Bouches-du-Rhône Archives.

[326]Burial records, Saint Louis Cathedral.

Français, was much better known. After having studied law in France where he married Elisabeth-Anne-Philippine de Peters,[327] he returned to Saint-Domingue where he amassed a nice little fortune. In 1794, he went to Philadelphia. In the year XI—1802-1803—he was once again at Cap-Français, where he became a public defender, *i.e.*, a lawyer, then a lower court judge. The *New York Herald,* in its August 18, 1809, edition, quoting an article from the *Baltimore Federal Republican,* claimed, without offering any proof, that he had been Toussaint L'Ouverture's secretary and grand master in a Masonic lodge for men of color.[328] He was in Santiago de Cuba on August 9, 1804.[329] With his wife and daughter, he left there to go to New Orleans, where his knowledge of English and Spanish earned him an almost immediate appointment by Claiborne as interpreter for the Orleans District and, in 1805, judge of Orleans Parish, a critically important post. He occupied the seat until 1811. With Edward Livingston and Pierre Derbigny, in 1806, he was chosen to establish the Louisiana Civil Code. In 1811, he was one of the founders and one of the regents of the first university in Louisiana, called the University of Orleans. He later served as a member of the House of Representatives, and finally as [state] senator. He died on December 4, 1832.[330]

His daughter, Elisabeth-Althéa-Julie, born at Cap-Français on July 1, 1790, married J-B. Rossignol des Dunes-Leclerc, born at Saint-Marc, the son of Jean-Baptiste and Marie-Madeleine Piémont, at New Orleans on February 7, 1832. She died there on February 7, 1832.[331]

Anne Becque, widow of Antoine-Théodore Ruotte, former member of the Cap-Français Superior Council, died on Febru-

---

[327]Who died in New Orleans in 1809.

[328]Stanely Faye, ed., "Louis Declouet's Memorial to the Spanish Government, December 7, 1814," *Louisiana Historical Quarterly*, XXII (1939), 813, repeats it but does not offer any proof.

[329]National Archives, Paris, Overseas section, Refugees from Saint-Domingue Papers, Consulat in Santigo de Cuba, T. 1.

[330]Burial records, Saint Louis Cathedral.

[331]Pierre-Paul de Gramont. Marriage records, Saint Louis Cathedral.

ary 18, 1804[332] at New Orleans, where his daughter married on March 19, 1812.

On May 28, 1803, Jean-Marc Bart,[333] a former colonist and *père de famille* who had been a clerk with Foäche, Morange, and Hardivilliers in Cap-Républicain, announced in the *Moniteur de la Louisiane* that he was establishing in New Orleans a school in which he would teach reading, writing, elementary calculus, history, geography, English, Spanish, French, simple mathematics, the art of commercial bookkeeping with single or double columns, correspondence, and theoretical and practical courses in commercial relations. He lived in Mr. Puytaven's house, next door to Mr. Jourdain. . . .[334] Louis-Paul Dauphin had left Cap-Républicain "with a great multitude of families," "fleeing the execrable tyranny the Negroes exercised there." He was born at Aix-en-Provence unto Jean-Baptiste Dauphin and Charlotte Dereine. On November 19, 1803, he died a bachelor at the age of fifty on Louis-Henri Desmahy's farm, a league and a half from New Orleans.[335] He was lucky enough to arrive there after a brief journey of only a few days.[336]

Marie-Louise-Victoire Chancerel, wife of Charles Carrère, had lived at Cap-Français. On August 6, 1804,[337] she was godmother to her granddaughter Prudence, the child of Charles Duval and Marie-Laurence Carrère. We do not know how long the family had been in Louisiana.

François Diart, born at Cap-Français, was a tailor. The son of François and Marie Diart, he married Eugénie Rapicault in New Orleans on May 29, 1803.

François de Saint-Just arrived in New Orleans in late 1803.

---

[332]Burial records, Saint Louis Cathedral.

[333]Son of Marc-Pascal Bart and Suzanne Falquière, landowners in Baynet *Etat de l'indemnité*, (1832), p. 548.

[334]*Moniteur de la Louisiane,* May 2 and June 6, 1803; AC, C 13a, 52:n.p.

[335]Burial records, Saint Louis Cathedral.

[336]Annotator's note: The author is apparently referring to the duration of Bart's voyage from the Antilles to New Orleans.

[337]Baptismal records, Saint Louis Cathedral.

During his first years in Louisiana, he tried to earn a living as an actor as he had done formerly in Saint-Domingue. He did not, however, have to work very hard: He was the brother of Denis de Saint-Just, a coffee grower in Dame-Marie in the far south.

Louis Chefdhomme and Rosalie Boutin, of Cap-Républicain, had one daughter, Marie-Louise-Catherine, born at Cap-Républicain, but baptized in New Orleans on March 31, 1802. A second one, Catherine, was born at Limonade and baptized at New Orleans on March 15, 1806.

Charlotte-Renée Mondion, married François Pillet, from Cap-Républicain. She had a daughter, Louise-Fortunée, who married Charles Gros at New Orleans in 1802.

Anne-Joséphine Dalban, daughter of Jean-Joseph and Anne Chavet, married Joseph Faurie, probably at Cap-Républicain, where she was born. They were still in New Orleans in 1802, after returning from Baltimore where their daughter Zoé was born.

May Louis Corna de La Livornière be considered a refugee? He was born at Nantes and had married Louise-Viviane Bunet, a Creole, at New Orleans on November 26, 1779. Louis-Michel de La Livornière, his father, had been captain of the fusiliers in the Cap-Français militia and owned two houses in that city. His son had lived with him for several years. The date of his return to New Orleans, where we find his signature dated April 9, 1803, is unknown.[338]

François-Auguste-Anne Hulin, from Rouen, son of François and Marie-Madeleine Duchêne, went to Cap-Républicain, where on May 3, 1800, he married Creole Mélanie Vitard. He was named second lieutenant in the New Orleans militia on May 1, 1806.[339] He may have been a refugee before 1800. He died on August 27, 1814. The *New Orleans Directory* of 1822 lists another François Hulin as a property owner. This was probably his

[338]Welcoming address of the inhabitants of New Orleans to Laussat, April 9, 1803. AC, C 13a, 52:290.

[339]"Register of Appointments in the Militia of the Territory of Orleans," Carter, ed., *Territorial Papers*, IX, 633.

father.

Marie-Claire Drouet, from Cap-Républicain, had a child on September 28, 1800. [The child] was baptized on May 21, 1802 in St. Louis [Cathedral], but his place of birth is missing from the baptismal certificate.

Marguerite Bordas, married Etienne Vaillé (?) on September 4, 1806. They were formerly from Cap-Républicain.

On July 27, 1801, Madeline, born at Cap-Républicain, the daughter of Antoine Griffogny and Catherine Neuviès, married at New Orleans Joseph Perrière from Antibes. Marguerite, their daughter, was born on July 20, 1803, and was baptized two days later.

Henry Bry, son of Henry and Julie Robert, came from Geneva to marry at New Orleans Marie-Agnès Seuzanneau from Saint-Domingue on October 1, 1804. He established himself as a planter in Ouachita county, and since he spoke English very well, Claiborne recommended him to President Madison for the Louisiana's Legislative Council on March 4, 1810.[340]

First named commander of the Iberville district on March 14, 1805,[341] Pierre Bailly, probably from Cap-Républicain, soon became judge of this same parish on May 29, 1805.[342]

Marguerite Bordas and Etienne Bailly seem to have attended the marriage of their daughter, born at Cap-Français, to Jacques Siméon on September 4, 1806.

Due to an unusual incident, we know that a poor fellow by the name of Matignon escaped from Saint-Domingue at the last minute, leaving behind his brother, a surgeon. In the October 22, 1806, edition of the *Moniteur de la Louisiane*, we learn that during his recent illness, he lost two twenty-year old letters his brother wrote to him from his home town.

The colonists established in proximity to Cap-Républicain do not appear to have taken refuge en masse in Louisiana, or else, only a few of their names are known.

[340]Claiborne to President Madison, March 4, 1810, *ibid.*, 864-87.

[341]Claiborne to Bailly, March 15, 1805, *ibid.*, 417.

[342]*Ibid.*; "Register of Civil Appointments in the Territory of Orleans," *ibid.*, 598.

Marie Savant and her husband, Jean Marsenat, were god-parents to Doctor Alliot's child in New Orleans on April 12, 1803. They were still living on April 26, 1820, when they attended their daughter's wedding.

Marie-Anne Roudanez and Emmanuel-Marius Pons-Bringier were married in New Orleans on April 5, 1804. She was the daughter of Pierre and Anne-Elisabeth Fleury, colonists in Dondon;[343] he was Marie-Françoise Durand's widower.

The widowed sisters Jeanne-Marie, formerly Mrs. Grand-Borie, and Marie-Elisabeth Laville, formerly Mrs. Pierre Chevrier, arrived in 1804. They were from Plaisance, about ten leagues south of Cap-Français. The latter married Henry Mélier in New Orleans.[344]

Pélagie Pain and Jean-Barthélémy Charbonnet were married in Louisiana around 1768 and then moved to Jérémie to establish a coffee plantation where they most likely died. François-Daniel Pain was godfather at St. Louis [Cathedral] to the Charbonnets' granddaughter.[345] This person may have been Louis-François Pain or his brother, natives of Saint-Louis du Nord. [Pain was the] son of Louis-Daniel Pain and Marie-Jeanne Hargant and husband of Marguerite-Marie Rangeard. Louis-François died at the age of fifty in New Orleans on August 9, 1809, and his wife on February 20, 1827. What complicates matters even more is that there were other colonists named Pain in Limbé, in Petite-Rivière du Nord,[346] in Léogane to the west,[347] and in Aux Cayes of Jacmel.[348]

A man called Rivière, either from Cap-Républicain or Quartier-Morin, wrote on March 10, 1803, to P. A. Mossu,

---

[343]Fleury was in Saint Louis for Marie-Anne and Henry's wedding in the *Etat de l'indemnité*, 1830, p. 30; and 1832, p. 36.

[344]National Archives, Paris. Overseas Section. Refugees papers of the consulate in Santiago de Cuba, June 23, 1807, T.1.

[345]Baptismal records, Saint Louis Cathedral, March 25, 1801.

[346]*Etat détaillé de l'indemnité*, 1832.

[347]*Ibid.*, 1834, pp. 248, 478.

[348]*Ibid.*, 1834, p. 426.

procurator for the Gallifet farms situated in Quartier-Morin, near Cap-Républicain that he has just arrived at New Orleans aboard a boat, whose captain has secretly introduced seventeen slaves from Saint-Domingue by paying $150 per slave to the Plaquemines commandant. Durousseau, the slaves' master, was vigorously prosecuted, which proves in Rivière's eyes the difficulty and danger of introducing slaves. Is it to be believed that Durousseau was a refugee?[349]

The burial of Marie-Françoise Béchau, wife of Pierre Cuvert Dessalines from Quartier-Morin, took place in St. Louis [Cathedral] on May 13, 1808.

From Port-de-Paix came J-B. Aumaillé, his wife Marianne Pouplié[350] and Thérèse-Eulalie-Gabrielle, their daughter, who would first marry François Grandmont, then Etienne, his brother,[351] and finally Georges Salles.

There was also the colonist Jean-Baptiste de la Hogue who had arrived in 1803.[352] That very same year, he is mentioned in the profile of New Orleans residents, prepared for President Jefferson, as being an untrustworthy, conspiring rogue. He nonetheless secured an appointment as the municipality's temporary secretary.[353] Was he related to the La Hogue who before 1789 had been commissioner of the French government to the governor of Santo-Domingo[354] or to the Mavoglès de Hogue who is found in Cuba in 1799?[355]

François-Marie Prévost was originally from southern France, where he was born at 1771. In 1800, he was a public health official on Port-de-Paix. The following year, he went to

---

[349]National Archives, Paris, 117 AP, Gallifet Papers.

[350]Who died before April 9, 1820.

[351]Dead at thirty-five on July 23, 1813, and buried at no cost.

[352]Carter, ed., *Territorial Papers*, IX, 257.

[353]*The Union: Orleans Advertiser and Price Current*, March 12, 1803.

[354] AC, E, box 219.

[355] Francisco Perez de La Riva, *El Café; Historía de su cultivo y explotación en Cuba* (Havana, 1944).

Louisiana, where he settled near Donaldsonville on the west bank of the Mississippi, 100 miles upstream from New Orleans where he performed Louisiana's first cesarean.

Anne-Marie Bourguignon wed Jean Salles in New Orleans on July 7, 1805. He was one of sixteen children born to J-B. Bonseigneur and Marguerite Pouplié, colonists from Port-de-Paix. His brothers do not appear to have arrived in Louisiana before 1809.

Jean-Joseph-Marie-Achille Desobry had a father, Hilaire-Joseph, colonist in Dondon and Morne-du-Cap, who had been massacred. He reached New Orleans on January 29, 1802, and he died there in 1819.

Marie-Marguerite Raingeard, a Creole from Saint-Louis du Nord, was the daughter of François and Marie-Jeanne Argault and the wife of Louis-François Pain.[356] They appear to have arrived in 1801.

Pierre Baron Desfontaines' act of burial, dated January 8, 1836, at St. Louis Cathedral, states that he had resided in New Orleans for about thirty-five years. Thus, he must have arrived around 1801. He came from Grande-Rivière du Nord. We know of several members of this family, all Creoles, who took refuge in Louisiana, all sons of Pierre and Marguerite Févé.

Pierre-Joseph went to live in Louisiana and was a witness to many marriages between 1820 and 1832. His act of burial has never been found.

Pierre married Judith Veillon in New Orleans but their marriage certificate is no longer extant. Their daughter, Elise, died at the age of six days.[357] He founded a bakery and died at the age of sixty-seven on January 7, 1836, his wife, the next day.

Adélaïde, their sister, spouse or widow of Mr. Harper, was a witness to several weddings between April 29, 1820, and September 15, 1822.

Anne-Marie-Rose, their other sister, the daughter of Pierre-Joseph, wed Samuel Boyer Davis on April 29, 1820. Among the witnesses of this marriage was Noël-Auguste Baron, also known

[356]Baptismal records, March 25, 1801, Saint Louis Cathedral.

[357]Burial records, November 15, 1815, Saint Louis Cathedral.

as Baron, *fils*, perhaps another brother of Pierre and Adélaïde. In 1822 he was a commissioner and broker associated with Pierre-François du Bourg de Sainte-Colombe.[358]

Louis-George-Casimir Bourcier was able to escape from Grande-Rivière du Nord, area known for its coffee-groves run by small planters. He was a native of Arcy-sur-Aube, son of Louis and Marie Oudin. He married Catherine-Geneviève de Silly, a Creole from the same neighborhood, on April 23, 1804.

Françoise-Sophie-Fortunée Hardi de Boisblanc was god-mother in New Orleans on October 15, 1805. Jean-Baptiste Cuvert du Boisblanc, from a totally different family, from Saint-Louis de la Petite-Anse parish in Quartier-Morin, and Marie-Françoise-Elisabeth de Laleu, his wife, had a daughter, Jeanne-Sophie-Fortunée, who married Joseph Peyrellade on March 12, 1806, and died the following July 12.[359]

Louis Borée, from Môle Saint-Nicolas, son of Joseph and Elisabeth Borée from Montpelier, married Anne-Sophie Maure. He died at the age of forty-five on August 16, 1806.[360]

In 1803, we see several Baristheauts from Môle Saint-Nicolas. There were at least three of them, maybe four: a so-called Baristheaut, *le jeune,* signed on April 9, 1803, the *Adresse de bienvenue des habitants de la Nouvelle-Orléans à Laussat.* Jean-Baptiste attended a refugees' wedding on September 16, 1806. The bride's name was Marie Baristheaut, but we do not know when she went to Louisiana. Nathalie, daughter of Jean-Baptiste and Marie Baristheaut died at the age of eighteen on December 29, 1804.[361]

Banger Boulle, husband to Marie-Joseph Guérin from Môle Saint-Nicolas, died on December 25, 1806.[362]

A native of Jean-Rabel, Elisabeth-Rose Cormier, married on December 4, 1829, Pierre-Marie Vincent, the son of Améda and

[358] *New Orleans Directory,* 1822.

[359] Burial records, Saint Louis Cathedral.

[360] *Ibid.*

[361] *Ibid.*

[362] *Ibid.*

Louise Isnard, in Saint Louis Cathedral, but she appears to have arrived in New Orleans well before 1809.

* * *

It was not easy to see why the refugees from the western sectors, Port-au-Prince, Gonaïves, Saint-Marc, Arcahaye, Cul-de-Sac and Léogane, are to be found in even smaller numbers in Louisiana. It is believed that the evacuation of these areas was conducted differently than in the North and South. Were there fewer [transport] ships or were the English able to seize many more refugees in the Gulf of Gonaïves and take them to Jamaica or send them back to France?

Pierre-David Bidet-Renoulleau, a former merchant marine captain, had opened a store in Port-au-Prince. He owned a plantation near town.[363] His wife, Marie-Françoise-Jeanne Laroque, was a Creole from Dondon. In 1802, they were in New Orleans, where their son Pierre-Daniel died on March 12, 1803, at the age of thirteen months. Through much effort, he was able to establish a tobacco mill. He had the word spread around that he was known for having run in Cap-Républicain the best factory in the Antilles.[364] In 1805, his address was No. 12, Place Publique;[365] in 1807, No. 12, Place St. Pierre.[366] In order to build his house, he borrowed $500 from Hyacinthe Courcelle of New Orleans on September 5, 1802.[367] He was one of the signers of a petition to Claiborne dated September 17, 1804, pleading for the relaxation of the American policy concerning the slave trade. In addition to his factory and his tobacco business, he was also in 1806 a gauger, weigher, measurer and merchant of dry goods.[368] A few years later, he would move to Pointe Coupée.

[363] AC, E 31 (1783-year IX).

[364] *Moniteur de la Louisiane*, September 19, 1803, and January 8, 1806.

[365] *New Orleans Directory*, 1805.

[366] *Ibid., 1807.*

[367] Notaries' Archives, Orleans Parish, January 7, 1803.

[368] *Moniteur de la Louisiane*, January 3, 1806.

Marie-Elisabeth Godineau, a Creole from Port-au-Prince, daughter of François and Elisabeth, married at New Orleans on February 7, 1803[369] Jean-Baptiste La Vallette Duverdier, born at Dax, the son of Jean and Anne Maisonneuve. The parents of Marie-Elisabeth owned houses in Port-au-Prince.[370]

Claude-Thomas, a former priest in Saint-Domingue, had at least passed through Port-au-Prince. From 1802 to 1818, he signed the burial acts at St. Louis Cathedral.

We do not know exactly when Mme. Trignant de Beaumont, *née* Victoire-Adélaïde Charlier, J-B. Harranibar and Angélique Galebert, his wife, arrived in New Orleans. Although she was originally from New Orleans, they lived in Port-au-Prince where they were landowners.[371] Mrs. Harranibar, widowed in 1805,[372] died at the age of thirty-five.[373] Jean-Casimir, her son and sole heir, does not appear in [the] New Orleans [records].

In 1803, J-B. Gérard Masson, Degas' maternal grandfather, probably went from Port-au-Prince, where he was born, to New Orleans.[374] He would marry Marie-Désirée Rilleux there in 1810.[375]

A certain Jalabert, probably François, born at Bordeaux, had lived at Port-au-Prince. He married—but we do not know where—Madeleine Greset, a Louisiana Creole. Their daughter Marie, born at Port-au-Prince on August 19, 1792, but baptized in St. Louis Cathedral on October 29, 1800, married J-B. Bozant, from Môle Saint-Nicolas, at New Orleans on April 28, 1821.

---

[369]Marriage records, Saint Louis Cathedral.

[370]*Etat de l'indemnité,* 1836, p. 406.

[371]*Ibid.,* 1832, p. 334.

[372]*New Orleans in 1805: A Directory and a Census* (New Orleans, 1836).

[373]Marriage records, May 28, 1810, Saint Louis Cathedral.

[374]A. Krebs, "Degas à la Nouvelle-Orleans," *Rapports France-Amérique* (August, 1952), 63.

[375]Carter, ed., *Territorial Papers,* IX, 826.

Maurice Bertin from Port-au-Prince was named chief surgeon of the New Orleans militia on September 20, 1808.[376]

Anne-Marie-Renée Goutard, born at Port-au-Prince, landowner in Mirebalais,[377] was the widow of Pierre Vincent. As a refugee in Louisiana, she married Gervais Le Roy whose son Jean-Baptiste, born at Mirebalais, died at New Orleans at the age of forty-five on November 25, 1815. They seem to have arrived in Louisiana in 1802.

Etienne Berret, receiver of a Port-au-Prince landgrant, a landowner also in Cavaillon, at the Prieur cross-roads, and also a farmer on the Dominicans' plantation, arrived in New Orleans in 1804.

On April 9, 1803, J-B. Verret signed the *Adresse de bienvenue des habitants de la Nouvelle-Orléans à l'arrivée de Laussat.*

Marie-Louise Boisbelleau, wife of Louis Rossignol des Dunes, signed her name to the baptismal certificates of the Boisbelleau, Rossignol and Remoussin children as their paternal grandmother in 1804.

Achille Bérard, most likely from Saint-Marc, was named militia lieutenant on November 27, 1807.[378]

Marie-Christine Blanchet died in New Orleans on June 27, 1805. She was the widow of Jean-Thomas Paigne and was from Petite-Rivière de l'Artibonite.[379]

Simon Millet, formerly an architect in Croix-des-Bouquets, was witness to the wedding of refugees at St. Louis Cathedral on February 25, 1821. He had arrived at the city as early as 1805.[380]

Jacques Rice Fitzgerald, originally from Donegal County, Ireland, had lived in New Orleans before becoming a businessman in Léogane, where he married Catherine-Victoire Descas. He returned to Louisiana in 1804 with Pierre Collette.

---

[376] *Ibid.*

[377] *Etat de l'indemnité,* 1834, p. 292.

[378] Carter, ed., *Territorial Papers,* IX, 637.

[379] Burial records, Saint Louis Cathedral.

[380] *New Orleans in 1805.*

His daughter, Victoire-Françoise-Adèle, born at Léogane, married in New Orleans a relative of Pierre Collette, J-B. Aimé Colheux of Longpré. We do not know if the Jacques Fitzgerald who died in New Orleans at the age of fifty-two on November 1, 1815, was the friend of Pierre Collette.

* * *

So many colonists left from Aux Cayes, the most important city in the southern part of the island, that they formed a veritable colony in New Orleans. We can only cite here those who took refuge there around 1803.

First there were the Davezac de Casteras, Creoles: Pierre-Valentin-Dominique-Julien, more commonly known as Jules, born January 17, 1769, was the son of an irrigation canal digger on Aux Cayes' plains and Marie-Thérèse-Geneviève de Linois. His friend, Moreau de Saint-Méry, built his father's reputation as a hydraulic engineer. His son would be General Jackson's *aide-de-camp* in 1815, after having been headmaster of the University of Orleans in 1811. In 1812, he was named secretary to the mayor of New Orleans. He died there unmarried on February 7, 1831.[381]

Marie-Rose-Valentine Telarie de Maragon, widow of Jean-Pierre-Valentin Davezac de Castera, also went to Louisiana. Her husband had been a deputy from Aquinas Parish to the colonial assembly held in Saint-Marc in 1790 and had been one of the eighty-five deputies who went to France the following August to defend their political independence before the *Constituante*. Upon returning to the colony, he was massacred in 1793 or 1794.

It is difficult to distinguish among the several Bourgeois, also from Aux Cayes: Charles(?), the widower of Marie-Elisabeth-Catherine Papier, left Saint-Domingue in October 1805[382] with his daughter Rose-Elisabeth, who was born at Aux Cayes and

---

[381] Burial records, Saint Louis Cathedral.

[382] Debien and Wright, "Les colons de Saint-Domingue à la Jamaïque."

who died at New Orleans in 1805 at the age of seventeen.[383] He was clerk of the municipality, and, the following July 21, would become secretary to the city council.[384]

In March 1794, a Bourgeois was incarcerated at Aux Cayes by order of the civil commissioner Polverel. He was set free the next month. He too would come to Louisiana in 1803.

The Buards were a remarkable family. Louis was named lieutenant in the New Orleans militia on November 27, 1805.[385] Adolphe was married to Catherine Martin. Their daughter Marie, born at Aux Cayes, died in 1811 at the age of eight.[386]

The following refugees from Aux Cayes appear only briefly [at New Orleans:] Julie Moreau, wife of Claude Trémé; and Marie-Denise Gabrielle Baudoin, born at Aux Cayes, widow of a Mr. Soulay, dead at the age of 62 on May 22, 1810. Was she related to Leger Baudoin, appointed militia lieutenant on February 22, 1806?[387]

Without their first names, it was impossible to find our way among all of the Béraults from Aux Cayes. A C. Bérault is said to have lost some letters bearing his address.[388] A Bérault, spouse of Marie Breton, died at New Orleans on March 20, 1810.

Jacques-François Poupard, a Creole from Aux Cayes, son of François, born at Argens (Finistère) and Marie-Anne Orfroy, married Célestin Bahi at New Orleans on June 18, 1807, in the presence of her father. In 1827, this Jacques-François would be identified as a watch-maker and grocer.[389] His father must have died an octogenarian on February 20, 1821.[390] He had a

---

[383] Burial records, May 21, 1812, Saint Louis Cathedral.

[384] Carter, ed., *Territorial Papers*, IX, 401, 483.

[385] *Ibid.*, 638.

[386] Free burial in November 27, 1811. Burial records, Saint Louis Cathedral.

[387] Carter, ed., *Territorial Papers*, IX, 633.

[388] March 22, 1806. *Ibid.*, 421,

[389] *New Orleans Directory.*

[390] Burial records, Saint Louis Cathedral.

homonym François Poupard, born at France, who died on July 4, 1832 at the age of eighty.[391] Were they related?

Louise-Adélaïde Bousquet, former resident of Aux Cayes, widow of François-Balthazar Bousquet, married M. Loutrel. She did not know how to sign her name. Her testimony was recorded to give support to Dormenon on March 28, 1809, at a time when the Saint-Domingue refugees in Cuba had not yet left Havana.[392]

We must also mention those persons permitted by General Rochambeau's proclamation to evacuate Aux Cayes in fall of 1803: Henri Olier and Elisabeth Bertrand, widow of an Olier.[393]

Also among this group were Philippe Jalabert and his two daughters, Marie and Céline, the former having been born at Abricots in 1794 and whose grave can still be seen in New Orleans Cemetery No. 2; Claude Delorgny; Jean-Baptiste Séné; and Simon Dupeu, who owned several homes in Aux Cayes.

The Charbonnets were a family who went to Jérémie from Louisiana at a time when quite a few Louisianians were migrating to southern Saint-Domingue. The first one was Jean-Barthélémy who had married Pélagie Pain, a Creole, around March 1768 in Natchitoches. At the same time, At[394] . . . [*sic*], his brother, married Marie-Antoinette Livaudais, but remained in Louisiana. Louis-Richard, son of Jean-Barthélémy, born at Jérémie, took refuge at New Orleans where he married Marie-Mélanie Fleuriau on April 29, 1799 and where he died on December 14, 1821. Their daughter, Mélanie-Jeanne-Céline, born at New Orleans, married her cousin from Jérémie, François-Simon Plicque on November 26, 1818. Marie-Jeanne-Claude-Antoinette, Louis-Richard's sister, also born at Jérémie, married

---

[391]*Ibid.*

[392]Pierre B. Dormenon, *Réponse à des calomnies* (New Orleans, 1809).

[393]National Archives, Paris, Overseas section. Saint-Domingue refugees' papers. New Orleans consulate, June 13, 1807.

[394]Annotator's note: Antoine Charbonnet, a New Orleans merchant, married Marie Antoinette Enould de Livaudais ca. 1769. Their daughter, Marie Anne, was baptized at New Orleans on November 20, 1769. Woods and Nolan, *Sacramental Records*, II, 49.

Aimable-Girod Plicque from Jérémie, massacred in 1804.[395] His widow took refuge at New Orleans in May 1804. Marie-Modeste, born at Jérémie around 1787, wife of Juste-Augustin-Roche Lebeau, a medical doctor who was still alive in 1818. She died around July 17, 1836. Aimable-Barthélélmy, born at Jérémie around 1787, married Marie-Françoise Languille. He was a clerk in New Orleans, a Freemason, and secretary-treasurer of the French Lodge, *l'Etoile polaire.*[396] He died in New Orleans on November 4, 1832.[397] Mélanie-Jeanne, born at New Orleans on February 2, 1801, was baptized on March 25, 1801.[398]

Nicolas Lescouflair and Julienne Brisson, his Creole wife from Abricots, colonists in Trou-Bonbon near Jérémie, boarded ship in this small port. She became the godmother of her grandson, Pierre Chameau, in 1805.[399] She died at the age of forty-eight on March 27, 1815.

Did Charles de Baligant, an heir of Charles-François de Baligant d'Heillecourt, a former landowner in Jérémie, come directly from Saint-Domingue? This refugee taught drawing. A former professor of sculpture and drawing from the port of Brest, he was completely trustworthy.[400] In 1806, his bust of Napoleon shown in Mr. Montégut's home caused much talk around town.[401]

Jean-Louis Lapauze was from Cavaillon and had lived there from 1800 to 1803. Joseph-Isaïe Le Carpentier, born at Torbeck, married Modeste Blache, a native of New Orleans and the daughter of François and Louise Blondeau, on August 16, 1808.

---

[395]Maurice Begouen-Demeaux, *Mémorial d'une famille du Havre*, 2 vols. (Le Havre, 1951), II, 248.

[396]*New Orleans Directory*, 1822.

[397]Burial records, Saint Louis Cathedral.

[398]Baptismal records, Saint Louis Cathedral.

[399]*Ibid.*

[400]*Moniteur de la Louisiane*, March 3, 1806.

[401] AC, C 13a, 52.

Louis Descambois, originally from Bordeaux and a former colonist from Abricots in the extreme south of the peninsula, was buried in St. Louis [Cemetery] on June 28, 1811.[402]

On September 2, 1806, Jean Cazeau married Marie-Catherine Boyé at New Orleans. They were both former inhabitants of Coteaux.[403]

Jean Leclerc, born at France in 1770, owned in Baynet a combination coffee and indigo farm, estimated at 200,000 *livres*.[404] With his wife. Elisabeth Carrière, he took refuge in New Orleans where in 1809, at the time of the arrival of the last refugees from Cuba, he founded *L'Ami des Lois*.[405] His witty but caustic pen has preserved his name.

Jean-Pierre Morgan was of Irish stock. This carpenter, brother of a process-server from Jérémie, ran half of a small coffee farm in Anse-à-Veau. When Cap-Républicain was evacuated, he and his daughter Elisabeth, then eight or nine years old, were saved from certain death by a young stowaway on a ship from Baltimore who was in harbor at that time. They were taken to New Orleans.[406]

Jean Marsenat and Marie Savant, his wife, had a rather unsettled life at the time of the Revolution. In a letter for Dormenon dated March 28, 1809, Marsenat states that he was from Aux Cayes of Jacmel[407] and claims to remember the massacres which took place in the Jacmel area, especially those perpetrated by Faubert and Gay at Jacmel and Sale-Trou in 1793. He was on Bernard Bret's plantation at the time. He was later arrested there and was deported in 1794.[408] Marsenat and

---

[402]*New Orleans in 1805.*

[403]Burial records, Saint Louis Cathedral.

[404]*Etat de l'indemnité,* 1832.

[405]Tinker, *Bibliography.*

[406]*Louisiana Gazette,* October 26, 1804.

[407]About 75 miles to the east of Aux Cayes.

[408]Dormenon, *Réponses à des calomnies.*

his wife were godparents to Marie Alliot, Dr. Alliot's[409] daughter. His name can be found in the *New Orleans Directory* of 1805, and again in the 1822 edition as a teacher in a school for people of color. On April 28, 1820, they married their daughter Adélaïde-Marcelline, born at New Orleans, to Jacques Sauyé.[410] We then lose track of their names.

J-B. Loménie de Marmé owned plantations in Petit-Trou and Fond des Nègres. He was the son of a captain employed by an independent shipping company. Fairly involved in the political discussions of the colonial reformers in 1788 and 1789, he was elected one of the representatives from the South to the Estates General, but was admitted only as a substitute. A member of the Massiac Club, he returned to the South in 1791. Writing in his *Mémoires* in 1803, Laussat calls him a refugee in New Orleans, along with Dugué Livaudais.

In reality, upon the arrival of the Saint-Domingue refugees in the United States, there was a certain desire to regroup, a need to reassemble their lives. Nowhere was it more obvious and persistent than in this movement towards Louisiana by those who had disembarked in the Eastern Atlantic States between 1788 and 1804.

On the top of this list we find Paul Lanusse, born around 1766, son of Pierre-Arnauld and Marie Lauret who were from Orthez. As well as his brother Jean, Paul went to Saint-Domingue where he established himself as a merchant. He was in Philadelphia in 1797[411] and at New Orleans in 1801. He was even a member of the *cabildo* and attorney general.[412] On August 6, 1802,[413] he married Marie-Céleste Macarty, daughter of Jean-Baptiste and Charlotte-Hélène Fazende, from Saint-Domingue. They would have ten children from 1804 to 1823, all born at New Orleans.

[409]Baptismal records, Saint Louis Cathedral.

[410]Marriage records, Saint Louis Cathedral.

[411]Notary Archives, Orleans Parish, Pierre Pedesclaux's acts, September 23, 1797.

[412]Cabildo Archives, July 10, 1801.

[413]Marriage records, Saint Louis Cathedral.

He was considered to be a wealthy businessman, becoming director of the Bank of Louisiana,[414] president of the chamber of commerce,[415] and one of the regents of the University of Orleans.[416] He died at Soto-la-Marina, Mexico, on October 10, 1825,[417] during a business trip taken to rebuild the fortune he had just lost.

His brother Jean, ten years younger, is more familiar to us. We do not know if he too went to Philadelphia, but he did take refuge in New Orleans. He died there on June 29, 1812.[418] He had married Hélène Dupèbe.

Claudin de Béleurgey was printer of the newspaper *La République et Affiches Américaines* in Port-au-Prince in 1793.[419] Two years later he published *Le Patriote Français* in Charleston. He next became a fencing instructor in New Orleans and then, in association with Jean Rouard, owner of the *Telegraph and Commercial Advertiser* which he sold in 1810 or 1811 to Jean Dacqueny.[420] In 1806, he was appointed lieutenant in the militia.[421]

Joséphine Dalban, born at Cap-Français, daughter of Jean-Joseph and Anne Chauvin, owners of a house there estimated at 160,000 *livres,* married—probably at Cap-Français—Joseph Faulic, born at Bordeaux around 1769, son of André and Pétronille Pénicaud. He had a daughter in Baltimore, Anne-Zoé.[422] Later, in New Orleans on June 21, 1802, he attended

[414]Carter, ed., *Territorial Papers*, IX, 368.

[415]*Moniteur de la Louisiane,* September 6, 1806.

[416]*Ibid.*, December 24, 1816.

[417]*Courier la Louisiane*, November 24, 1825.

[418]Marriage records, Saint Louis Cathedral.

[419]Miss M-J. Menier and G. Debien, "Journaux de Saint-Domingue," *Revue d'histoire des colonies françaises* (1950), 409.

[420]Tinker, *Bibliography*, p. 75.

[421]Carter, ed., *Territorial Papers*, IX, 633.

[422]Who was to marry Emile Jones in New Orleans on February 12, 1820.

Christophe Gros and Louise-Fortunée Pillet's wedding. The household was to contain at least two children: Jean-Joseph-Hippolyte, born on May 4, 1802, baptized on October 21, 1802; and Emilia-Elisabeth, born on March 6, 1804, baptized November 27, 1804. Christophe died on September 4, 1807, at the age of thirty-eight, and his wife died at the age of sixty-two on June 9, 1833.

Morange, of the firm Stanislas Foäche, Morange, and Hardvilliers, took refuge at New York. He wrote to Foäche on May 31, 1804: "Madame Plicque—widow of a wholesaler from Jérémie who had been killed the preceding year—is getting ready to leave for Louisiana to live there with her family. Many other Frenchmen are going there also but it was believed that they would not find this country to their liking."[423] Her nephew and his wife, having left from New York in 1806, were lost in a shipwreck.[424]

Barthélémy Simon and Anne-Augustine Morgan, refugees at Charleston, had one son, Antoine, born on May 25, 1800. He was taken to New Orleans as a child. He married Marie-Antoinette Lemarlier there. He died on January 17, 1832.

In announcing the play *Commerce de nuit,* the *Moniteur de la Louisiane* in its May 25, 1808, issue praised Rifaux, also from Charleston, for his "special talent for all the Creole *patois* that he possesses to a high degree and who received some acclaim in Saint-Domingue and other places."

Also from Charleston was Jean-Antoine Dacqueny,[425] where he had married Angélique La Chapelle from Grenada on November 3, 1799. In New Orleans, he founded, with J-B-S. Thierry, *Le Courier de la Louisiane.*[426] He died in that city on September 1, 1814.

Joseph Belzans, former wholesaler from Saint Domingue, was in Charleston on December 12, 1794. In 1806, he opened an

---

[423] Begouen-Demeaux, *Une famille du Havre,* II, 152.

[424] *Ibid.,* II, 272.

[425] Born in Honfleur, Saint Catherine Parish, on December 7, 1777, to Joseph Simon and Marie-Anne Galouin.

[426] *Revue de la Société haïtienne d'histoire* (1931), 41.

art school in his residence at 63 North Bourbon Street.[427]

We know of J-B. Villeneuve and Jean-Claude-Auguste Follin, who married Marie-Joseph Hébert.[428]

Auguste-Dominique Tureaud was a refugee first in Baltimore.[429] He had made several trips across the United States, including Louisiana, when, in 1803, he settled in New Orleans, marrying Elisabeth Bringier, daughter of Emmanuel Pons. He engaged in business there and served as a godfather on November 22, 1804, in St. Louis Cathedral.

René-Nicolas Théart was not a Saint-Domingue colonist, but was an architect, a Catholic, and a royalist. From there, he went to New York; the circumstances surrounding this trip are unknown. He married there, probably before 1798, Marie-Rose Robert, a Creole from Cap-Français, daughter of Joseph-Robert and Marie-Jeanne Mary, planters from Petite-Anse. Their son René-Nicolas was baptized in St. Louis Cathedral on April 14, 1799. They then settled in Assumption Parish, where Mrs. Théart died.[430]

Finally, we have Jean-Marie Lamothe, a Creole from Saint-Marc, son of Pierre and Marie Couvertier. He first sought refuge at Philadelphia. On February 19, 1809, he married in St. Louis Cathedral Marie-Ann Séguin from Philadelphia, daughter of Marie-Jacqueline-Marguerite Michaud and Pierre, from Saint-Domingue.

* * *

There was most probably an incessant flow of refugees between Jamaica and Louisiana from 1793 to 1800. The English colonial authorities, after having accorded some help to them, "asked" the young men who did not want to enroll in the occupying army to go to Cuba or Louisiana.

---

[427]*Moniteur de la Louisiane*, September 20, 1806.

[428]From La Rochelle, son of Jacques and Françoise Guillon.

[429]King, *Creole Families*, pp. 419-422.

[430]AC, E 31; Tinker, *Bibliography*.

Then there were those who, in 1798, evacuated Saint-Domingue with the English troops or who had been captured at sea by English corsairs and taken to Jamaica, only to leave for Louisiana as soon as they were able.

Among those who had left Saint-Domingue in 1798 were Joseph Villars Dubreuil with his children, and the Louis d'Aquin family who founded a large bakery on Royal Street in New Orleans. The business prospered and was put up for sale in 1806.[431] Shortly thereafter, however, a fire destroyed the business, forcing Mr. D'Aquin to remain a baker at least until 1824, this time at 130 Chartres Street.[432]

Freshly arrived from Jamaica in 1803, Dr. A. Rolin notified the public in issue 372 of the *Moniteur de la Louisiane*, that "his health and weak constitution not permitting him to treat chronic and acute diseases that demand frequent visits, . . . will have to limit himself to those affecting principally the young and to skin diseases. . . . He lives on Government Street."

Julie-Félicité Rossignol was born at Jamaica, as well as her three sisters: Marie-Marguerite in 1796; Marie-Louise, 1800; and Marguerite, 1802. They were the children of Jean-Baptiste-Constant and Madeleine Piémont, refugees. Since only the youngest daughter was baptized in New Orleans,[433] one may reasonably assume that they had just arrived in New Orleans.

One of Jules Davezac de Casteras' sisters, Louise, born in 1782, widow of Moreau de Lassy, a former officer, refugee, and colonist in Jamaica, went from Kingston to New Orleans in 1803 or 1804. In 1805, she married Edward Livingston, one of the city's most prominent lawyers.

Tullius Saint-Cérano, born at Kingston in August 1802, was still a child when, in 1805, he accompanied his parents as they departed southern Saint-Domingue after their plantation burned. He was to become a professor and a poet.[434] His grave is

---

[431]*Moniteur de la Louisiane*, June 26, 1806.

[432]*New Orleans Directory.*

[433]Baptismal records, November 24, 1804, Saint Louis Cathedral.

[434]Tinker, *Ecrits*, p. 451.

in [St. Louis] Cemetery No. 2.

The D'Aquin family was famous for its peregrinations across the Antilles. Antoine-Pierre, born at Mobile in 1721, was the head of the family. He went to Saint-Domingue and became a colonist at Artibonite. He married Marguerite-Pierrette-Charlotte Bizoton de La Motte at Saint-Marc. In 1786, he was commissioner of the colonies.[435] Among their children were:

1.) Charles-Pierre, *dit* d'Aquin des Cahots, married Marie-Louise le Bon de La Pointe. His son Charles, born at Kingston, married Marie-Anne-Elisabeth Daron des Mortiers and died at around the age of thirty-five.[436]

2.) Pierre, *dit* d'Aquin des Petits-Bois.

3.) Thomas, born at Saint-Marc, married Anne Robinet de Saint-Gérard de La Laigne, a Creole from the same neighborhood. Their children include: François, *dit* Bizoton, born June 16, 1804; and Aimée, who died at the age of two on September 23, 1812, and was buried in a potter's field.[437]

4.) Elisabeth-Charlotte, *dite* Bonne, was born around 1745. She married Jean-Louis des Dunes de Poincy at Saint-Marc on August 12, 1777.[438] He died on November 18, 1833.

5.) François, born at Saint-Marc, was in Kingston in 1803. He died at New Orleans around the age of thirty-five. His wife, Françoise-Barbe, died on August 30, 1809. On February 16, 1804, he was godfather to his nephew François; his daughter Marie-Elisabeth, born at Jamaica, married Jean Againe in New Orleans on May 25, 1819. He had been named lieutenant in the militia on February 20, 1806,[439] and then promoted to the rank

---

[435]AC, E 107.

[436]Burial records, November 22, 1836, Saint Louis Cathedral.

[437]François, *dit* Bizoton, married: 1.) Léocadie d'Aquin, his cousin: 2.) Eugénie Rossignol des Dunes. Arriving from France in 1852, he died in Paris on May 7, 1855. His daughter Hélène, born in 1833, wed Dr. Frédéric Allain in New Orleans. In 1869, after the death of her husband, she went to France where she died at the age of ninety-four in January 1927. She was the author of *Les souvenirs d'Amérique et de France par une créole* (Paris, 1882).

[438]Confirmation of this marriage on April 18, 1811, and November 30, 1820. Marriage records, Saint Louis Cathedral.

[439]Carter, ed., *Territorial Papers*, IX, 634.

of captain on January 1, 1809.[440]

6.) Louis, born at Saint-Marc, married Adélaïde d'Eynaut and was at first a colonist in Petite-Rivière de l'Artibonite and was to be found in Kingston in 1803.[441] We do not have the baptismal records of his children, but we know the date of his son Charles' death at the age of approximately four[442] and his daughter Marie-Thérèse, born at New Orleans, died on June 15, 1810. Joséphine Althée, born at New Orleans, married James Puech, and died on May 9, 1822. Louis d'Aquin died on April 24, 1834, at the age of fifty-seven. During the war against the English, he led a militia battalion composed of Frenchmen and white Creoles.[443] In December of 1814, another battalion was formed recruited from the men of color by Charles Savary, a man of color himself. Louis d'Aquin commanded this second battalion, which distinguished itself in the Battle of New Orleans.[444] He was the one who owned a bakery.

Three Charest de Lauzons, who had owned coffee groves in the hills of Acul near Cap-Français, also arrived from Jamaica: François, former militia officer from the Marmelade sector, his wife Perrine de Gournay and his sister-in-law, also a Creole, the widow of Etienne de Lauzon.

Among the many Désobrys who took refuge in the United States—either in Baltimore or in New York—only one seems to have gone to Louisiana—Jean-Joseph-Marie-Achille. Arriving in 1802, he died unmarried on June 18, 1809. His death certificate declares that he was born at Saint-Domingue, but we do not know his occupation, his age, nor his parents' names. His heirs turned up in New York, while the widow of his brother Hilaire-Felix, Marie-Rose Abellard, was a refugee at Baracoa, Cuba.

---

[440]Rowland,ed., *Official Letter Books*, IV, 384.

[441]S. P. Delany, *A History of the Catholic Church in Jamaica, From 1494 to 1929* (New York, 1930).

[442]Burial records, October 24, 1807, Saint Louis Cathedral.

[443]Gayarré, *History of Louisiana*.

[444]*Ibid.*, III, 402.

She went from there to New Orleans in 1809.[445]

* * *

One may rightfully conclude that the colonists who went first to Cuba arrived at Louisiana before 1804 in more or less the same numbers as those who went there from Jamaica, the difference being that the Cubans did not arrive in large groups. Almost all of these colonists went there[446] of their own free will, in search of a better way of life.

J-B. Canonge, from Marseilles, was a colonist in Jérémie, where he lived with his mother and seven brothers and sisters. It was rumored that he plotted to turn the island over to Napoleon, but it is not known if this was the reason he left the island for Philadelphia. He studied law there and ended up in New Orleans. He made a career as a lawyer and a jurist. One of his sons, Louis-Placide, became a famous journalist, playwright, and, for a while, director of the New Orleans French Opera.[447]

François Bocquet, accompanied by a slave, went to New Orleans *via* Havana in the spring of 1803. In *Le Moniteur de la Louisiane* (March 23, 1803), he identified himself as a painter and as an engraver of "large and miniature scale with calligraphic numbers." He worked as a tutor on Burgundy Street, behind the church. He had been a musician in the Cap-Français theater in 1784,[448] but he only gave lessons in French, Spanish, and English.[449] He must not have done this for very long. He then opened a school,[450] apparently without great success for he went to Havana from whence he returned in 1809.

---

[445]His heirs did not accept his succession until inventory could be taken. (Notarial act passed by Narcisse Broutin on February 12, 1810.)

[446]Annotator's note: New Orleans.

[447]Tinker, *Ecrits*, p. 66.

[448]Fouchard, *Artistes et repertoires*, p. 9.

[449]*Moniteur de la Louisiane*, May 28, 1808; *The Union: Orleans Advertiser and Price Current*, December 27, 1803.

[450]*La Gazette de la Louisiane*, November 16, 1804.

J.-B. Brouet witnessed a wedding on September 16, 1806. He had procured a coffee farm in Cuba.[451]

Louis Blanchard, who had also been the owner of a coffee farm in Cuba before settling in Louisiana,[452] was appointed militia lieutenant in New Orleans on November 27, 1805. He submitted his resignation on May 8, 1806,[453] and was later named justice of the peace of Saint Charles Parish on July 17, 1808.[454]

Paul Boyer, who had been Louis Bourgeois' partner in a Cuban coffee farm venture,[455] was in New Orleans in 1805.

* * *

The list of those whose place of residence in Saint-Domingue was unknown to us was a long one.

Baptiste Baron signed a petition on November 9, 1804, in Pointe Coupée.[456]

Pierre Baron.[457]

Gaspard Barrier, born at Lalbenque in Quercy, married Elisabeth de la Biche in New Orleans on August 4, 1806. She was a native of Aux Cayes. He also witnessed a marriage of refugees on March 2, 1812.

On February 14, 1804, at New Orleans, Alexandre Baudin signed a letter to Jefferson complaining about Claiborne who had deprived the planters of the privileges accorded to them by the by-laws of the West India Company.[458]

---

[451] *New Orleans in 1805*; and Debien and Wright, "Les colons de Saint-Domingue passés à Cuba," 600.

[452] Debien and Wright, "Les colons de Saint-Domingue passés à Cuba," 601.

[453] Carter, ed., *Territorial Papers*, IX, 635.

[454] *Ibid.*, 824.

[455] Dormenon, *Réponse à des calmonies.*

[456] Carter, ed., *Territorial Papers*, IX, 327.

[457] *New Orleans in 1805.*

[458] *Ibid.*

Ignace Baudon.[459]

Grégoire Belhomé.[460]

Marie Belhomé was a godmother at St. Louis Cathedral on January 5, 1801.

Etienne Berret, a surgeon from Collabrieux in Provence, emigrated from Saint-Domingue and died on December 23, 1806 at about the age of sixty-eight.

Billon, a health official, announced in the *Louisiana Gazette* on June 18, 1805, that he had successfully treated yellow fever both in Saint-Domingue and New Orleans.

François Blanche.[461]

Alexandre Blanche, named militia captain in late 1806.[462]

Marie Boché, wife of Charles-Urbain Ducasse, July 20, 1805.

Antoine Bodé.[463]

Marianne Bontemps, wife of Jean de Rivière, from Cap-Français, attended at a baptism on October 15, 1805.

Paul Briant witnessed a wedding on July 5, 1804.

Isaac Boyé.[464]

Mr. Dufilho, a pharmacist, identified as a recent arrival from Saint-Domingue.[465]

Pierre-Jean-Nicolas-Louis-Arthur, son of Nicolas de Finiols, was born at New Orleans on August 20, 1803, and baptized on October 15, 1805.[466]

Michel-André Laîné, a native of Le Havre, married Maria del Pinar Hernandez.

Marianne Lemonnier, daughter of Yves, from Rennes, and

[459]*Ibid.*

[460]*Ibid.*

[461]*Ibid.*

[462]Carter, ed., *Territorial Papers,* IX, 699.

[463]*New Orleans in 1805.*

[464]*Ibid.*

[465]*Moniteur de la Louisiane,* June 25, 1803.

[466]King, *Creole Families,* p. 419.

Marie Saint-Martin, refugees of 1801, was baptized on October 2, 1802.

Marie-Claire de Rohan had a son in New Orleans in 1802, who was baptized on November 17, 1803.

Henri Verdereau, a native of La Rochelle, married Jeanne-Marguerite Chessé from New Orleans on July 30, 1805. The witnesses were Antoine-Augustin Raboteau, a colonist from Gonaïves, François Pichon, Jacques Rice Fitzgerald, and Armand Magnan.

Marianne Bertin, spouse of J-J. Pécon, was born at Saint-Domingue and attended a baptism on March 24, 1803.

* * *

All of these names, some of which we specifically sought out, others which came to our attention in the course of our research, show us that the great majority of the refugees who went to Louisiana [from the sugar islands] were from Saint-Domingue. Besides them, we notice people coming from Martinique, not very numerous undoubtedly, but important enough to mention. We did not record their names systematically. Nonetheless, here are some of them:

Pierre Humbert, a native of Martinique, son of Pierre and a mother whose name we have not been able to locate, died a bachelor at the age of twenty-six at Mr. Masicot's home in St. Charles Parish.[467]

Jeanne Taton, wife of Pierre Hardi de Boisblanc,[468] was grandmother to a Hardy child in 1793[469] and godmother to a Mérieux child on March 30, 1799. We are certain that we read Taton but Mr. Sidney Villeré assures us that the name was Catin. She was born at Fort-Royal.[470]

Jean-Baptiste Francis, a dancer and choreographer of ballets,

---

[467]Burial records, Saint Louis Cathedral.

[468]Born in Saint-Jean d'Angély.

[469]Baptismal records, Saint Louis Cathedral.

[470]Present-day Fort-de-France.

went from Bordeaux to Saint-Pierre. He was a lead dancer in 1788. He appeared in a show in Saint-Domingue in April of 1789; in Charleston in 1794; in New York in 1796; in Boston in 1797; and in Philadelphia in 1798. His name first appeared in New Orleans in September 1799, where he remained until 1808. He went there with his wife, whose name was not recorded.

Charles Tizonneaux, born at Fort Saint-Pierre, son of Jean-Baptiste from Cadillac in Gironde, and Françoise Tauche, a Creole from Martinique, was husband to Marie-Rose Larche in New Orleans, her place of nativity. He died at the age of sixty-one.[471]

J-B. Thibeaud, from Saint-Pierre, son of Jean and Elisabeth Labat, married Marie-Antoinette Charest de Lauzon, a Saint-Domingue Creole, at New Orleans on April 13, 1804. The couple went to Cuba before February 1, 1819, at which time Thibeaud died. His widow returned to New Orleans, where she died on March 2, 1827, at the age of thirty-five.[472]

Emmanuel-Marius-Pons Bringier, from Aubagne, son of Pierre and Agnès Arnoul, had married in France Marie-Françoise Durand, from Marseilles. They went to Martinique in 1780. Fifteen years later, they were living in New Orleans, but we do not know if they went there as refugees. Their daughters married refugees: Fanny, married Augustin-Dominique Tureaud in 1803; and Françoise married Christophe Colomb.[473] Bringier was named regimental adjutant in the militia.[474] Widowed, Mrs. Bringier married Marc-Antoine Ronderez, a former colonist from Dondon, on April 4, 1806.

* * *

By grouping these names that we have collected, it must be noted that we are seriously distorting reality. Until 1803, the

[471]Burial records, Saint Louis Cathedral, November 16, 1792.

[472]King, *Creole Families*, pp. 408-409.

[473]*Ibid.*, p. 417.

[474]Carter, ed., *Territorial Papers*, IX, 636.

refugees disembarked at New Orleans individually or in small, isolated family groups. It was only after that time [1803] that they travelled in large groups, almost by droves. As long it was an almost imperceptible infiltration, their problems did not cause the city's administration any concern. Until 1804, the *cabildo's* silence toward them was very significant. But when the Americans took possession of Louisiana, the refugees, who had begun to arrive in greater numbers, came to be seen as a problem, because they would have to be assimilated alongside the Louisiana Creoles.

Unfortunately, we have little more than the official documents with which to reconstruct this problem. The only individual correspondence in our possession recounting the voyage of these ill-fated refugees and the first arduous months of their life in a new land are the letters in the Stanislas Foäche and Bégouen Demeaux papers in the possession of Laurent Bégouen Demeaux of Paris.[475]

Pierre Collette's letters summarize the circumstances of his voyage. He was a coffee planter in the Jean-Rabel sector in northwestern Saint-Domingue, almost at the very end of the northern peninsula. With his mother, he owned three large plantations in the hills with a warehouse, a store, and a landing on the coast. In a remarkable article, Georges-A. Chevalier describes their creation.[476] Nearly 600 slaves worked on their coffee farms. In the worst years of the French Revolution, they did not suffer too much, as can be seen from the fact that the numbers of slaves declined only slightly—to about 500 in 1802. Collette's continued presence in the area until this date partially explains this stability.

He must have begun thinking about leaving Saint-Domingue as early as late 1802. Thus his departure could be carefully prepared. He confided most of his papers to his nephew who went to Baltimore where he remained a long time. He abandoned

---

[475]Its microfilm is in the Archives of the Seine-et-Marne.

[476]G.A. Chevalier, "Etude sur la colonisation française en Haïti. Origins et développement des propriétés Collette," *Revue d'histoire et de géographie d'Haïti* (October, 1938-April, 1939).

Cap-Français in October 1803, a few weeks before the surrender by General Rochambeau and the remnants of the Leclerc expedition (November 1803), taking with him treasury drafts, probably payment for coffee delivered to the state-owned store or requisitioned cattle. Family tradition also says that he had some diamonds sewn into his belt. About twenty slaves, almost all domestics, accompanied him.

His intention was to reach Porto-Plata, to the east, on the Spanish part of the island, in order to stay as close as possible to his homeland to keep an eye on events. The English blockade forced him to return to Cap-Français for a short time before setting out again. He had arrived at Baracoa by December [1803] and, in early 1804, he was in Santiago de Cuba, where he did not seem to be happy. He thought he would fare much better in New York. He ultimately decided to land at Louisiana in the summer of 1804. He was accompanied by his friend James Rice Fitzgerald, former cashier for the Banque de la Louisiane, his wife, Victoire, *née* Dessars, their daughter, and their retinue: Guinoterre Pincemaille, his black house-keeper, two children who must have been his, and eighteen domestics.[477]

His first days in New Orleans were trying, even though he was received as well as possible and lived with friends. The cost of living was much higher than in Saint-Domingue. He could not afford to reside in the city and rented a small house on the outskirts for 10 *gourdes* per month. He lived meagerly by renting his slaves and by his winnings from gambling.

Several of his slaves died, which reduced his income even further, and initiated his slide toward poverty. He began to accumulate debts:

P. Collette to Stanislas Foäche.
New Orleans, November 16, 1804.

My honorable friend, having left Cap-Français in time to avoid becoming a victim of the cannibalistic masters of Saint-Domingue, I have been taken against

---

[477] One of these children was a girl named Adèle, who died in 1832.

my will to Santiago de Cuba, not wishing to leave that island [Hispañola], if possible. The poor condition of the sailing vessel which I boarded did not permit it to remain under sail; it was necessary to turn back to Cuba.

My stay on this island [Cuba], which lasted nine months, convinced me that my apprehensions about going to the Spanish possessions were only too well founded; besides the inconvenience that they try to cause the French, the regime and the government put so many obstacles in one's way that one would have to be born Spanish to be able to tolerate them; add to that the most base and crass ignorance and superstition and you would be able to form your own idea of these people who are truly hideous.

The crops are the most pitiful things in the world; rumor has it that they are beautiful around Havana; that may be; but surely this beautiful colony lacks any important crop. The French are establishing coffee groves there. If ever Saint-Domingue reclaims its former glory, they [the Cubans] would not last long; all that I have seen on these lands and all of the information that I have gathered have demonstrated to me that the lands in general are significantly inferior to those of Saint-Domingue. The island is quite arid; there are no alluvial plains that produce the incomparable wealth of Saint-Domingue.

Cast upon Cuba with a few domestics as my only resource, not sure of being able to keep them for long because to the ease with which the Negroes can escape from their masters, no longer being able to rent them, life, as miserable as it was here, was still very expensive. Shanties command exorbitant rents because of the great number of refugees. All of this finally led me to cast my lot with other counties and [I began to] seek the one that would suit me the best. I believed that Louisiana was the one offering the greatest advantages to unfortunate colonists forced to flee their island. First of all, the same language is spoken there, [and] the remnants of our Negroes are worth a lot more money, for they command much higher rental fees. Ownership of them is more secure. Second, the same habits are to be found there. You are more or less known by Frenchmen, either personally or by reputation; there are more or less the same crops; and a climate that is not very different from ours. I was not mistaken. I found here what I was hoping to find, and my only regret was not having come sooner; I would not now find myself in a bind.

They hastened to show me the farms; everywhere I saw astounding vegetation; this country has remained in the undeveloped state the Spanish governor forces it to retain, but, despite the discontent many individuals will derive from being under American rule, it is certainly destined to become very considerable under that country's domination, unless it persists in banning the introduction of slaves. The latter have the special advantage of being the only ones who can successfully plant and cultivate sugarcane in this latitude, despite the fact that it grows beautifully here, it produces neither the quantity nor the quality [of sucrose] necessary to compete with the sugar colonies. There exists only the advantage of exporting it duty free to the United States, which always assures a good price, since the other sugar producers pay tariffs of three and a half *gourdes* per quintal.

I spoke to you about the vegetation; it is truly astounding. One would never believe that one can find five or six month old cane three, four or even five feet high, whereas at that age in Saint-Domingue it was only beginning to sprout; but, on the other hand, the land is promptly exhausted; after five or six years it no longer produces cane. When that happens, the farmers have the option of planting Otahity cane which works perfectly well and gives sugar which, without having the same grain as Creole cane, is nonetheless pretty and light. It is to be feared, and there is no doubt about it, that in a few years it will have the same fate as the Creole cane, for it has been proven that it exhausts the land even more quickly.

Manure is a sound remedy that has not been used, but in my opinion, the best means [of restoring the soil] would be to alternate cane and rice. Furthermore, in view of the fact that, during the overflows, they irrigate the fields with river water, leaving such a large quantity of loam that three, four, or five inches of new land are deposited, the land could thus be renewed annually. But this unfortunately would mean having to plant every year; a row must be dug and the cane planted so that they[478] would all be touching along the line. This crop is unquestionably unsuited to this climate, in which there are, at the most, only two months to grind the cane that grows in four or five months time and where it has to be protected from a hard freeze by a layer of straw. However, it is still lucrative enough to produce great profits, indeed fortunes, for the planters; cotton is [nevertheless] much more widespread and [economically] significant. Caterpillars are causing great damage this year and is a source of concern for the farmers.

The species which grows the best is our wild cotton,[479] but from which they derive no advantage because the seed is very sticky and which cannot pass through the rods [of the cotton gins]. The machine one uses here solves this problem. It is true that it cuts the cotton [fibers], but it does as much work as forty Negroes. With some precaution and seeds that are easier to handle, I think that the cotton would be less damaged. If ever I should return to Saint-Domingue, this is the machine I would use; I have never seen wild cotton eaten by caterpillars.

Rice is the crop best suited [to the Louisiana

---

[478]Annotator's note: The seed cane stalks.

[479]Annotator's note: Brown cotton.

environment] and at 5 *gourdes* per quintal, if it [the price]
should stay that high, it should become the primary crop.
It is the one that I would emphasize if I were forced to
forget Saint-Domingue and to establish myself here.

Oranges attain an incredible size, thanks to all the
vegetation here. I saw some enormous ones on my way
from Balise to New Orleans. Saint-Domingue oranges are
midgets by comparison. Some attempts have been made
to grow coffee, but without any success, mainly due to the
proximity of water.

This should be enough news about this land.

Nine days later, November 20, he wrote to Stanislas Foäche:

. . . the landowners scattered throughout the different
countries of America are too far away to derive any
advantages from Saint-Domingue. Whatever their
situation may be, they can only anticipate and await [the
arrival of] any army and the emperor's stated intention
of reestablishing the colonial regime. Those who are here
burn with the desire to return there and that is what
has prevented them from forming settlements that would
assure their tranquility and their [financial] well-being
if they had turned their backs on Saint-Domingue. It is
essential that they determine the government's intentions
regarding this grave matter.

Then Collette got older, continuing, in the words of Mr.
Foäche, to "Creolize," to gamble and to go deeper into debt."
One by one his slaves disappeared. He died at New Orleans on
November 24, 1818, at the age of seventy-eight.[480]

* * *

It is difficult to develop a broad overview [of the refugees] by

---

[480]G-A. Chevalier, "Un colon de Saint-Domingue pendant la Révolution: Pierre Collette,
planteur de Jean-Rabel," *Revue d'histoire et de géographie d'Haïti*, XXXIX (January,
1940-January, 1941).

working exclusively with a series of names that one cannot always identify. This is only a work by and for beginners, hardly more than an enumeration, an attempt at compiling a compendium [of names]. How many names of refugees must have escaped our attention that others would discover and be able to furnish more ample commentary and explanations!

But, first of all, how many colonists from Saint-Domingue actually arrived before 1809 in Louisiana, to which the refugees in Cuba were deported during the Spanish War? The disappearance of the registers recording the arrivals at New Orleans for that year prevent us from answering that question.

The official census of 1788 made by Governor Miró counted in Louisiana 19,445 whites, 1,701 free blacks, and 21,465 slaves, for a total of 42,611 people, 5,338 of whom lived in New Orleans. A hundred or so refugees seem to have arrived from Saint-Domingue between 1791 and 1797 and twice that many between 1797 and 1802. It is estimated that over a thousand were able to enter in 1803 and 1804, but we have no idea how many of those returned to France.

In 1809-1810, several thousands from Cuba disembarked. *Le Moniteur de la Louisiane* (January 27, 1810) speaks of 2,731 whites, 3,102 colored people, and 3,226 slaves, among whom there were 2,763 adult males, 3,410 females, and 3,226 slaves. This time, the proportion of colored people, women and children was much more important than with previous arrivals. These 9,059 new-comers more than doubled the Creole-speaking population [of Louisiana], but the massive arrival of Americans from the East Coast negated their impact.

Despite their rather small numbers, the refugees prior to 1809 played a large role in the organization of New Orleans' first theater and in the success of its first seasons. Since one of us[481] has already taken interest in this subject and has published the results of his research, it is not appropriate to repeat it here, no new findings being available.[482]

By the same token, we say nothing about the appearance and

---

[481]Annotator's note: René J. Legardeur, Jr.

[482]Le Gardeur, *The First New Orleans Theater*.

development of the sugar industry on South Louisiana, where one has assigned an important role to the Saint-Domingue refugees, skillful technicians in the growing of sugarcane and in the fabrication of sugar. Mr. Le Gardeur has dedicated himself to clarifying its complex origins, something the documents from that period do not do. When Mr. Le Gardeur died in 1973, he was completing a study of Louisiana's first sugar-mills, its first sugar refineries, and their problems. Despite its incomplete form, it was published.[483] It clearly shows that in this domain, the refugees' activities have been greatly exaggerated. They did not have the initiative they were once thought to have. All they did was to follow a movement that had been started in Louisiana before they began arriving in great numbers.

A study of the first twenty years of newspaper publishing in New Orleans would be an interesting chapter. On this point, there can be no possible discussion. The refugees took part in the founding of most of them. *Le Moniteur de la Louisiane*, which appeared in 1794, was edited J-B. Lesueur-Fontaine, a refugee. On October 14, 1804, J-B. Thierry, with his brother Jean, having recently arrived from Saint-Domingue, started *Le Courrier de la Louisiane*. On December 14, 1804, Claudin de Beleurgey, a refugee, printed *Le Télégraph* and the bilingual *Commercial Advertiser*. He went from Charleston where he had created *Le Patriote Français* ; and there were others.[484]

There should also be a chapter dedicated to the establishment of the schools the refugees maintained in Louisiana. Most of them were probably short-lived, for their primary objective was to make a living for the refugees who started them, and they were not always very competent [teachers].[485] Nonetheless, it is something that has never been attempted, and it would probably

[483] Center for Louisiana Studies, *Green Fields: A Catalog Complementing the Pictorial Exhibit Green Fields, Two Hundred Years of Louisiana Sugar* (Lafayette, LA., 1980), pp. 1-28.

[484] Tinker, *Bibliography*, pp. 47, 75.

[485] Stuart G. Noble and Arthur G. Nuhrah, "Education in Colonial Louisiana," *Louisiana Historical Quarterly*, XXXII (1949), 759.

develop along the lines concluded below by an anonymous Louisiana colonist not having any apparent ties to the refugees.

> Nobody knows better than you just how little education the Louisianians of my generation have received and how little opportunity one had twenty years ago to procure teachers. You are perhaps the only exception among the Creole ladies. I cannot conceive that someone like yourself, reared in New Orleans at a time much more difficult than now in terms of education, can possess so much knowledge. Louisiana today offers almost as many resources as any other state in the American Union for the education of its youth. The misfortunes of the French Revolution have cast upon this country so many talented men. This factor has also produced a considerable increase in the population and wealth. The evacuation of Saint-Domingue and lately that of the island of Cuba, coupled with the immigration of the people from the East Coast, have tripled in eight years the population of this rich colony, which has just been elevated to the status of statehood by virtue of a general governmental decree.[486]

And that is not all for it would be necessary to focus upon those Saint-Domingue Creoles who lived in New Orleans among the refugees and exchanged their ideas with [those of] the Louisiana Creoles. [One would also have to] address the history of the free men of color exiled to Louisiana. They were there in sufficiently large numbers to have left their mark on history. But, in these early days, it is difficult to identify them correctly, and their names do not always figure in the Saint Louis Parish records. Still another chapter in Louisiana's past left untouched.

Insofar as the refugees consciously chose to seek asylum in Louisiana, we can more or less accurately determine their motivation [for going there].

---

[486]Surirey Papers.

The refugees spoke of the similarities of language, religion, customs and climate as they imagined, expected or at least believed them to be between Louisiana and Saint-Domingue.

Laussat, having come as colonial prefect to take possession of Louisiana and having stayed eight months at New Orleans from 1803 to 1804,[487] noted in his *Mémoires* (p. 157) on a page written not long after his return to France before the arrival of the refugees to Cuba:

> I imagine that, of all our colonies, Saint-Domingue was the one from which that Louisiana has borrowed the most customs and ideas. Frequent relations existed between them. Even today when the Negroes, turned masters, chase us from Haiti, these refugees seek asylum here preferably. One finds many older people who have been taken in by relatives, friends, and who have in general only feeling of affection and goodness towards the blacks. There was also a small number of slaves who have followed their masters, reduced to a shadow of their former selves, into the resources of industry and work, in a word, into misery.

As Laussat well noted, they found the same colonial spirit, the same Creole spirit, the same way of dealing with the question of color. Here was where they felt least homesick. They were sheltered from the threat of a slave uprising. As in Cuba, the government resisted revolutionary ideas and the [activities of the] Friends of the Blacks, something [white] colonists never stopped fearing.

One must speak of the immensity of available lands in Saint-Domingue, of all of the land available for growing cotton which was starting to be developed on the island in the days preceding the Revolution. When, in 1793, one was already hoping for the retrocession of Louisiana to France, one was also expecting to see 600 colonists arriving from Saint-Domingue.[488] On February

[487]Laussat remained in New Orleans until April 21, 1804.

[488]State Department Archives, United States, political correspondence, volume 7, p. 21.

28, 1794, the Marquis de Rouvray advised those who wanted to expatriate themselves to request land grants in Louisiana.

The Saint-Domingue colonists knew that indigo was being phased out, but after 1795, optimism was pervasive for they must have gotten wind of the successful beginnings of the fabrication of sugar. Was not the cultivation of coffee also a possibility?

We are not led to believe that the transition from one colony to another was easy. Even in a land that presented social characteristics analogous to those in Saint-Domingue, this exile was a tremendous shock. For the most part, a new society was forming on the banks of the Mississippi. The change of status among the large Creole families who went to the continent is ample proof of this fact. As a rule of thumb, the large, rich families who played an important role in Saint-Domingue, are nowhere to be found in Louisiana. They no longer enjoyed the social status afforded by a large number of slaves or vast plantations. Most of them carried only the memory of past wealth. On the other hand, most of the refugees who left their mark on nineteenth-century Louisiana were drawn from families of low status in Saint-Domingue.

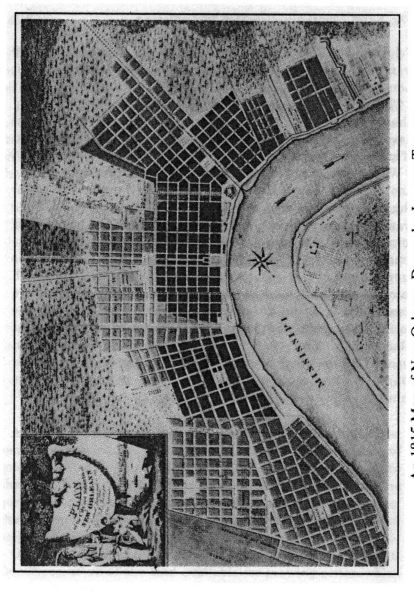

An 1815 Map of New Orleans, Drawn by Jacques Tanesse.

The 1809 Immigration of Saint-Domingue Refugees to New Orleans: Reception, Integration and Impact[1]

by Paul Lachance

Refugees often encounter a mixed reception in societies where they seek asylum. At one pole, the response is humanitarian. Refugees are by definition involuntary migrants. Fleeing political or religious persecution in their homeland, at risk of prison or death if forced to return, they are said to be entitled to special consideration, perhaps even to enjoy a "right of asylum." If necessary, exception should be made to laws governing immigration to facilitate their entry. The opposite pole of response is defensive. Only the number of refugees for whom there is a place should be admitted. Every precaution must be taken to distinguish bona fide from bogus refugees, and especially to exclude those who might present a danger, either as carriers of an alien ideology or because the size of the refugee movement would strain the institutions of the receiving society.[2]

When refugees form a large group arriving within a short span of time, the consequences of granting them asylum can become an issue of public controversy. Those who would limit their entry, if not exclude them entirely, foresee a negative impact in the absence of strict controls, while advocates of a humanitarian policy of unimpeded entry either downplay the potential impact of refugees or point to benefits for the host

[1] A Social Sciences and Humanities Research Council of Canada Leave Fellowship supported this study. This article originally appeared in *Louisiana History*, XXIX (1988), 109-141.

[2] As these lines are written (1988), the arrival in Nova Scotia of 174 East Indians claiming to be refugees is producing just such a mixed reaction in Canada.

society. In this article, I focus on the reception accorded 10,000 Saint-Domingue refugees who arrived in New Orleans by way of Cuba in 1809. At that time, the population of New Orleans was scarcely larger than the refugee movement itself. Reactions to it were typically mixed. Both proponents and opponents of a humanitarian policy anticipated the consequences of the refugees settling in Louisiana. These contemporary anticipations will be compared with the actual impact of the refugees, immediately and over the long run, as it can be established with the advantage of historical hindsight.

The itinerary of the refugees began in Saint-Domingue, the richest of the Caribbean sugar islands in the eighteenth century. Parallel to the revolution in France, a struggle for power between planters, *petits blancs,* free persons of color, and slaves took place in the colony from 1791 to 1804. Ultimately victorious, black insurgents formed the first independent nation of ex-slaves in the Americas, which they renamed Haiti.[3] Each phase of the Saint-Domingue, or Haitian, revolution led to the emigration of displaced colonials, sometimes accompanied by slaves. The largest movements were to the East Coast of the United States in 1793, Jamaica in 1798, and Cuba in 1803.[4]

Louisiana was, as a rule, a secondary destination of Saint-Domingue refugees. In the last decade of Spanish rule, several hundred made their way to New Orleans from Philadelphia, Baltimore, and other Atlantic seaports. Nearly a thousand arrived from Jamaica at the time of the Louisiana Purchase.[5] Then, in 1809, the expulsion from Cuba of French colonials who

[3]The Haitian Revolution is recounted in the classic histories of T. Lothrop Stoddard, *The French Revolution in San Domingo* (Boston and New York, 1914); and of C. L. R. James, *The Black Jacobins: Toussaint L'Ouverture and the San Domingo Revolution,* 2nd ed. (New York, 1963).

[4]An overall view of refugee movements resulting from the revolution is John Baur, "International Repercussions of the Haitian Revolution," *Americas,* XXVI (1970), 394-418.

[5]Gabriel Debien and René LeGardeur, "Les colons de Saint-Domingue réfugiés à la Louisiane (1792-1804)," *Revue de Louisiane/Louisiana Review,* X (1981), 119, 132. Debien and LeGardeur estimate 100 arrivals between 1791 and 1797, 200 between 1797 and 1802, and over1,000 in 1803-1804, adding that it is impossible to determine how many of these settled permanently in New Orleans.

had originally sought asylum there generated the last and largest wave of refugees to reach New Orleans.[6] The mayor of New Orleans counted 9,059 arrivals between May, 1809, and January, 1810.[7] Almost all were from Santiago de Cuba and Baracoa. Only one boat transporting refugees to New Orleans left from Havana.[8] Additional arrivals in the first months of 1810 brought the total number of refugees in this migration to more than 10,000.[9]

The three castes of the former colonial society in Saint-Domingue—whites, free persons of color, and slaves—were about equally represented in the refugee movement of 1809.

TABLE I

Age and Sex of Saint-Domingue Refugees
Immigrating from Cuba to New Orleans
in 1809, by Racial Caste

	Men 15+	Women 15+	Children	Total
Whites	1,373	703	655	2,731
FPC	428	1,377	1,297	3,102
Slaves	962	1,330	934	3,226
Total	2,763	3,410	2,886	9,059

Source: Mayor's Report, January 18, 1810, published in the *Moniteur*, January 27, 1810.

[6]The following historians have discussed the 1809 migration in some detail: Charles Gayarré, *History of Louisiana*, 4 vols. (1885; reprint ed., New Orleans, 1972), IV, 204ff; George Washington Cable, "Historical Sketch [of New Orleans]," in George Waring, Jr., *Report on the Social Statistics of Cities*, Part II, *The Southern and the Western States* (Washington, 1887), pp. 243-244; and Luiz Perez, "French Refugees to New Orleans in 1809," *Publications of the Southern History Association*, IX (1905), 293-310.

[7]Rapport du maire de la Nouvelle-Orléans au Gouverneur Claiborne, le 18 janvier 1810, published in the *Moniteur de la Louisiane* (hereafter *Moniteur*), January 27, 1810.

[8]See the "Extract from the Lists of Passengers Reported at the Mayor's Office by the Captains of Vessels Who Have Come to This Port from the Island of Cuba," July 18, August 7, 1809, in Dunbar Rowland, ed., *Official Letter Books of W. C. C. Claiborne, 1801-1816*, 6 vols. (Jackson, Miss., 1917), IV, 381-382, 409; hereafter cited as *Letter Books*.

[9]*Moniteur*, January 27, 1810, referring to Cuban refugees detained in Jamaica before continuing on to Louisiana.

The sex ratios among adults of the three groups were imbalanced, with a preponderance of males among white refugees and of females among non-whites, free or slave. Children made up a larger proportion of free persons of color (42 percent) than of slaves (29 percent) or whites (24 percent).

The number of refugees was large relative to the population of Orleans Parish in the first decade of the nineteenth century.

TABLE II
*Refugee Movement of 1809 Compared to the Population
of Orleans Parish in 1806 and 1810,
by Racial Caste*

	Whites	FPC	Slaves	Total
Orleans Parish, 1806	6,311	2,312	8,378	17,001
Refugees, 1809	2,731	3,102	3,226	9,059
Orleans Parish, 1810	8,001	5,727	10,824	24,552

Sources: Mayor's Report, January 18, 1810, published in the *Moniteur*, January 27, 1810; "Recensement général du Territoire d'Orléans au 1er de janvier 1807," item 1 in Joseph Dubreuil de Villars Papers, William R. Perkins Library, Duke University; Population Schedule for the Territory of Orleans of the Third Census of the United States, 1810, f. 468-470.

More refugees were counted by the mayor in 1809 than the total increase of white and slave populations in Orleans Parish from 1806 to 1810, and they represented 90 percent of the increase in free persons of color. Measured against the urban population of the parish, 10,000 to 12,000 in 1806, 17,242 in 1810, the migration appears even larger. Its immediate effect was to double the population of New Orleans proper.

News of the events leading to the expulsion of the refugees from Cuba reached Louisiana in April. Cubans refused to accept Napoleon's substitution of his older brother Joseph for Ferdinand VII as king of Spain. On March 12, 1809, the Marqués de Someruelos, captain-general of Cuba, issued a proclamation calling for vigilance committees in every town and parish to investigate the conduct and opinions of Frenchmen in Cuba and to expel those whose presence might prove dangerous.[10]   The first boatload of refugees from Cuba arrived at Fort Plaquemines by May 12.[11]   On May 17, the mayor of New Orleans, James Mather, acting on rumors of the imminent arrival of up to 6,000 white refugees, called on the municipal council to provide measures of temporary relief, including removal of the fish market to a vacant lot and use of its five storerooms as accommodation for refugee families, collection of blankets for the destitute, and formation of a welfare committee to procure pecuniary aid and work for refugees.[12]   The council passed a resolution to this effect at its meeting of May 24.[13]   By August, the welfare committee had collected and distributed $5,000 in aid and was calling for a second subscription for needy refugees who continued to arrive in the city.[14]   By way of comparison, residents of New Orleans paid $7,650 in taxes on real estate and slaves in the fiscal year beginning May 1, 1809.[15]

In addition to the local government, the principal French-language newspapers, the *Moniteur* and the *Courrier,* served as conduits of aid to the refugees.   They printed letters and editorials evoking sympathy for the refugees by picturing them as "victims of the horrors of war . . . . unfortunate planters, whose conduct [in Cuba] was an example of industry, of equanimity in adversity, and of submission to the laws of the country where they had found an asylum."[16]   On the practical

---

[10]See the *Moniteur,* April 12, 1809, for the proclamation. News of the application of the decrees of expulsion appeared in the *Moniteur* on May 10, 13, and 17, 1809. It probably arrived on the same boats carrying the first refugees.

[11]Claiborne to Lieutenant Walsh, May 12, 1809, in *Letter Books,* IV, 351.

[12]James Mather to the Municipal Council, May 17, 1809, Mayor's Messages to the City Council, City Archives, New Orleans Public Library, III (January 11, 1803-December 13, 1809), pp. 132-133.

[13]Proceedings of Council Meetings, City Archives, New Orleans Public Library, May 24, 1809, II, 65.

[14]*Moniteur,* August 23, 1809.

[15]*Ibid.,* August 22, 1810, "Etat sommaire des recettes et dépenses de la Paroisse d'Orléans, exercice de 1809 (May 1, 1809, to August 30, 1810)." The tax rate was $1 for every $1,000 in property.

[16]*Le Courrier de la Louisiane* (hereafter cited as *Courrier*), May 24, 1809.

side, editors allowed refugees in search of employment to advertise
their talents free of charge and printed propositions addressed
by Louisianians to the refugees, such as offers to employ them
or their slaves, to exchange property in Louisiana for property
abandoned in Cuba, to let them farm land not currently under
cultivation, or to sell them real estate in the city on generous
terms.[17]   The newspapers also announced events organized in
the refugees' behalf, like the special performance at the Théâtre
St. Pierre for an "ill-fated" family.[18]

These initiatives were intended for white refugees. Some
were truly dependent on the generosity of residents of New
Orleans. The mayor called attention to the presence

> among the white Refugees [of] many poor women both
> old and young, and some old or disabled men who can
> not provide for themselves, and will remain a burthen on
> the Community so long as there will be no alms house at
> New Orleans, and our charity Hospital shall remain in
> its present unimproved state.[19]

Free persons of color aided refugees of their caste. On June 17,
the mayor signed an appeal calling on them to contribute to a
fund to "save from poverty certain persons of their own class," in
particular, "several women of color, recently arrived from Cuba,
and burdened with children of a young age." Two free men of
color, Charlot Brulé and Batiste Hardi, assumed responsibility
for this collection.[20]

---

[17]See the *Courrier*, June 5, 1809, and the *Moniteur*, June 10, 1809, for offers to allow
refugees to advertise for employment without charge; the *Courrier*, June 12, 1809, for an
offer to employ a refugee as a cook for a family and to make and sell pastry on his own
account; the real estate advertisements of A. Bonamy in the *Courrier*, June 1, 5, 1809;
and offers of farms or land to farm, particularly in outlying Opelousas and Natchitoches
parishes, in the *Moniteur*, June 14, 1809, and the *Courrier*, July 24, 1809.

[18]*Moniteur*, June 14, 1809.

[19]Mather to Claiborne, August 7, 1809, *Letter Books*, IV, 405.

[20]*Moniteur*, June 24, 1809.

Finally, residents of New Orleans put pressure on William Claiborne, the federally appointed governor of the Territory of Orleans, to allow slaves accompanying the refugees to disembark. In 1808, the federal law prohibiting entry of foreign slaves into the United States had gone into effect. Accordingly, Claiborne at first ordered that slaves accompanying the refugees be detained on the ships transporting them and that the ships be impounded.[21] This not only deprived slave-owning refugees of an important means of support; it also had the consequence that they were forced to leave furniture, small parcels of merchandise, and packets of sugar and coffee on board the impounded ships.[22] As early as May 15, Claiborne forwarded to Washington a petition in which citizens of New Orleans asked the federal government not to apply the law of 1808 to the slaves brought in by refugees from Cuba.[23]

Aid to the refugees was justified on humanitarian grounds. The mayor appealed to the population's "inclination for charity" in asking it to provide for the "relief of suffering humanity."[24] The preamble to the resolution of the welfare committee read:

> Considering that a great number of persons who have been forced to leave the isle of Cuba, came to seek shelter among us; and considering that the majority of these persons arrives in an absolute want of objects of prime necessity, and are unable to procure them if they are not helped. . . .[25]

[21]Claiborne to Walsh, May 12, 1809, in *Letter Books,* IV, 351. See also pages 364, 392.

[22]Claiborne to Poydras, June 4, 1809, in National Archives, Washington, D. C., House File: Territory of Orleans, 11A-F2.2, June 6, 1809, R.G. 233, Records of the U. S. House of Representatives, 11th Congress, 1st session.

[23]*Letter Books,* IV, 354.

[24]Mayor's Messages, May 24, 1809.

[25]Council Proceedings, May 24, 1809. See also the appeal for contributions to the Société de Bienfaisance in the *Moniteur,* June 17, 1809.

Even the demand to let the slaves disembark was couched in humanitarian terms: "Undoubtedly the laws of the country forbid the introduction of slaves, but the divine law, the laws of humanity make it our duty not to repell those wretches from our shores."[26]

In general, the Gallic community, composed of native Louisianians, immigrants from France, Belgium, Savoy, and French cantons in Switzerland, Saint-Domingue refugees already present in the city, and other immigrants whose second language was French, responded sympathetically to the refugees. Governor Claiborne reported to the secretary of state in Washington, "The foreign Frenchmen residing among us take great interest in favour of their countrymen, and the sympathies of the Creoles of the Country (the descendants of the French) seem also to be much excited."[27] However, the reception by other elements of the population was less friendly. Claiborne added, "The native Americans, and the English part of our society . . . (with some few exceptions) appear to be prejudiced against these strangers, and express great dissatisfaction that an Asylum in this territory was afforded them."[28] A week later, he again mentioned that "many good Americans are dissatisfied with so great an influx of foreigners," but the "most clamorous" were residents "whose hearts are either wholly English or wholly Spanish."[29] The shadow of Napoleon followed the refugees to New Orleans. There, too, they became the target of the animosity towards Napoleonic France of partisans of England and Ferdinand VII.

American hostility to Saint-Domingue refugees antedated 1809. Some Americans identified the refugees with the very revolution they sought to escape. James Brown described the town guard created by the municipal council in 1805 as "a

---

[26]*Courrier*, May 24, 1809.

[27]Claiborne to Smith, July 29, 1809, in *Letter Books*, IV, 392.

[28]*Ibid.*

[29]Claiborne to Smith, August 5, 1809, in *ibid.*, IV, 400.

French Maréchaussée of St. Domingo cut-throats" who frequented taverns and drank with free Negroes or slaves.[30] In a polemic against the Civil Code, Jeremiah Brown held the "swarm of refugee lawyers from the bloodletting on S. Domingo" responsible for "nearly all the rancor manifested . . . against the common law." He singled out Louis Moreau-Lislet as "the St. Domingo Lycurgus" who was attempting to impose the Napoleonic Code on the Territory.[31]

Attacks on American shipping by French privateers in the Caribbean fanned American opposition to the refugees. In the summer that the refugees arrived, two privateers, Antoine Bouchet and Jean-Marie Arbeau, were put on trial in New Orleans. They were defended by none other than Moreau-Lislet and acquitted.[32] According to one account of the proceedings, Daniel Clark, a member of the grand jury, swore to have the privateers hanged to avenge the hospitality of the American government to the emigrants from Cuba.[33] There was a basis in fact to the association of refugees with privateering. Until the expulsion of the French, Santiago de Cuba and Baracoa had been important bases of French privateers. Dominique You commanded privateers operating out of Cuba before joining the Baratarians;[34] and the records of the French *agences de prises* in Cuba show that other refugees, like Henri de Ste. Gême, had invested heavily in privateering expeditions.[35]

[30]James Brown to John Breckinridge, September 17, 1805, in Clarence Carter, ed., *The Territorial Papers of the United States*, 28 vols. (Washington, D. C., 1934-1975), IX, 510.

[31]Jeremiah Brown, *A Short Letter to a Member of Congress Concerning the Territory of Orleans* (Washington, D. C., 1806), p. 21, cited in George Dargo, *Jefferson's Louisiana: Politics and the Clash of Legal Traditions* (Cambridge, Mass., 1975), pp. 151-152.

[32]Claiborne to Smith, July 29, 1809, in *Letter Books*, IV, 391-392, and enclosures, 393-399.

[33]*Courrier*, July 24, 1809.

[34]French privateers sailing out of Cuba operated, like the Baratarians, under Guadeloupe commissions. Stanley Faye, "Privateers of Guadeloupe and Their Establishment in Barataria," *Louisiana Historical Quarterly*, XXIII (1940), 431-433.

[35]Archives Nationales, Paris, France, Archives des Colonies, Série AC, Correspondance à l'extérieur, 1807, Ferrand to Ste. Gême, February 10, 1807.

A diatribe against the refugees from Cuba written by "An American" and printed by the *New Orleans Gazette,* an English-language newspaper, painted a lurid picture of barbarous acts of piracy by Santiago privateers against American commerce.[36] In addition, it accused Saint-Domingue refugees of setting up gambling houses in New Orleans and of forging death certificates to recover bonds they had posted for the release of their slaves. Since the American consul in Cuba had informed the refugees of the law prohibiting the introduction of slaves from abroad into the United States, the refugees should expect no special treatment on this account. The existing legislation should be strictly enforced.

In the context of chronic tension between English-speakers and French-speakers in New Orleans since the Louisiana Purchase, the apparent reinforcement of the Gallic population by the refugees was a major factor in the negative reaction of Anglo-Americans. From the start, the latter had counted on immigration to make English-speakers a majority of the population.[37] For those who entertained such hopes for the rapid Americanization of Louisiana, the influx of refugees in 1809 seemed a major setback. It more than cancelled out previous gains in the American population.

Several Americans articulated their deception. W. B. Robertson, the governor's secretary, felt the refugees would "rivet upon us a decided and irresistible preponderance of French influence, and thus prevent us, for many years to come, from considering this [Louisiana] in heart and sentiment as an American country."[38] James Brown lamented, "we are at this

[36]A "Frenchman" responded to these accusations in the *Courrier,* July 12, 1809. I have been unable to locate the issue of the *Gazette* in which the original attack on the refugees was printed.

[37]As one American said in 1804, "If the increase of American population should continue for three years to come to equal what it has been for the last nine months they must inevitably constitute the majority." John Gurley to Gideon Granger, July 14, 1804, Jefferson Papers, Library of Congress, cited in Dargo, *Jefferson's Louisiana,* p. 10.

[38]Robertson to the Secretary of State (Robert Smith), May 24, 1809, in *Territorial Papers,* IX, 841.

moment a French province." He commented on how the refugee movement of 1809 offset American immigration since the Louisiana Purchase:

> Our American population since the Cession has perhaps increased about 2,000 whilst we are indebted to the last 12 months alone for the introduction of from 10 to 15000 French. The refugees from all the Islands who had sheltered themselves in the different American States or French colonies, have collected in this City & Territory where they find their own manners, laws, and I may add government.

Like many Americans, Brown looked on the refugees as the "forces of Bonaparte."[39]

Equivalent declarations from the Gallic community of how it stood to gain from the refugee movement are not to be found. Instead of envisaging the consequences of the migration in ethnic terms, friends of the refugees called attention to the 500 plantations they had established in Cuba and their potential to contribute similarly to the economic development of Louisiana. As one apologist for the refugees pointed out, there was enough land in Louisiana for 100,000 families to cultivate.[40] Another compared the expulsion from Cuba to the revocation of the Edict of Nantes, as a result of which Huguenot refugees transplanted French arts and manufactures to the North of Europe.[41]

---

[39]James Brown to Henry Clay, February 26, 1810, in James Podgett, ed., "Letters of James Brown to Henry Clay, 1804-1835," *Louisiana Historical Quarterly,* XXIV (1941), 931-932.

[40]*Courrier,* May 22, 1809.

[41]*Ibid.,* May 24, 1809. In the same vein, the appeal for aid to the refugees from the mayor of New Orleans described them as arriving "with their capital and their industries, which will develop the arts and agriculture in this Country." Not without a measure of contradiction as to the condition of the refugees on arrival, he argued: "Considering that the relief of suffering humanity is not the only motive which must cause you to act; and if, on the one hand the misfortunes of a large population related to us by common origin, are of a nature to arouse in us strong feelings, there are some political reasons suggesting that you should not leave to the horrors of need, a multitude of persons whom you may render useful to their country." Mayor's Messages, May 17, 24, 1809.

Considerations of utility were also a reason given for making an exception to the law prohibiting entry of foreign slaves. To admit the refugees without their slaves was to "deprive them of the means of procuring subsistence, and they may become a burthen to the country, to which, if admitted with their slaves, they would be useful."[42]

Governor Claiborne oscillated between the negative and positive poles of response to the Saint-Domingue refugees. When corresponding with Anglo-Americans, he appears to be partial to their point of view:

> I regret the cause which has thrown upon our Shores so great a number of foreigners—I would much rather, that the Space in this society, which these emigrants will fill, had been preserved for the native Citizens of the United States.[43]

On the other hand, in a letter to Julien Poydras, a wealthy French planter serving as delegate of the Territory of Orleans to Congress, humanitarian considerations seem foremost. Concerning his initial decision to detain slaves accompanying the refugees, he explained to Poydras:

> I should myself be well pleased if Congress would relax the Law forbidding the importation of slaves as related to these *miserable* exiles.—I witness *their* distress, and would most readily alleviate it, if in my powers.[44]

Eventually, even before officially authorized to do so, he gave in to pressures to allow the slaves to land.[45]

[42]*Courrier*, May 22, 1809.

[43]Claiborne to John Graham, July 19, 1809, in *Letter Books*, IV, 390.

[44]Claiborne to Poydras, June 4, 1809, in House File (see above, note 22).

[45]Claiborne to Graham, July 19, 1809, in *Letter Books*, IV, 390-391. He justified his initiative in the following manner: "To have them sent out of the Territory, would have been attended with an expense which I had not the means of meeting nor was it easy to select a proper place; To have confined them in Prison, would have been an inhuman act, it would moreover have been attended with an expense which I was neither authorized or prepared to incur; to have deprived the owners of the present use of the negro's [*sic*]

The House of Representatives debated on June 28, 1809, a bill for the remission of fines and penalties related to slaves belonging to the refugees from Cuba. Thomas Newton argued in favor of passage on humanitarian grounds: "Let us say to these unfortunates, as Dido to Aeneas, when he was exiled from Troy: 'I have suffered misfortune myself, and therefore know how to extend the hand of relief to others.'" Representatives Nathaniel Macon of North Carolina and John Montgomery of Maryland supported it on the hard-nosed grounds that only by authorizing entry of the slaves could their departure from Louisiana with their masters be effected, the slaves being the main resource of the refugees. The bill passed unanimously.[46]

The text of the law was printed in a special broadside of the *Moniteur* on July 30, along with a French translation of a letter to the bill's sponsor from Edward Livingston, one Anglo-American in New Orleans who did not share the hostility of his compatriots to the Gallic community. Claiborne scrawled at the bottom of a copy of the broadside he sent to Washington: "In this way it is, that this man [Livingston] feeds his popularity—he and his partisans here wish to make it believed to the French that to the influence of this Letter alone may be attributed the passage of the Law."[47] One detects another reason Claiborne let the refugees' slaves land pending the decision by Congress. Increasingly vexed by the opposition of many Americans in New Orleans to his government, he was bidding for support in the Creole population. For letting the slaves disembark, he was

---

would have been to have thrown them [the owners] as Paupers upon this Community, who are already sufficiently burthened with contributions for the poor, the sick and the aged Emigrants."

[46]"House debate on emigrants from Cuba," June 28, 1809. The debate is digested in Gales and Seaton, *Annals of Congress,* 11th Congress, p. 463.

[47]*Moniteur,* extra, July 30, 1809, with Claiborne's annotation, in National Archives, Washington, D. C., State Territorial Papers, Orleans Series, T-260, No. 10, R.G. 59.

denounced by xenophobic Americans "as a Frenchman." Now, he risked losing to another political rival the credit he had hoped to obtain in the Gallic community for his action on the slave issue.

The refugees arrived at a time when United States officials lacked confidence in the willingness of the cosmopolitan and faction-ridden population of New Orleans to defend Louisiana in the event of attack by a foreign power. The territorial governor and his subordinates were worried by the presence in the city of partisans of Napoleon, England and Spain, not to mention the Burrites.[48] Linguistic differences were an obstacle to organization of an effective militia.[49] The influx of Saint-Domingue refugees compounded these problems. In 1814, only months before the Battle of New Orleans, Claiborne still complained of

> the invincible repugnance of the Creole and French population to be enlisted in the service of the United States under officers not of their own choosing, and their apprehension of being sent out of the State, for which alone they were disposed at that time to shed their blood.[50]

In addition, as the slave revolt of 1811 was to confirm, there were reasons to fear for the internal security of the territory. Claiborne confided in January, 1810,

> [W]ith a population so mixed, and becoming more so every day by the press of emigration from Cuba and elsewhere, I must confess I am not without apprehensions that disorders and disturbances may

---

[48]Claiborne to Smith, January 1, 1809, cited in Gayarré, *History of Louisiana*, IV, 204-205.

[49]Henry Hopkins to Claiborne, October 28, 1809, *Territorial Papers*, IX, 854-857. "Walk the streets of the city. There is not one where you will not meet at the same moment Americans, Louisianians, Frenchmen, Spaniards, Germans, Italians, etc. There is not a language in which orders would be understood by everyone in the company."

[50]Cited in Gayarré, *History of Louisiana*, IV, 226-227.

arise. The free men of color, in and near New Orleans, including those recently arrived from Cuba, capable of bearing arms, cannot be less than 800. Their conduct has hitherto been correct. But in a country like this, where the negro [*sic*] population is so considerable, they should be carefully watched.[51]

Such considerations help to explain why the governor continued to try to dissuade refugees from coming to New Orleans. In August, 1809, he asked the American consul in Santiago to direct the French who had not yet departed from Cuba to seek an asylum elsewhere in the United States.[52] In November he made the same request of the American commercial agent in Jamaica. Claiborne was particularly insistent that free people of color be discouraged from immigrating to the Territory of Orleans: "We have at this time a much greater proportion of that kind of population than comports with our interests."[53]

Whether on the part of the government or of private citizens, whether humanitarian or defensive, contemporaries reacted especially to the size of the 1809 migration. In fact, the impact of the refugees was less a function of their number on arrival than of how many stayed in New Orleans and the place they took in its social structure. Evidence of persistence of the refugees must be examined to judge whether their actual impact was as great as contemporaries predicted at the moment of arrival.

At first, many refugees lacked the means to leave New Orleans. As the mayor observed in a report to the governor at the beginning of August, 1809, the "Refugees have been till now necessarily detained in Town on account of their slaves; And the longer they will be compelled to stay in Town, the less they will feel disposed to settle in the more distant parts of this

[51]*Ibid.*

[52]Claiborne to Maurice Rogers, American consul at Santiago de Cuba, August 9, 1809, in *Letter Books*, IV, 401-402.

[53]Claiborne to William Savage, commercial agent of the United States for Jamaica, November 10, 1809, and to Vincent Gray, American consul at Havana, August 9, 1809, in *ibid.*, V, 3-6.

Territory."[54] The special act of Congress remitting the penalties incurred for the introduction of slaves from Cuba removed this obstacle to emigration; but far from having the intended effect of facilitating the departure of the refugees with their slaves, the law made it easier for them to integrate themselves into New Orleans society.

A first indication that many refugees chose to settle in New Orleans is their failure to take advantage of efforts undertaken to facilitate their departure. In addition to allowing an exception to the 1808 law prohibiting importation of foreign slaves, Congress also made an exception to the Non-Intercourse Act in the interest of the refugees. Notwithstanding the ban on trade with France then in effect, it authorized the president to make arrangements with the minister plenipotentiary of France to transport the refugees to France or a French colony.[55] In September, a 278-ton ship, the *Cérès,* was dispatched from Philadelphia to New Orleans for this purpose. On November 13, 1809, Genestet Faisandieu placed an advertisement in the *Moniteur* that the *Cérès* had arrived in New Orleans and would depart *en parlementaire* for Bordeaux in 45 days. He advised those who wished to take advantage of the opportunity to arrange for passage on a first-come, first-served basis. In January, 1810, the ship was still in port. On February 10, and 24, a last advertisement announced definite departure on the twentieth, with space still available.[56] The difficulty in filling even one ship suggests that most refugees were in no hurry to sail for France.[57]

Early in 1810, the legislature of the Territory of Orleans

[54]Mather to Claiborne, August 7, 1809, in *ibid.,* IV, 406.

[55]Section II of the "Act for the remission of certain penalties and forfeitures, and for other purposes," approved June 28, 1809, *Annals,* 11th Congress, appendix, 2508.

[56]*Moniteur,* November 15, 1809, January 10, February 10, 24, 1810.

[57]As late as 1819, the French navy sent a ship to transport 40 impecunious refugees in different states back to France. Baron Portaly (minister of Marine and Colonies) to Hyde de Neuville (ambassador to the United States), Paris, March 10, 1819, Archives du Ministère des Affaires Etrangères, Paris, France, Correspondance politique: Etats Unis, No. 34 (1815-1820).

passed an act returning to the refugees the bonds they had posted for their slaves and allowing them to dispose of the slaves on the same terms as legally imported slaves.[58] The slaves were an important resource. On May 31, 1810, for example, the refugee Yves LeMonnier sold Jean-Baptiste, a 20-year-old slave he had inherited ten years before in Saint-Domingue, to Théodore Macarty for $600.[59] That was enough money to procure passage out of New Orleans, but it was also more than enough to buy a lot in the new suburbs developing on land formerly occupied by the plantations of François Livaudais or Bernard Marigny. Even a penniless refugee could buy a lot in the Faubourg *La Course* from Livaudais for $200 to $800, no money down, the first payment due in a year, and up to five years to pay at an interest rate of 6 percent per annum.[60]

The dispatches of the French consul in New Orleans from the years corresponding to the War of 1812 often mention the refugees. In October, 1812, he divided the "large number of Frenchmen" resident in his jurisdiction into four categories: planters and merchants who retained French citizenship after the Louisiana Purchase, the French from the first direct emigration from Saint-Domingue, those expelled from Cuba, and Frenchmen who came directly from France, but were unable to return to France for one reason or another. The second and third categories, he added, were a "special case." They "await here the circumstances that will permit them to return to Saint-Domingue."[61] If this allusion bespeaks a lingering hope that asylum

---

[58]Acte concernant les esclaves importés dans ce Territoire contre les dispositions de l'acte du Congrès du deux mars 1807, et pour d'autres objets," approved March 16, 1810, and printed in the *Moniteur*, March 21, 1810.

[59]Notarial acts, S. de Quiñones, No. 11, pp. 363-364.

[60]In addition, for two years, the purchaser had the right to use wood from the cypress swamps for construction and firewood and to put two animals to pasture for each lot purchased. Advertisement in *Courrier*, June 21, 1809; for similar terms from Marigny, see his advertisement in the *Moniteur*, March 21, 1810.

[61]Louis Tousard to Sérurier (ministre plénipotentiaire of France in the United States), October 6, 1812, Archives du Ministère Etrangères, Correspondance politique: Etats-Unis (supplément), No. 33 (1809-1814), f. 161; hereafter cited as AE, Etats-Unis (supplément).

in Louisiana would prove temporary, it soon became evident to
some refugees it was likely to be permanent. The necrology in
the *Moniteur* for Louis Duffourg, who died in January, 1813,
described him as a "Saint-Domingue Creole, forced out of his
native land like so many others, who searched and found a new
homeland [*patrie*] in the hospitable regions of America."[62]

The removal of legal barriers to the entry of Saint-Domingue
slaves presumably led to the absorption of some into the slave
population of New Orleans, especially artisans, domestics and
their children. Among 96 natives of Saint-Domingue whose
names were registered in 1841 on the mayor's list of free
persons of color entitled to remain in Louisiana, 71 were former
slaves manumitted in New Orleans.[63] However, other slaves
belonging to Saint-Domingue refugees quickly made their way
to the countryside, judging from advertisements addressed
to the refugees from Cuba to hire teams of slaves for work on
plantations outside the city.[64]

Unlike slaves, free men of color above the age of fifteen were
never officially exempted from legislation forbidding them to
settle in the Territory of Orleans.[65] Governor Claiborne wanted
this law enforced. On August 4, 1809, he asked the mayor of
New Orleans, "Have you been enabled to execute the Law of
the Territory as relates to the freemen of Colour?—Are they
retiring from the Territory, and to what place, do they seem to
give a preference?"[66] Mather replied that to date 64 free men of
color above 15 had given security for their departure from the

[62]*Moniteur*, January 16, 1813.

[63]Register of Free Colored Persons Entitled to Remain in the State, Mayor's Office, I
(1840-1857), New Orleans Public Library, City Archives.

[64]*Courrier*, July 21, 26, 1809.

[65]The territorial legislature forbade by an act adopted on June 7, 1806, the entry of free
men of color fifteen years old and above from Hispañola and the other French islands.
An act of April 14, 1807, extended the prohibition to all free persons of color regardless
of origin. See Donald Everett, "Emigrés and Militiamen: Free Persons of Color in New
Orleans, 1803-1815," *Journal of Negro History*, XXXVIII (1953), 384-385.

[66]Claiborne to Mather, August 4, 1809, in *Letter Books*, IV, 404.

Territory, as required by law. Others who had been granted a delay to produce proof of freedom or procure securities had not returned and could not be found. He knew "but of few men of color who had left this place."[67] In January, 1810, the mayor complained that the law did not give him sufficient authority to obtain evidence leading to expulsion of free men of color; but he also pointed out their good behavior. No person of color had been arrested or brought before the courts.[68] In other words, the legislation seems to have served as a means of control over free men of color rather than to force their immediate emigration.[69]

The French consul noted the presence in November, 1813, of at least 500 free men of color from Saint-Domingue. That was the number of mulattoes that Lieutenant Colonel Savary, an officer from the former French garrison of Santo Domingo, himself a mulatto, promised to put under the command of the renegade republican French general, Humbert, who had just arrived in the city.[70] This plan came to naught; but a year later, they joined a second battalion of free men of color officially authorized by the Louisiana legislature. It was placed under the command of Major Daquin, a white refugee, with Savary holding the rank of captain.[71]

Thirteen years after the influx of 1809, the "Notes on New Orleans" in Paxton's city directory referred to the refugees as the single most important factor in the increase of the population of the city since the Louisiana Purchase: "The population was much increased by the unfortunate French emigrants from St. Domingo, and afterwards in 1809, by those who were compelled to flee from the island of Cuba, to the number of about 10,000."[72]

[67]Mather to Claiborne, August 7, 1809, in *ibid.*, IV, 407.

[68]Mather to Claiborne, January 18, 1810, printed in *Moniteur*, January 27, 1810.

[69]The skewed sex ratio of adult free refugees of color may also reflect some age falsification to circumvent the discriminatory legislation.

[70]Tousard to Sérurier, November 8, 1813, AE, Etats-Unis, supplément, No. 33 (1809-1814), f. 223.

[71]Roland C. McConnell, *Negro Troops of Antebellum Louisiana: A History of the Battalion of Free Men of Color* (Baton Rouge, 1968), pp. 67-71.

[72]John Adems Paxton, comp., *The New Orleans Directory and Register* (New Orleans,

By 1837, memories had dimmed. The directory of that year inaccurately reported both the date of the influx from Cuba as 1807 and its size at "several thousand" refugees.[73] Thus, for more than a decade, but for something less that three decades, Saint-Domingue refugees formed a visible sub-group of the New Orleans population.

A more precise view of how long the refugees maintained a visible presence in New Orleans is provided by the registers of St. Louis Cathedral and the Ursuline Chapel, where the vital events of almost all French-speakers were recorded up to 1840. In the course of his research on Saint-Domingue refugees, the late René LeGardeur systematically searched the St. Louis Cathedral funeral registers for individuals with some connection to Saint-Domingue. Of 355 entries in the register for whites from July, 1809, to May, 1810, 183 (52 percent) were for refugees, as one would expect from the number of whites in the 1809 migration relative to the white population of New Orleans at the moment of arrival.[74] From 1815 to 1828, refugees accounted for 600 of 4,600 acts (13 percent),[75] reflecting a decline in the proportion of refugees in the white Catholic population due to the departure of some refugees, the arrival of other immigrants to replace them, and natural increase of the resident population.

LeGardeur calculated the frequency of refugee funerals relative to funerals for white Catholics of all origins, non-French as well as French. In my research in the marriage registers of St. Louis Cathedral and the Ursulines chapel, I distinguished French-speaking from non-French-speaking spouses, subdivided French-speakers into Creoles, or natives of Louisiana, Frenchmen born in Europe, and Saint-Domingue refugees, and examined the registers for persons of color as well as for

1822), p. 45.

[73]*Gibson's Guide and Directory of the State of Louisiana and the Cities of New Orleans and Lafayette* (New Orleans, 1838), pp. 229-230.

[74]LeGardeur to Debien, February 13, 1960.

[75]LeGardeur to Debien, November 1, 1960.

whites.[76] The number of white refugee spouses increased from 2 in the 1790s to 63 in the 1800s, peaked at 258 from 1810 to 1819, before declining to 173 in the 1820s and 59 in the 1830s.

TABLE III

Number of Refugee Spouses and Percentage
of All French-Speaking Spouses Who Were Refugees,
by Caste and Decade

	WHITES		FPC's	
Decade	% of all French-Nspeaking spouses		%of all French-Nspeaking spouses	
1790-1799	2	0.5	6	6.0
1800-09	63	7.7	7	5.1
1810-19	258	18.4	63	25.0
1820-29	173	13.5	147	33.3
1830-39	59	3.3	127	15.1
TOTAL	555	9.7	349	19.9

Source: Marriages listed in registers of St. Louis Cathedral and the Ursulines Chapel, 1790-1839, Archives of the Archdiocese of New Orleans.

Refugees furnished 18 percent of all white French-speaking spouses in the second decade of the nineteenth century, and 14 percent in the third decade.

Meanwhile, non-white refugees marrying in New Orleans jumped from less than ten before 1810 to 63 from 1810 to 1819, 147

[76]Paul Lachance, "Intermarriage and French Cultural Persistence in Late Spanish and Early American New Orleans," *Histoire Sociale/Social History*, XV (1982), 50-52. In that study as in this article, I counted Saint-Domingue refugees born in Europe as part of the European French. In Saint-Domingue as in Louisiana, a clear distinction was made between Frenchmen born in the metropole and in the colonies. On the other hand, unlike the *Histoire Sociale* article, where I counted *all* persons born in Jamaica or Cuba marrying in New Orleans *after* 1810 as refugees, I was able for this article to distinguish Cuban- and Jamaican-born spouses with French names from those with Spanish or British names. This has practically no effect on statistics for free persons of color; but it decreases the proportion of refugees among all French-speaking spouses after 1820. It tends to sharpen the trends observed in the 1982 study.

in the 1820s and 127 in the 1830s. That represents 15 percent of non-white French-speaking spouses from 1810 to 1819, 13 percent from 1820 to 1829, and 15 percent in the 1830s. The timing of the demographic impact of Saint-Domingue refugees on the free-black component of the Gallic community differed from that of the white component. It reached a peak in the 1820s rather than in the preceding decade and tapered off less sharply in the 1830s. The most probable explanation is the younger age composition of refugees of color. It will be recalled that 42 percent were younger than 15, compared to only 24 percent of white refugees.

From the proportion of Saint-Domingue refugees in the Gallic community and the size of that community in 1820, a decade after the last large migration of refugees, the approximate number of refugees who settled in New Orleans can be estimated. According to the federal census of 1820, the population of the city was 27,176, of whom 13,584 were whites and 6,237 were free persons of color.[77] At that date, 8,000 to 9,000 of the whites and 4,500 to 5,000 of the free persons of color belonged to the Gallic community.[78] At close to a fifth of white French-speakers and a third of French-speaking free persons of color, proportions compatible with the marriage data, approximately 1,700 white refugees and 1,600 non-white refugees (excluding slaves) remained in the city as of 1820. That equals almost two-thirds of the whites and half of the free persons of color in the mayor's statistics for arrivals from Cuba in 1809. Since some of the refugees still present in New Orleans in 1820 had arrived before or after 1809, the rates of persistence of Saint-Domingue refugees from Cuba may have been somewhat lower, but not much.

The age structure of the 1809 migration yields a similar estimate of the refugees' persistence. By 1815, the age group of 15

---

[77]Fourth Census of the United States, 1820, p. 81.

[78]This estimate is based on contemporary calculations that three-fifths to four-fifths of the white population was French-speaking in 1806 and on the rate of increase of white French-speaking spouses since 1806. Evidence from the register of free persons of color in 1841 suggests that few Anglo-Americans of that caste arrived before 1820. The 1820 federal census enumerated 6,237 free persons of color in New Orleans. If my estimate of the size of the Gallic community errs, it does so on the conservative side.

or younger in the 1809 statistics began to marry. After 1820, most marriages involved refugees who had been children in 1809. Counting 100 of the 258 white Saint-Domingue spouses from 1810 to 1819, and 200 of the 232 from 1820 to 1839, as from this age group, almost half of the 655 white refugee children in 1809 could conceivably have married in New Orleans. Allowing for greater mortality and mobility in the older age groups, particularly among the surplus of white adult male refugees, the rate of persistence of white refugees in New Orleans was still high by contemporary norms. Joseph Ingraham remarked in his travel account of 1832 that half the population of the city renewed itself every few years.[79] Mortality was also high in New Orleans. In this context, it seems reasonable to conclude that a relatively large fraction of the Saint-Domingue refugees did settle in New Orleans, potentially enough to constitute a distinct ethnic group for two decades after the major influx of 1809, but of declining importance after 1830.

The impact of the refugees depended not only on how many settled in New Orleans, but also on where they fit in the city's socio-economic structure. The primary social cleavage was racial. Under French and Spanish domination, New Orleans had developed into a typical Caribbean three-caste society composed of whites, free persons of color and slaves, like that which had existed in Saint-Domingue prior to the revolution and which the refugees had recreated in Santiago de Cuba.[80] The racial mix of the 1809 migration meshed with that of the host society. In this respect, Saint-Domingue refugees differed from the uniquely white German and Irish immigrants who displaced free persons of color and slaves after 1840.[81] The

---

[79]Joseph Ingraham, *The South-West by a Yankee*, 2 vols. (New York, 1835), I, 115-116.

[80]Laura Foner, "The Free People of Color in Louisiana and St. Domingue: A Comparative Portrait of Two Three-Caste Societies," *Journal of Social History*, III (1970), 406, 423-430; Thomas Fiehrer, "The African Presence in Colonial Louisiana: An Essay on the Continuity of Caribbean Culture," in Robert R. Macdonald, et al., eds., *Louisiana's Black Heritage* (New Orleans, 1979), pp. 19-25. For the racial composition of the refugee population in Cuba, see Bohumil Badura, "Los Franceses en Santiago de Cuba a mediados del ano 1808," *Ibero-americana Pragnensia* (1971), 157-160.

[81]Earl Niehaus, *The Irish in New Orleans, 1800-1860* (1965; reprint ed., New York, 1976); John Frederick Nau, *The German People of New Orleans, 1850-1900* (Leiden, 1958). Parallel with the increase in German and Irish immigration after 1840, a signifi-

Saint-Domingue influx had the opposite effect: it reinforced the existing racial structure.

The refugees not only augmented the size of all three castes in New Orleans; they also transferred there the barriers, and modes of interaction across barriers, characteristic of three-caste societies. In the pleas of refugees to Claiborne to allow their slaves to disembark, one catches a glimpse of the quasi-familial relationship between some masters and slaves: "A Father of a family will assure me, that one & sometimes two or three faithful slaves constitute his only means of support—& a Lady will pray me to have pity on her Infant Child whose nurse is not permitted to leave the vessel."[82] Other refugees recounted stories about faithful domestics who enabled them to escape from insurgent slaves in Saint-Domingue intent on the massacre of all whites.[83] On the other hand, advertisements for the return of fugitives and legal suits to regain possession of slaves claiming to be free suggest that not all slaves accompanying the refugees were "faithful domestics."[84] The harsher side of slavery is evident in characteristics cited to identify runaways, like the derogatory term "Malard" branded onto the breast of a pregnant slave named Plaisir or the scars on Dominique's chest.[85]

What most clearly distinguishes a three-caste from a two-

cant reduction of the non-white castes set in. The number of free persons of color fell from 19,376 in 1840 to 11,133 in 1860, while slaves declined from 24,042 to 15,204 over the same twenty years.

[82]Claiborne to Poydras, May 28, 1809, in *Letter Books,* IV, 372.

[83]One such story was handed down to and recounted by Anne Labranche, "History of the Augustin Family" (n.d.), p. 2, typed manuscript in Augustin-Wogan-Labranche Family Papers (1803-1923), Howard-Tilton Memorial Library, Tulane University.

[84]Advertisements for Plaisir in the *Courrier,* June 26, 1809, for Fillette by Mme. Peuch and Dominique by P. P. André in the *Courrier,* September 4, 1809, for Agathe by Dupérai in the *Moniteur,* November 1, 1809, and for Marie by Duconge in the *Moniteur,* November 11, 1809. Superior Court, #3382, *Betsy Sires, fwc* v. *Marianne Delaunay, fwc,* and *Jean Mayet* v. *Marianne Delaunay and Betsy;* #3443, *Jeanette, fwc* v. *the Sheriff of this court, G. W. Morgan.*

[85]Advertisements for Plaisir and Dominique cited in preceding note.

caste racial structure is the special status accorded free persons of color in the three-caste system. The refugees, accustomed to legal distinctions delimiting the rights of each caste, adapted easily to similar rules in Louisiana. Such rules served more to define permissible forms of social interaction between castes than confine each in a separate sphere. Jean Boze kept Henri de Ste. Gême, who returned to France after the Battle of New Orleans, regularly informed about his children by a free woman of color whom he left behind in Louisiana.[86] At the same time, the refugees rigorously respected the law forbidding whites and free persons of color, and free persons of color and slaves, from intermarrying.[87] Interestingly, Boze remarked approvingly that Ste. Gême's children attended balls organized for young men and women of color rather than the quadroon balls leading to *plaçage,* although the children were themselves the product of a miscegenous union.[88]

Besides race, occupation and wealth served to differentiate the population of early nineteenth-century New Orleans. Its occupational structure resembled that of port cities on the Atlantic coast like Philadelphia, New York and Boston.[89] Of 1,251 men whose occupations are cited in the 1811 directory, about 20 percent manufactured products—from bread and chocolate to shoes, hats, tin, and watches—that they sold locally; 60 percent provided services to the local community as professionals, retail shopkeepers, grocers, publicans and the like; 15 percent were involved in different capacities in maritime transportation and

---

[86]For example, Boze to Ste. Gême, September 26, 1833, Henri de Ste. Gême Papers, MSS. 100, The Historic New Orleans Collection; hereafter cited as THNOC.

[87]Joseph Dainow, ed., *Compiled Edition of the Civil Code of Louisiana,* 17 vols. (St. Paul, Minn., 1947-1973), XVI, 55. The statute was Article 8 of the 1808 Digest of the Civil Code and Article 95 of the 1825 Louisiana Civil Code.

[88]Boze to Ste. Gême, March 10, 1830, THNOC.

[89]Jacob Price, "Economic Function and the Growth of American Port Towns in the Eighteenth Century," *Perspectives in American History,* VIII (1974), 128-137. In Table I, 137, the percentages of the populations of Boston in 1790, Philadelphia in 1774 and 1780-1783, and New York in 1795 in the governmental, service, industrial and maritime sectors are similar to the percentages in New Orleans in 1811, as given in the text.

external commercial exchange; and about 5 percent were government officials.[90] The assets declared in marriage contracts by men from different occupational groups reveal a definite social hierarchy.[91] At the top were merchants who brought on average $19,226 to their marriages, followed by planters with $13,737, and professionals with $9,562. In the middle were retailers and government officials with average declarations of $6,336 and $4,899 respectively. The bottom rank was comprised of artisans and mariners whose declarations averaged $2,679.[92]

Where did refugees fit in this hierarchy? The advertisements for employment they placed in newspapers soon after arrival suggest they entered at various levels. A free colored woman from Baracoa wished to be employed in nursing a white child,[93] while an elderly lady from Santiago de Cuba proposed to buy an interest in a tavern or coffee house.[94] Among male refugees from Cuba offering their services to the public were a watchmaker;[95] a joiner, painter and glazier;[96] two doctors, both

[90]Thomas H. Whitney, comp., *New Orleans Directory, and Louisiana and Mississippi Almanac for the Year 1811* (New Orleans, 1810).

[91]The marriage contracts are located in the Notarial Archives, Civil District Court, New Orleans, where they are bound with other acts in the books of the following notaries public: Narcissus Broutin (1804-1819), Christoval de Armas (1815-1819), Michel de Armas (1809-1819), Stephen de Quiñones (1805-1816), Marc Lafitte (1810-1819), Hugues Lavergne (1819), John Lynd (1805-1819), Pierre Pedesclaux (1817-1819), Carlisle Pollock (1817-1819), and Benedicte van Pradelles (1806-1808).

[92]These averages are based on the 190 cases in which the occupation of the bridegroom was either mentioned in the marriage contract or cited in the 1811 or 1822 directory for New Orleans and whose assets were described in the marriage contract. Such was the case for 41 merchants, 27 planters, 16 professionals, 45 retailers, 11 government officials, 45 artisans, some in the service and others in the industrial sector, and 5 mariners.

[93]*Courrier*, September 11, 1809.

[94]*Ibid.*, August 11, 1809.

[95]*Ibid.*, August 30, 1809. He also proposed to rent out a slave whom he described as an "excellent steady cook."

[96]*Ibid.*, July 26, 1809.

with thirty years experience;[97] and a young refugee from Havana
with experience as an overseer, pharmacist, and store clerk.[98]

The two types of employment sought most frequently
through advertisements were work on plantations and teaching.
One refugee asked to be employed in the administration of an
estate or the fabrication of sugar, if only for the season, offering
the labor of three Negroes experienced in sugar production to
the planter who hired him.[99] Another declared himself ready
to work on a trial basis without compensation as a refiner of
sugar or in a distillery.[100] A third refugee capable of managing
a sugar, indigo, cotton, or tobacco plantation, experienced in the
sawing of wood, and the owner of four slaves, proposed to form
a partnership.[101] Others sought employment on plantations as
architects, carpenters, mechanics and engineers, often claiming
special expertise in sugar production.[102] To the extent they were
successful, these refugees left the city.

At least fifteen refugees from Cuba advertised themselves
as teachers. Pierre Lambert offered to give classes every day of
the week except Thursday and Sunday in arithmetic, algebra,
geometry, infinitesmal calculus and navigation for $16 a month.[103]
François Bocquet announced the opening on July 1, 1809, of a
school with hours from 8:30 to 11:00 and 2:30 to 5:00 where,
"following a method as easy as it was natural," children would be
taught reading, writing, French, Spanish and English, history,
arithmetic and geography.[104] A father and son started a school

[97]*Ibid.*, June 12, 1809 (Bernard); *Moniteur*, October 14, 1809 (Poursine).

[98]*Courrier*, October 9, 1809.

[99]*Ibid.*, July 12, 1809.

[100]*Ibid.*, July 14, 1809.

[101]*Ibid.*, August 30, 1809.

[102]*Ibid.*, June 9, 1809 (P. Thuet); *Moniteur*, June 17, 1809 (Gigaud), June 24, 1809 (François Roboam; Croisat, *l'aîné;* Atanace Savignac).

[103]*Courrier*, September 15, 1809.

[104]*Ibid.*, June 23, 1809. He had also advertised in the *Louisiana Gazette,* October 25, 1808, identifying himself as "lately from Havana." Thus he arrived prior to the influx of 1809.

for white youth of both sexes on the plantation of Madame
Kernion in Gentilly, adding they could take in several students
at half-pension. The wife and mother of the two directors was
to take charge of the young ladies.[105] Four different refugees
proposed to give instruction in the playing of various musical
instruments, vocal music and dancing.[106] Some advertisements
listed private lessons as one of several acceptable forms of work,
like the following notice printed in the *Courrier:* "A man from
Cuba knowing the English, French and Spanish languages,
book-keeping at double entry, drawing and mathematics, is
desirous of finding employment either in a counting-room to
do the writings, or in a public office as a translator, or even
in a private house for teaching youth."[107] The refugees Pierre
Lambert, Jules Davezac and Jean Augustin made up three-
fifths of the original faculty of the Collège d'Orléans, which
began operation in 1813.[108]

The rapid movement of refugees into the active population
was observed by the mayor in August, 1809, when over half of
the refugees from Cuba had arrived. He divided white refugees
into two categories: those able to live off the labor of their
slaves and those forced to depend on their own talents.

> Out of the whole number of male grown persons *two
> thirds of them possess some trade.*—Several among them
> who once possessed estates, or belonged to wealthy
> families in the Island of St. Domingo, now follow the
> occupations of Cabinet Makers, Turners, bakers,

[105]*Moniteur,* November 4, 1809.

[106]*Courrier,* June 23, 1809 (advertisement of Lahens, *l'ainé*); *ibid.,* July 3, 1809 (advertisement of Couerderoy); *Moniteur,* July 5, 1809 (advertisement of François de St.
Just).

[107]*Courrier,* June 9, 1809; see also similar advertisement in *ibid.,* June 5, (Bazanac),
June 28, July 14, September 15 (Justin Laroque), 1809.

[108]*L'Ami des lois,* October 27, 1813, in Lambert Family Papers (1798-1862), Louisiana
Collection, Howard-Tilton Memorial Library, 244, box 1, folder 23.

> Glaziers, upholsterers; and I will venture to assert that in the above, and twenty other different trades, there are not less than six hundred men from Cuba usefully employed among us, at the present time.[109]

Non-white refugees also quickly made a place for themselves in the occupational structure by helping to meet the demand for more housing resulting from the refugee influx. In January, 1810, the mayor commented on their "uncommon industry. Many houses have been built in little time and at less cost than before."[110]

Bakers are one trade in which the immediate effect of the refugee influx on business activity is measurable. Every baker had to declare at the end of each month how much flour he had used. In May, 1809, 24 bakers used 520 barrels of flour. By September, the number of bakers making declarations had jumped to 34, and the quantity of flour consumed to over 700 barrels.[111] Of 43 bakers making declarations between October, 1806, and January, 1813, whose birthplace I have been able to determine, 8 were born in Saint-Domingue and 12 were Frenchmen who immigrated to New Orleans by way of Saint-Domingue.

The occupations of 32 Saint-Domingue bridegrooms who signed marriage contracts in New Orleans between 1804 and 1819 provide an overview of the sectors into which white refugees moved. Compared to the 1811 directory, high-status sectors are over-represented and low-status sectors are under-represented in the marriage contract data; but the contracts remain useful for the impression they provide of the relative standing of the refugees.

[109]Mather to Claiborne, August 9, 1809, in *Letter Books,* IV, 405.

[110]Letter of James Mather, January 18, 1810, published in the *Moniteur,* January 27, 1810.

[111]Calculated from monthly declarations printed in *ibid.*

TABLE IV
Occupational Sectors of White Refugees Compared to All Signers of Marriage Contracts, 1804-1819, and to Individuals Named in the 1811 Directory

| Sector | Marriage Contracts | | | | 1811 Directory | |
| | Refugees | | All Signers | | | |
	N	%	N	%	N	%
Government	1	3.1	15	6.9	57	4.6
Service	18	56.3	125	56.8	743	59.4
Professional	3	9.4	27	12.3	133	10.6
Retailers	10	31.3	57	25.9	213	17.0
Crafts, etc.*	5	15.6	41	18.6	397	31.7
Industrial	3	9.4	22	10.0	254	20.3
Maritime						
commerce	10	31.3	58	26.4	197	15.7
Mariners	2	6.3	8	3.6	24	1.9
Merchants	8	25.0	50	22.7	173	13.8
SUBTOTAL	32	100.0	220	100.0	1,251	100.0
Planters**	0	0.0	30	12.0	8	0.5
Undetermined***	31	49.2	126	33.5	774	24.9
TOTAL	63		376		2,033	

Sources: Marriage contracts in New Orleans notarial archives; Whitney, *New Orleans Directory . . . for the Year 1811.* The scheme of classification is taken form Jacob Price, "Economic Function and the Growth of American Port Towns in the Eighteenth Century," *Perspectives in American History,* VIII (1974), 128-137.

*Retail crafts, building crafts, travel and transportation, other services.

**Percentage of all cases with occupation identified, including planters.

***All cases, whether or not occupation identified. The 1811 directory also lists 49 women for a total of 1,661 names.

In contrast to the 12 percent of all contract-signers with known occupations who were planters, none of the refugee bridegrooms was in this high prestige category. Otherwise, about the same proportion of white refugees are to be found in each occupational sector as among contract-signers in general. In the short run at least, they reinforced the existing urban occupational structure by adding to all sectors proportionately.

However, in sectors where they were numerous enough to make statistical analysis meaningful, white refugees declared less wealth on average than Anglo-Americans, Creoles, and the European French. The average assets at marriage of Saint-Domingue merchants, for example, amounted to $2,953, compared to well over $10,000 for merchants of other nationalities. Refugee shopkeepers declared on average $4,833 in their contracts, only two-thirds the average declaration of European French retailers and an even smaller fraction of the average for other groups in the same occupational category. White refugee artisans averaged only $1,100, again well below the average of almost $3,000 for other white artisans. Collectively, the average declaration of white Saint-Domingue refugees was $3,136, or less than half the average for European French bridegrooms ($7,663) and less than a third the average for Creoles ($10,309). No refugees were among the richest 10 percent of bridegrooms. These statistics are calculated from data from the decade of arrival and the decade following arrival of the refugees. As such, they may reflect losses suffered in the forced migrations from Saint-Domingue and Cuba.

The occupations of eleven free men of color born in Saint-Domingue who signed marriage contracts in New Orleans between 1807 and 1819 have also been determined. Nine were artisans, one was a butcher and the other was a barge captain. Compared to all contract-signers, they were over-represented in the manufacturing sector and completely absent from the mercantile and professional sectors; but so were free men of color native to Louisiana. On average, non-white refugee bridegrooms brought only $1,116 into their marriages, compared to $2,161 by Creole free men of color.[112] Thus, like their white counterparts, free men of color in the refugee population entered

---

[112]Exactly the reverse was the case for the non-white refugee brides, whose average declaration of $2,010 was twice the $941 declared by Creole brides.

the sectors in the occupational structure open to them at the bottom.

Cutting across both racial and socio-economic cleavages was the language divide. Using birthplace as an indication of primary language, and intermarriage as a measure of the strength of linguistic identity, the marriage registers of St. Louis Cathedral and the Ursuline Chapel show the absorption of Saint-Domingue refugees into the Gallic community. Up to 1840, fully 91 percent of white female refugees born in Saint-Domingue or Cuba and 85 percent of white female refugees took French-speaking spouses. Among free persons of color in the refugee population, 97 percent of the males and 95 percent of the females married French-speakers. If it is true that children tend to be raised in their mother's language, even the families of the 15 percent of white female refugees married to Anglo-Americans and non-French immigrants were not necessarily lost to the Gallic community.

The pattern of intermarriage among white French-speakers reveals the extent to which the refugees formed a distinct subgroup within the Gallic community. From 1800 to 1839, there was frequent intermarriage between Saint-Domingue refugees, the European French, and Louisiana Creoles. On the female side, 46 percent of the white refugees married French-speaking immigrants from Europe and 14 percent married Louisiana Creoles. On the male side, 45 percent of the white refugees married Creoles and 4 percent took European French brides. The high percentage of exogamous marriages was in part the consequence of imbalanced sex ratios and the unequal number of potential spouses in the subgroups of the Gallic population. The index of homogamy is a measure of preference for spouses from the same group which controls for these demographic factors. It is more revealing than simple percentages.[113]

---

[113]See my explanation of the index of homogamy in "Intermarriage and French Cultural Persistence," 60-62.

TABLE V
Decennial Indices of Homogamy for Subgroups
of the White French-Speaking Population

Decade	Louisiana Creole	European French	Saint-Domingue Refugees
1800-09	.252	.203	.361
1810-19	.323	.232	.266
1820-29	.363	.316	.236
1830-39	.410	.413	.157

Source: Marriages listed in registers of St. Louis Cathedral and the Ursuline Chapel, 1790-1839, Archives of the Archdiocese of New Orleans.

Note: The index of homogamy ranges from -1 to +1. A negative value means a tendency towards exogamy over and above that expected from demographic factors. A positive value reveals a tendency towards endogamy. The higher the value, the greater the propensity in either direction.

In the first decade of the nineteenth century, the coefficient of homogamy was higher for Saint-Domingue refugees than for the European French and for Creoles. This reflects the distinct identity of the group on arrival in New Orleans.[114]

Over the next decades, though, the propensity of Saint-Domingue refugees to marry one another progressively diminished, in contrast to Creoles and the European French who became more clannish in their choices. By the 1830s, the refugees showed little preference for each other over outsiders as marriage partners. Marriages in this decade involved children born to Saint-Domingue families during the last years

[114]From 1800 to 1809, refugee brides outnumbered refugee bridegrooms by 41 to 22; and from 1810 to 1819 by 172 to 84. It will be recalled that the mayor's report on 9,059 refugees in the Cuban migration revealed exactly the opposite imbalance, namely, 1,373 white males against 703 white females over the age of fifteen. The mayor counted French-born refugees as refugees, while I classify them as European French. Many of the 104 European Frenchmen whom Saint-Domingue women married before 1820 may be supposed to be Frenchmen who arrived in New Orleans by way of Saint-Domingue and the route of the refugees. If I had classified them as refugees rather than as European French, the homogamy of refugees in the first decades of the nineteenth century would be greater, possibly much greater, than in the table. That would make the increasing readiness to marry outside the group observed after 1820 all the more striking.

of the Haitian Revolution or soon afterwards in Cuba. Growing up in Louisiana, their formative experiences were the same as native Louisianians of the same generation; and they increasingly chose Creoles as partners over immigrants from France. By the 1830s, 69 percent of Saint-Domingue males married native Louisianians, up from around 40 percent in the three preceding decades. Half of the Saint-Domingue females continued to marry the European French; but the proportion marrying Creoles increased from 7 percent before 1810 to 15 percent in the following decades. This may be interpreted as evidence of integration into the Creole side of the Gallic community.[115]

The coefficient of homogamy for free persons of color born in Saint-Domingue decreased from .581 in the first decade after the arrivals of 1809 to .447 in the 1820s and .323 in the 1830s. This reflects increasing intermarriage with Creole free persons of color; but the lowest coefficient for non-white refugees (.323) was greater than all but the first coefficient for white refugees (.361). Apparently, Saint-Domingue refugees remained a distinct subgroup longer among free persons of color than among whites in the Gallic community.

In general, the settlement of Saint-Domingue refugees in New Orleans added members to all three racial castes in the city without altering significantly the proportion of each in the population as a whole, nor the nature of race relations in a three-caste society. Similarly, they contributed additional artisans, shopkeepers, professionals and merchants to the city's active population without altering the sectoral distribution of occupations, nor racial differences in employment. Only by adding to the French majority at the expense of Anglo-Americans did they alter the existing *rapport de force* between

---

[115]However frequent intermarriage between refugees born in France and in the colonies in the decade following the influx of 1809, such marriages declined over time relative to marriages between refugees who were children at the time of the migration and few of whom were born in France. Their entry into the marriage market is reflected in a more balanced ratio of male to female spouses in the refugee subgroup after 1820. What is interesting is that endogamous marriages did *not* increase as the sexual imbalance lessened. On the contrary, white refugees showed less and less inclination to choose each other as spouses, confirming the loss of identity by the 1830s.

two social groups. The positive reception accorded the refugees by the Gallic community undoubtedly influenced the decision of many of them to remain in New Orleans; and although unarticulated, one reason French-speakers responded to the 1809 migration in humanitarian fashion may have been their hope that it would add to the numerical strength of the Gallic community. From the opposite perspective, did the refugees have the negative impact that hostile Anglo-Americans anticipated? Did the enlargement of one of the "foreign" elements in the already cosmopolitan population of New Orleans put American sovereignty in jeopardy? Did the refugees "rivet" upon the city "a decided and irresistible French preponderance . . . for many years to come"?

In retrospect, such fears appear exaggerated. First, doubts regarding the loyalty of the French population in general, and of the refugees in particular, turned out to be groundless. Admittedly, up to the British invasion of December, 1814, the right of French citizens in Louisiana to exemption from militia duty was a subject of diplomatic contention between France and the United States.[116] Most of the 75 names on two lists of Frenchmen entitled to exemption drawn up by the French consul in New Orleans belonged to refugees.[117] Nevertheless, by the admission of the consul himself, when called to arms by General Jackson, "All the French men marched, and I have only one who claimed exemption."[118]

The participation of Saint-Domingue refugees in the defense of New Orleans is evident from the composition of units that fought under Andrew Jackson's command. Among the white veterans of the Battalion of New Orleans whose birthplace

[116]A reference to this contention is made at the beginning of the letter of Sérurier to James Monroe, April 26, 1815, AE, Correspondance politique: Etats-Unis, vol. 72, f. 86.

[117]"Letters of Louis Tousard, French consul at New Orleans to Governor William C. C. Claiborne, pertaining to French citizens who claimed they should be exempt from U. S. military service," January 6, 10, 1814, in Howard-Tilton Memorial Library.

[118]Anne Louis de Tousard to John Clement Stocker, January 6, 1815, in Norman Wilkinson, ed., "The Assaults on New Orleans, 1814-1815," *Louisiana History,* III (1962), 49.

Ronald Morazan has been able to determine, 28 percent were Saint-Domingue refugees;[119] and the second battalion of 256 free men of color was composed of non-white refugees.[120] Many of the Baratarians were also refugees. The dispatch of the French ambassador recounting the American victory described the privateers of Barataria as "former French filibusters driven from our islands by British conquest or by insurrections excited by the British; intrepid men, hardened to fatigue and experienced in the work and dangers of war. They furnished to the General 800 soldiers and especially excellent gunners."[121]

Some refugees fought for exactly the reason that Anglo-Americans felt they could not be trusted. For staunch supporters of Napoleon who blamed the loss of Saint-Domingue and their expulsion from Cuba on the British, the Battle of New Orleans represented one last chance to wage war against their arch-enemy.[122] However, contrary to Anglo-American suspicions, not all refugees were Bonapartists. In the West Florida Revolution of 1810, a pitch had been made for French support. Acting as intermediary for the Anglo-American organizers of the revolt, a former French colonial officer in Cuba told the refugees that "any attachment to Bonaparte should be no offense to the Country." Their response was that "they had used Bonaparte's name to please the Spaniards who had vexed them, but as Citizens of their new Country they'd Rather Remain independent than to submit to any master."[123]

---

[119]The remaining 22 percent of veterans were divided about equally between Anglo-Americans and immigrants from non-French-speaking countries in Europe and the Caribbean. Ronald Morazan, comp., *Biographical Sketches of the Veterans of the Battalion of New Orleans, 1814-1815* (Baton Rouge, 1979). Morazan identifies the birthplace of 109, or approximately one out of every six, veterans.

[120]McConnell, *Negro Troops*, pp. 67-71.

[121]Sérurier's account of the American victory in the Battle of New Orleans, February 7, 1815, AE, Correspondance politique: Etats Unis, vol. 72, f. 25-26.

[122]For the example of a refugee who blamed the British for the expulsion from Cuba as well as for the loss of Saint-Domingue, see the letter of a "Réfugié de St. Yague de Cuba," July 9, 1809, printed in the *Courrier*, July 10, 1809.

[123]Audibert to Skipwith, September 4, 1810, in James A. Podgett, ed., "The West Florida Revolution of 1810, As Told in the Letters of John Rhea, Fulwar Skipwith, Reuben Kemper, and Others," *Louisiana Historical Quarterly*, XXI (1938), 87-88. Audibert then

It was not necessary to be Bonapartist to be anti-British. Even among refugees with little or no attachment to Napoleon, traditional Gallic anglophobia was probably the main reason they fought on the side of the Americans in the Battle of New Orleans. Some, however, may have been motivated by gratitude to the country that had afforded them asylum. At least such was the hope of Henry Hopkins, adjutant-general of the American militia, who said of the refugees arriving in 1809: "Several undoubtedly will take up residence and will consequently be incorporated into the militia. We can expect that sentiments of gratitude will attach them to the country welcoming them into its bosom."[124] Finally, the martial atmosphere in New Orleans as it awaited the major British offensive of January 8, 1815, put pressure on those who otherwise might have remained neutral. The French consul wrote to his brother-in-law in Philadelphia two days before the climactic battle, "General Jackson will be the Savior of this country. He has now from 15,000 to 18,000 men all burning with eagerness to cross swords with the English. Nationalities no longer count; we are all Americans."[125]

The prediction that the refugees would fasten a French influence on New Orleans for years to come corresponded better with what was to happen historically. French-speakers remained a majority of the white population for about two decades after the influx of 1809. Only in the 1830s, with the large increase in immigration from Ireland and Germany, was the Gallic community reduced to a definite minority.[126] Thus the years of French preponderance in New Orleans coincided with

---

remarked, "I think if the Convention Would promise . . . to the Ruined inhabitants of St. Domingo by the Spaniards, some little Share in the Vacant lands for their personal Military Service, that the Convention should soon have a collection of Good Soldiers who made a Continental War in St. Domingo against all portion White, Black, and Mulattoes."

[124]Hopkins to Claiborne, October 28, 1809, *Territorial Papers*, IX, 854-857.

[125]Tousard to Stocker, January 6, 1815, in Wilkinson, "Assault on New Orleans," 46.

[126]As of 1840, it may have slipped to less than a fourth of the total white population.

those in which the impact of the refugees was strongest; and it is certain that the influx of 1809 did reinforce the Gallic community, both in terms of numbers and of institutional completeness.

Nevertheless, at the time of the 1809 migration, French was already the language of somewhere between three and four out of every five white residents of New Orleans, and English of but one out of ten at most. The ratio was so much in favor of the French that French preponderance was almost inevitable for another decade, with or without the refugees.[127] Furthermore, in addition to Saint-Domingue refugees, the natural increase of Creoles and continuing immigration from France contributed to the growth of the Gallic community. From 1810 to 1829, when the refugee impact on marriages was strongest, refugees accounted for 16 percent of white French-speaking spouses, while the European French furnished 24 percent and Creoles 60 percent.[128]

The long-term impact of the refugees was limited by an important characteristic of refugee movements, namely, not to be renewed by subsequent migration. After 1809, a few refugees who had entered the United States through other ports moved to New Orleans, but probably less than left the city. In spite of the relatively high persistence of refugees, some did emigrate to the countryside, back to France, or even back to Cuba when the

[127]As the refugees began to arrive in 1809, Claiborne estimated the growth of the white population of the Territory since 1806 at three to four thousand, two-thirds of whom were native Americans. Adding them to the 3,500 natives of the United States in the Territory as of 1806 makes for 6,000 Americans in a total white population of 30,000 before the arrival of the refugees from Cuba. Claiborne to Smith, May 18, 1809, in *Letter Books*, IV, 361. Even if a less sympathetic response had discouraged many refugees from settling in Louisiana, it would have made little difference in the timing of the displacement of the French majority.

[128]These statistics understate somewhat the impact of white refugees. The European French include natives of France who immigrated to Louisiana by way of Saint-Domingue. If they were counted instead in the refugee category, it may well have been larger than that of the European French in the decade following the influx of 1809. Moreover, Creole spouses include children born to refugees in New Orleans who began to marry in the 1820s. Nevertheless, the migration from Cuba was only one of several demographic factors contributing to French preponderance up to 1830.

special measures against the French were rescinded.[129] The consequence of few new arrivals was constant attrition of the original refugee population through emigration and mortality.   The effect of minimal subsequent immigration does not show up until the 1830s in the marriage data, but then it is striking. In that decade, as the youngest cohort of refugees was married off, spouses born in Saint-Domingue or in Cuba of refugee parents fell to 3 percent of white French-speaking spouses, while the European French marrying in New Orleans, reflecting an increase in immigration from France in the 1830s, rose to 31 percent. Over the long run, continuing immigration from France was more important than the temporarily circumscribed refugee influx in sustaining the Gallic community in New Orleans.

In anticipating the impact of refugees on the relative strength of linguistic groups in New Orleans, Anglo-Americans ignored free persons of color and slaves. For that matter, so did most white French-speakers. When non-white elements of the refugee population were taken into account, it was usually in racial, not linguistic, contexts, for example, whether or not they added to the potential danger of slave insurrection. However, the Gallic community was multi-racial; and refugees accounted for a larger proportion of the increase in French-speaking free persons of color after 1810 than of whites, due to the absence of French-speaking immigrants of color from other countries. For the same reason, slaves accompanying the refugees were the only important foreign addition to that component of the Gallic community after 1808.

By their integration into all racial castes and occupational sectors, Saint-Domingue refugees strengthened the French presence throughout New Orleans society. By contrast, the first American immigrants to settle in New Orleans tended to be white merchants and professionals, especially lawyers, emigrating from milieux that were much more ethnically homogeneous than New Orleans. The fear of French preponderance

---

[129]*Moniteur*, April 29, 1813, for the proclamation of the captain-general of Cuba restoring Frenchmen in the possession of property sequestered in 1809.

expressed in hostile reactions to the refugees was characteristic of those Anglo-Americans unable or unwilling to adjust to the cosmopolitan character of New Orleans society. They directed against the refugees their frustration with finding themselves a minority in a city that did not yet fit the American mold.

Index

CPSIA information can be obtained
at www.ICGtesting.com
Printed in the USA
FSOW02n1832151016
26108FS